A REALLY
BIG LUNCH

A REALLY BIG LUNCH

JIM HARRISON

With an Introduction by
Mario Batali

Grove Press
New York

First Grove Atlantic hardcover edition: March 2017

Published simultaneously in Canada
Printed in the United States of America

FIRST EDITION

ISBN 978-0-8021-2646-7
eISBN 978-0-8021-8944-8

Library of Congress Cataloging-in-Publication data is available for this title.

Grove Press
an imprint of Grove Atlantic
154 West 14th Street
New York, NY 10011

Distributed by Publishers Group West

groveatlantic.com

17 18 19 20   10 9 8 7 6 5 4 3 2 1

CONTENTS

INTRODUCTION

One night back in 2000, a beleaguered author not so hot on the idea of *any* book tour, but who was nevertheless *on* a book tour, appeared at my restaurant Babbo in New York. Jim Harrison and I had written letters to each other, but had never met, and little did I know then how he would go on to become one of my closest friends. In tow were a few members of his publishing team, a book editor from the *New York Times*, and a handful of other lucky food lovers from NYC. Jim was hungry, thirsty, joyously friendly, and characteristically overeager for the first course to come out of the kitchen. Jim's appetite was legendary, and nothing makes a cook quite so happy as someone who exists entirely to eat—and when not eating, to talk about eating, to hunt and fish for things to eat, or to spend time after eating talking about what we just ate.

That night we ate just about every non-grocery-store cut of every animal I served. The meal ran to fifteen courses: from one of Jim's favorites, our Babbo-made testa, with my dad's finocchiona and culatello, to lamb's tongue vinaigrette, tripe in the style of Parma, and both beef cheek and calf's brains raviolis; from light love letters of goose liver, crispy sweetbreads dusted in fennel pollen and finished with duck bacon and membrillo vinaigrette, on to squab with barlotto, quail with salsify, and duck with brovada; finishing with a whole series of desserts. Jim relished in the unabashed frivolity of this meal; he would talk about "tripe," sure enough, there it came, and a tale of hunting would beget the birds shot in the story. We drank '82 and '85 Barolos, both in magnum, then a double mag of Le Pergole Torte then back to the north for some Gaja Barbaresco with which we ate a couple robiolas and a mountain gorgonzola with housemade black truffle honey.

Our friendship moved from pen pals to real pals that night, and I knew I had finally shaken hands, shared *abrazos fuertes* and broken bread with not only an eternal friend but a mentor, a spiritual leader, a confidant, and a man who shared my passion for all things above and beyond the world of food, and who wrote sentences that stretched beyond the wildest poetry of my imagination, resonating with stories of the friends and associates who eat well, drink Lambrusco and vin de pays as well as Bordeaux from the fifties and sixties, work hard, play hard, and experience the natural world in full.

A couple of years later, after a mere ten-course meal celebrating the magnificent white truffle at Babbo, I walked Jim back to his hotel. He stayed regularly at the Inn at Irving Place near Gramercy Park, a charming hotel that allowed smoking—a deal breaker for Jim—and was close to the Spanish restaurant that our team opened in 2003, Casa Mono. It was after 11 pm, closing time, and we had consumed as much food as was humanly possible. We discussed his obsession with Antonio Machado the entire walk home. As we turned the corner to his hotel, Jim peered into the candlelit Casa Mono and then leaned in. "Mario, do you think we could just get a little taste of those fabulous oxtails in piquillo peppers you do here on a little bread, just for the taste in my mouth, please? Just a taste," he bashfully whispered, "it reminds me of Lorca."

"You bet, Jimmy," I said. And a quick little bottle of Priorat to wash it all down, five American Spirits on the stoop, and off to bed. I have never seen a man so happy in his pursuit of pleasure that evening. And from that moment on, we were friends for life.

Jim and I shared many qualities: an unending appetite, inhaling life to the full chorizo, finding hilarious and playful nuance in every breath and every moment, but I always was and remain the student. Jim was sharper, more in tune with the distant cry of the loon over the lake while fishing on a lazy Tuesday morning, more sensitive to the moonlight over Washington Square Park on a dusk walk toward the Babbo apartment, where he sometimes stayed. Jim lived art not as a method to distill his thoughts, but as a categorical way of understanding life, a quest to quench an insatiable thirst for all it put before him. And to share that understanding with any and every one he met.

But Jim was not all Zen, and certainly not patient. We once shared a slightly overlong supper at the Michelin three-star restaurant Eleven Madison Park in New York, where he fidgeted through most of the complex meal, announcing early on in his loud baritone to the entire dining room, "Maaaario, you know I am much more of a trattoria kind of guy," and finally sending his chicken back to the kitchen, because the chef had somehow denied him "THE FUCKING LEGS . . . where are THE FUCKING LEGS . . . ?" When we cooked together he was often at my shoulder with cooking tips and timing questions. "Are you going to stir that?" or "Remember I like it medium rare, not a degree over, damn it," while cooking a three-inch-thick rib eye from Carnevino on his parrilla in Arizona. By the time we were seated he grudgingly admitted to the deliciousness of the meal and to the success of yet another of our collaborations . . . It always gave me infinite joy.

In January of 2016, two months before Jim left us all lonely, we gathered again. This time we were memorializing Linda, Jim's beloved wife of fifty-six years, at their *casita* in Patagonia, in Arizona near the Mexican border town Nogales. With a handful of intimate friends and family of Jim and Linda to feed, I set off with a plane full of food and two of Jim's favorite chefs, Anthony Sasso from Casa Mono and Chris Bianco from Phoenix. We cooked rib eyes, sausage and peppers, paella, and *fideuà*, ate an entire kilo of Oscietra caviar with an entire *jamón de Jabugo*, we made drinks for brunch with giant local pomelos. I surprised him with his favorite lunch of all, a glorious Bollito Misto with testa, zampone, brisket, osso buco, tongue, and fresh sausage, all served up with his sauce love, a tangy salsa verde of capers, herbs, chopped cornichons and mustard, the hot one from France he dreamed of daily. Jim was sad; life was hard without his lovely Linda. We ate, we talked, he complained, as he always did, about my taste in music and the volume I played it at while prepping or cleaning up after dinner. We lived hardily that weekend, and we did our best to heal Jim with what we knew he loved most. We spoke of his imminent trip to Paris, of our plans to really dig into our pet project of the last decade called *The Search for the Genuine*. He plumbed a gem or two from his poetry mind suggesting that cooking for himself was going to lead him "to learn to love again," but his heart cried for Linda . . . He was in a dream state, a fugue, a funk . . . I watched him drift off on the patio toward the creek, the birds, grief, and then he'd snap right to when I'd say *Jim* and hand him a mound of mascarpone, jamón, and caviar; the food and my love helped draw him back toward life. That last weekend I saw him filled my heart with his joy, his immense and remarkable love, his visceral way with words both loving and cross, tangy and salty, sweet, gentle and filled with love of the physical plane.

Jim once wrote of a character, "He's literally taking bites out of the sun, moon, and earth," which is what he himself spent a lifetime doing. Damn he was my hero.

—Mario Batali
January, 2017

EAT YOUR HEART OUT

As your ass't food editor and private WATS line to the *terre d'edibles* I wanted to alert you to certain new developments in the area of hot sauces. (Just yelled at my yellow Labrador who is in the garden eating corn on the cob without salt and butter. Yesterday it was a dozen eggs and a pound of butter left out on the counter.) But before we get to the hot sauce let me make a few divergent points.

1. No one is allowed to use cocaine before the meal when I cook. Afterward, OK. Cocaine creates a sort of bubble-gum nimbus that slaughters the palate and sensuous capacities, in addition to shrinking the wee-wee and tearing holes in the social fabric.
2. A warning to certain of your left-leaning, spit-dribbling, eco-freak readers: I kill much of what I eat; ducks, quail,

deer, grouse, woodcock, trout, salmon, bluegills, the lowly
carp (Hunanese hot and crispy carp). These people should
know that technically speaking their bean sprouts scream
when they are jerked out by their roots. Everything living
ends up as a turd of sorts.

3. Numerologically I can't end up on an even number (2) for
private reasons. Spend as much as possible on good food
and wine. Last night I drank a 1949 Latour and a 1953
Richebourg because I was depressed about returning to
Glitzville (Hollywood). I wept over a Save the Children
ad. Then as the great wine surged through my proud veins
and emptied into my brainpan I had a long satisfying fantasy
about Meryl Streep. "How can I help but love you, Jim,"
she said, "I've read your ten books and eaten your ten best
meals. I guess you could say I'm yours." Then I slipped on
my fifty-dollar Key West pig mask and stalked her pealing
laughter through the penthouse etc. . . . Her husband was
conveniently absent, having become waylaid on a turnip
expedition in Washington Heights. O Meryl!

Anyway, hot sauce *au point*: Richard Schweid's magnificent *Hot
Peppers* (Madrona Publishers, $6.95) is worth a hundred times its
price. Yes the book is worth six hundred ninety five dollars, the
exact amount of a quarter ounce of you-know-what. Luckily I got
my copy free. Unfortunately, Schweid, the sage of Cajuns and *Cap-
sicum*, is ignorant of Clancy's Fancy, a hot sauce manufactured by
Colleen Clancy, 630 Oxford, Ann Arbor, MI 48108. Ms. Clancy is
a lass steeped in exotic Acadiana. I've never met her but her sauce
is stopper and neck above the hundreds of sauces I've collected from
Ethiopia to Ecuador, from cold Leningrad to the steamy fuck-crazed
alleys of Bangkok where slant oysters are far more numerous than
the fabled Belons, Bon Secours, or the champ Apalachicolas. Jimmy
Buffett, the minstrel, uses it in his duck-crab-shrimp gumbo. Sam
Lawrence, the publishing tycoon, uses Clancy's during Key West
exercise routines. I use it copiously. Example—a Caribbean stew.

3 lb PORK SPARERIBS (cut to 1-rib pieces)
1 CHICKEN (cut into serving pieces)
2 lb HOT ITALIAN SAUSAGE
½ cup TOMATO PASTE
7 cloves of GARLIC
3 tbsp FAUCHON BASIL VINEGAR
7 tsp CLANCY'S FANCY
1 cup CHICKEN STOCK
3 tsp LEMON JUICE
1 tsp SUGAR
7 dashes WORCESTERSHIRE SAUCE
1 tbsp CHILI POWDER
1 tbsp PAPRIKA

1. Place spareribs in large Dutch oven and cover with water. Cook for 20 minutes, discard water.

2. Place chicken pieces in bottom of Dutch oven and cover with spareribs and pieces of sausage. Add onions.

3. Mix all other ingredients in a bowl and pour over mélange.

4. Bake covered for 1 hour and 45 minutes at 300. Spoon off excess fat or suck it off with a straw.

Do not change or substitute! Above my desk hang a crow wing and a pink rubber piglet with a green drake trout fly stuck in its ass, and a coyote tooth in its mouth. I've written a new novel called *Warlock*. You tamper with my recipes at your peril!

FOOD FOR THOUGHT

Dear Mike,*

I am so confused and distraught that this will have to serve as my
food letter for the upcoming issue. Let's face it, the twin specters of
food and politics loom large these days. On a recent trip to Central
America, to cover for my own curiosity the multifaceted revolutions
in that area, I frankly ate very well. One particular lunch for instance
I had squid stewed in their own ink, braised quail on toast, a soup
made entirely of miniature crustaceans, plus a skewer of several lob-
sters and two bottles of wine. This was extraordinarily cheap because
of our advantage in the exchange rate. The cooking was prodigiously
adept compared to my recent ten-day trip to New York City where
food, lodging, and pharmaceuticals ran about $8,000. I want you to

* Mike Golden, editor of *Smoke Signals*

be the first to know that when my next novel is published I'm heading straight to Costa Rica.

You said you were curious about my meals with Orson Welles, who of course, is a bit of a trencherman. The most memorable was at Ma Maison (the restaurant with the unlisted phone number out there in Glitzville). The two of us were accompanied by a beautiful Hungarian countess who left in either boredom or disgust halfway through the meal. You see, Mike, she was slender and could not comprehend our great, sad hearts choked as they are with fatty deposits. Orson began by clearing his palate with a half dozen bull shots in quick succession. As we were hungry the first course was a half pound of fresh caviar with an iced bottle of Stolichnaya. (Politics again! In Palm Beach two years ago a liquor store clerk refused to supply me Stolichnaya because of what the Russians were doing in Afghanistan. I explained to him that the residents of that sorry country of Afghanistan are Muslims and don't drink vodka. My account was such that I got my vodka.) The next course was a wonderful ragù of sweetbreads in pastry covered by a half quart of black truffle sauce, accompanied by a rare old Burgundy the name of which would mean nothing to the impoverished hippies who read your magazine. Then without a moment's rest arrived a whole poached Atlantic salmon in a sorrel sauce and a white Bordeaux. At this point the countess wrapped herself in her cape and spun into the night. Her departure enabled me to ask Orson how he managed to snag Rita Hayworth at the top of her form. He said he was in Rio at the time her picture appeared on the cover of *Life* magazine; he took the next plane to L.A. and literally browbeat her into the marriage bed within ten days. It seems, though, that romantically the great man's true weakness was for hatcheck girls.

To tell you the truth, I was beginning to lose some of my appetite at this point, my life at the time being submerged in a number of business and romantic failures. My spirits arose however when the next course arrived: an immense platter of slices of rare duck breasts in green peppercorn sauce accompanied by beautifully braised and sculpted root vegetables. With this, quite naturally, we had a very rare Romanée-Conti. I was astounded that Mr. Welles

had remembered from the day before over an ample lunch that this
was my favorite item, perfected by the great Paul Bocuse before
he submerged himself in the *cuisine minceur*, a method even more
fraudulent than psychiatry. This last course nearly put me under and
I looked down happily at the record of the meal left on my shirt-
front. I rejected the platter of desserts and rushed to the bathroom.
A certain unnamed actress had given me a vial of white powder,
which she told me I should use to keep awake. I know you can
vouch for the fact that I don't use drugs but this seemed an excep-
tional occasion. I poured the whole gram on my palm and snorted
heavily so that anyone coming in the bathroom might think I was
washing my face. I have no memory really about what we talked
about other than food and sex.

But back to food and politics. I won't drink Polish vodka because
of the long record of anti-Semitism in that country. I generally avoid
German restaurants for the same reason. So I am not without my politics, am I? I avoid the cooking of my motherland, Sweden, because
it is a land without garlic, a land without sunshine. I avoid Jewish
cooking because it is basically lousy. A certain tribe mentioned in
Lévi-Strauss's *The Savage Mind* eats bear shit for constipation not
political reasons. Perhaps when no one is looking Nancy Reagan licks
her new china. I do know that of all Mother Westwind's children,
the mammalian group, man alone cooks. Man alone is capable of
looking over a girl's shoulder while he fucks her at the coffee table
laden with fifteen appetizers. He stares into the blank eyes of the
Dungeness crab that will be transformed from a delicate sea creature
into a mere turd.

How can I answer any of the questions on your questionnaire? All of
my dooms are small dooms, the ones, to quote myself, "that seem to
lurk behind each fence post." Yet your questionnaire is not contemptible nor is my refusal Audenesque; all that fake liberalism warring
against the state when it's still the same fake liberal paying his taxes
and marching right along with the other civil servants. I barely ever

think of the government anymore even though a few years ago I paid taxes equaling the salaries of four senators. Why they took this money that could have been spent on food, wine, and floozies— exotic travel—beats me. As an instance of the banality of it all I read in this morning's paper that when confronted with this $100 billion deficit, Reagan told a cute joke about some Negro buying a bottle of vodka with food stamps. This, I think, indicates a constitutional hopelessness in leadership. Another instance I reflected on when I was in Central America: I wondered if there was a single legislator who was familiar in any deeper sense with the history of Latin America. I thought then—probably nope. But enough of this sententiousness. Don't you find it strange that the true symbol for God, the Buddhist circle, is also the exact shape of a dinner plate. Has this ever occurred to you? The all-knowing father-mother has made us machines of devouring and he has given us heads to figure out what we are going to eat next. Let's not be ignorant, in terms of mythography, that the sacrament of the Eucharist makes us all vampires. Yes, vampires by proxy. Mike, you should remember that within the unyielding anguish of the writer, it's always night and you're always flying solo, and then usually over the Mato Grosso.

Yes, Golden, I went without protein for four days . . . without any form of protein, eating rice and fruit like a Jain. Golden, even that name. Do you realize that if you could get $350 an ounce for your body you would be worth what Barry Manilow makes in one night at a concert? Anyway, I went without any protein for four days, I fell into a depressing trance, I could barely move, my head ached, I was depressed, of course, this the average third world experience. I dreamed of ham, western ham, northern ham, southern ham, not eastern ham. Redeye gravy, the sweet vinegar clove gravy, mashed potatoes, more ham, slabs of ham, juicy ham, dry ham, ham sandwiches, ham croquettes, ham on rye, hamburgers—anything. I wanted it, I wanted it with a desperation akin only to sexual desire. I wanted it like a fifteen-year-old farmboy in 1952 wanted Ava Gardner. All those big words of yours and your questionnaire are meaningless to me. Such polysyllabic words such as God and world are too much for me to handle at this late date. Do you not on your logo express the strange wisdom of the ages, both the Orient and the Occident, not to speak of the other regions by saying, "Zen bones, Zen bones, Zen hambones"?

THE DEAD FOOD SCROLLS

Dear Mike,
"Whither food?" you asked in a recent letter. That question set me to thinking. Food, you see, is something that is so obviously dead and that we have in large, large quantities. We don't, of course, bother bearing this deadness in mind because quite naturally you eat it, everybody eats it—dogs, cats, everything on earth. Everything that lives eats it. Certain things worry me though, certain thoughts— tonight I am in a white heat and all around me is snow, and I sit awake with my sleeping animals who always keep a weather eye half open in case I go to the refrigerator. I'm angry enough to turn over a car myself, something I did on a bet with a Model-A way back when my back was in good shape. Yes, I tipped over a Model-A by myself. What I'm trying to say tonight is there's nothing to eat, in fact my bank account is low, which is another source of anger. Mike, to be frank,

I feel myself on the verge of a change. Perhaps a great leap backward into a smaller size. All too frequently I find that women, when they say to me you're too big, they're not referring to my primal fundament but my overall body size! When I ask friends do you think I'm too big they say no, and use polite euphemisms such as burly, pulpy—not insulting words, just a shade short of grotesque. But certainly you, Mike, who live in New York, which is rife with such schemes, know there is nothing so boring as somebody else's self-improvement plan. The oddity here is that I am not trying to improve on anything. What I'm thinking is much more positive than the cheapness, the drabness of self-improvement plans. What I am thinking is what if a man just said to himself in the privacy of his haunted nights, I swear on Mom, the Lord, and everything holy, I'm only going to eat live food. Enough of this dead food that has been taxing my system and taxing my popularity with the opposite gender. I don't mean those sorts of decadent experiments of the Middle Ages when the French were given to eating a swan while it was still alive. They would cook a swan while it was still alive and start eating at it while it was still squawking. I don't mean torture, neither do I mean that I'm going to become one of those bliss-ninny grazers they call vegetarians. Mike, you probably think I'm setting you up for something here; I'm not, I am perfectly serious. Of course I know that a woman, Ms. Distaff as it were, is alive, and a woman's you-know-what is very much alive, but checking with my local optometrist, the only real medical man in the area (he's also gay), a woman's you-know-what is totally without nutritional value, unless you catch her right after she's spilled the bowl of soup in her lap.

Luckily for me the inception, the beginning of this experiment— and as the experiment unwinds I'll let you know—is that I'm going south to do a little hunting, after an onerous, secret project that I'm not at liberty to divulge to anyone of course. I'm going to Louisiana to hunt the fabled woodcock and I'm going to do some quail hunting in north Florida so I will be close to the Cedar Key oyster and the Bon Secours oyster. I will be interested to hear from any of your readers of any other live food that I can have. I love sushi but you know there is a point at which you really don't want to sink your teeth into a fish that's still flopping, and I'm not again talking about the greens that can be technically alive. I could go out and dig under two feet of snow and find some reasonably green parsley, rip it up, and stuff it in my mouth—that's not what I mean.

I'm a little worried that I've changed certain brain waves by not drinking enough alcohol which I've cut down on vastly. Mostly because I find the less I drink, the more I get to dream and dreaming (up here in the great white north where not a lot happens) gives you something interesting to do at night. Anyway, of late I've been strapping weights all over my body and dancing to reggae music for an hour a day to combat winter. I'm wondering if this isn't changing my brain in some ways because I used to eat beef and now I'm suddenly going for more pork products. I have a passion, which I've only been able to solve lately by going to Kentucky and eating ample quantities of pork skin and pit barbecue with a sauce so hot that every hair on my body including seven hairs on my chest is wet. So that might be a consideration. Then again I'm not going to take this live food thing too far if it endangers my health. For instance, I've agreed to do a project with the French actress Jeanne Moreau: the project is of course top secret as is everything I do. Anyway I was thinking of lying there on the forest floor in France with a trained pig; admittedly this would cost bucks. The minute the truffle is torn from the ground I will pop it in my mouth while it is still alive like a big black, pitch black, coal black, raw apple. It isn't that I've killed too much; I must say that I've enjoyed eating several hundred woodcock, quail, geese, and venison this fall. These animals are top-drawer nutrition-wise as they spend their lives in what your humble readers in New York would think a natural environment. There is nothing quite so natural as the big slab of deer liver fresh from the steaming cavity.

Incidentally, I sent McGuane Schweid's now famous book, at least it's famous in my own mind, *Hot Peppers*. I think, of course, it's superior in grace and beauty to any novels I've read coming out last

year. There is a beautiful meal enclosed in a new book by William
Least Heat-Moon: the book is called *Blue Highways*. Look for the
great meal in there.

    This reggae music might just be poisoning me. I looked for
Jamaica on the map to make sure I knew just where it was. But I
have a tendency to jig around in odd places when I shouldn't be
jigging around, like the lobby of the Carlyle Hotel, or at the Keeneland auction—the horse sale. At the horse sale which I attended
the top mare went for $3.8 million: think of socking that into a
wine cellar! As my cousin, Thurman, who is a block layer, says—a
house with an empty refrigerator is like a dildo without a battery.
It's pretty catchy. In other words, if your clothes are too tight, get
bigger clothes.

I fear this reggae is infecting everything I do now. Once Buffett
brought me a gallon of fresh shucked oysters and we went out to
have a few cold ones, put them in my studio fridge, and when we
got back I put them out on my desk next to some books—my books
looked so fragile compared to this great mass of fresh shucked oysters and, as if not knowing what I was doing, I thrust both hands
into this gallon of oysters and began to eat greedily, because I was
so dazed with grief at the time I knew this live food would help—
of course they weren't swimming because oysters don't swim—they
were moving counterclockwise at a rate which you didn't see them
directly, you just saw it out of the

*Try to explain eagerly to a
starving child that you just
gave up spending a couple
of hundred bucks a week on
cocaine; the starving child
sits there with those huge
eyes like a Keane painting
and whispers, "Congrats."*

corner of your eye. I wanted to congratulate you for quitting smoking but have you thought perhaps you quit smoking for the same
reason that you started smoking, another desperate ploy of the ego?

It's like trying to explain eagerly to a starving child that you just gave up spending a couple of hundred bucks a week on cocaine; the starving child sits there with those huge eyes like a Keane painting and whispers, "Congrats." I suppose with the same distance that a writer necessarily has from the world, I will always be a rather lonely detective of food, uncritical, an observer between meals . . . it's a job.

Addendum

Dear Folks,

I am back to eating dead food. In Florida I put a small live frog in my mouth but I could not swallow it. The same thing happened with a minnow. Perhaps, this whole concept of live food should remain just that, a concept. My next Dead Food Scroll will be about "the food of lust and violence."

I hope you are well, Mike. I have been dancing an hour each day not with a girl but with a heavy dumbbell in each hand. I am getting to be a very strong fat guy.

A Letter to the Editor

Dear Mike:

Hang on to Jim Harrison. Don't let that big fish off the hook. He's the best food editor in the US of A. He makes James Beard look sick. In fact any robust male makes James Beard looks sick. Keep Harrison at all costs. Spare no expense. Send him cases of Echezeaux, Romanée-Conti, Montrachet, Roederer Cristal. Spoil him. Pamper him. Give that glutton anything he wants. And watch your distribution soar. Before you know it Smoke Signals will be right up there with Family Circle and Good Housekeeping. He will make you golden, Mike.

Faithfully yours,
Sam Lawrence
Boston, Mass.

THE VIVID DIET

Dictated while mildly deranged by grief and hope

One wonders, doesn't one, why we are insufficiently wily in foreign affairs. Without question it is because we do not eat vividly. We are always being euchred out by people with superior diets with more interesting food, technically speaking of course. Mitterrand made mincemeat of Reagan in Europe mostly because of the kind of superior foods he eats. Let's face it Mitterrand drinks superior Bordeaux, Burgundy, eats garlic, truffles, goose livers, various forms of tripe, sweetbreads, intestines, jellied calves feet for midnight snacks. By contrast the sluggish Germans what do they eat or more importantly look at Reagan's diet, it's a nightmare, though he stops short of the ketchup and cottage cheese trip that Nixon had which isn't as bad as some people say it is, it's just not something you'd want to eat more than once in your life but Reagan's into a lot of bran flakes, very lean dryish turkey breasts, probably no garlic whatsoever, lean fish. So maybe we should start thinking about it.

I'm making this presumption that you want to live vividly. Everyone knows that D. H. Lawrence said that the only aristocracy is that of consciousness. Rather than shlep through life on this Reagan diet eat vividly. Or what does William Buckley eat? I understand his wife is a famous hostess. William Buckley shows signs of eating far too many club sandwiches. Anyone who can eat a quarter of a club sandwich without expiring from torpor is beyond me. Buckley no doubt has a food perversion, a food that perhaps his wife doesn't even know about. Something like Franco-American on toast or Kraft Instant Macaroni and Cheese. My daughter likes the latter and I've tasted it, and it's proper for a fourteen-year-old girl. Maybe Buckley secretly cheats because most of his philosophical viewpoints are formed by his efforts to justify being rich. Who cares if he's rich? If you want a philosophical justification of it you can't pull this white Christian trip because you'll never find a man in the history of mankind who was less impressed by the moola than Jesus. What is a diet of vividness but to live vividly, to see vividly, to write vividly, to make love vividly or as the French say it "to fricoter," which is a new French hip term.

We start at base with garlic. Without garlic forget it. Garlic should be bought in odd numbers. You should get one pound, three pounds, five pounds, seven pounds of garlic. Roast these heads like they do at Mustard's famous restaurant near Yountville, California. Use a little olive oil, fresh rosemary, thyme, beef stock. You cut the top off the garlic, a little flat spot on top so you can baste it. Eat several heads, as I have on numerous occasions. Just squish them out or go at them with an oyster fork. Drink a pint mug of Cabernet with this, anything less is cowardly and you won't be vivid. Nowhere in the United States that I have traveled with my band, Vince Van No Go and His Poor but Proud Crowd, have I seen people that live more vividly than in Cajun country. Of course much is being made of this diet but essentially what you get in New York is a very watered-down variety except Texarkana and the great chef Abe de la Houssaye.

Down there they're not afraid of your basic hot peppers. Go over to Nogales it's the same thing. The best menudo in the country can be gotten across from the Historical Museum in Nogales. They serve these wild little chiles. There are wild Sonora chiles on the side, freshly chopped cilantro, and there are nice fatty morsels of calves' feet in there with the tripe. It's just splendid. Myself and the grizzly expert, Douglas Peacock, go there.

How to eat vividly? Of late I have been following this diet because I decided I don't want to die. It's called *Eat to Win* by Doctor Bob Haas. Of course the question is win what? Now I don't recommend this as a vivid diet but the principles are correct—to reduce the amount of fat in your diet and simple carbs, and go for complex carbs and protein. Get the sludge out of your veins. I've been meaning to write Dr. Bob, who will be known henceforth as Bob, a comforting name. Bob being the most popular name in the United States, naturally there are some good Bobs and some bad Bobs but mostly indifferent Bobs, not to speak of the old-fashioned BeBob-a-re-Bob. I've been thinking of writing Bob about improving this diet because there are too many recipes in there that are torpid.

The best salt substitute, the only salt substitute that's adequate, is plenty of hot peppers. My grizzly man sent me a care package from Arizona of about thirty different kinds of ground and whole chiles. Other than the fact that the place is hot and stupid, why doesn't one live in Arizona where all these chiles are available? I don't know, I just love "here" and it's never occurred to me to move down there. My soul is drawn toward these Apaches and Hopis and Navajo. I watched the sacred Yaqui Deer Dance and had some snacks at this Yaqui Festival. Let me tell you these Indians aren't afraid of a little hot pepper. They adore them, they hang wreaths, strings, and medallions of peppers all over their little adobe huts. I've made wild rabbit tacos with plenty of hot peppers. You could actually make a giant burrito with a whole squirrel but I don't really care for squirrel. It reminds me of a really extravagantly premature baby.

Some of the key to this diet I might eventually publish along with a Frenchman and a Montana painter in a cookbook which is to be called *Sporting Food.* It's the kind of food that Balzac would eat without getting pissed off. It's not boring food. How am I going to stop such foods from killing me? Well I learned a secret in Brazil last winter and this secret had nothing to do with the extraordinarily cheap pharmaceuticals there. That threw me off my feet for a while, those softball-sized sacks did nobody any good. As it's known locally, that kind of snort is known as "bone-be-gone." If you want to turn your pecker cold as stone just keep it up, boys, keep it up. Down in Brazil I was at a churrascaria and their beef down there is grass fed so it's not full of fat, like ours. You'd see vast tonnages of meat roasting on wood fires and they would hack you

I don't really care for squirrel. It reminds me of a really extravagantly premature baby.

off what you want. They would wheel it around on carts that took several peasants to push. Along with these meats there were extraordinarily hot salsas. My favorite cut of meat was a little fatty. It was the hump of a zebu cattle, it's about the texture of a brisket but much more delicious. There is a marvelous racial mix in Brazil. I'm thinking this diet of rice and beans and fruit and vegetables and fish might be what gives these women on the beach bottoms that were designed by their ineluctably superior diet. Go to Brazil, it's quite inexpensive, skip any drugs because foreign jails are really dreary. And then there is the danger to any attractive male like myself. Go to Brazil, eat vividly. If you're a girl you'll be that thirteen-year-old staring up at that picture of James Dean or Monty Clift again, you'll have hot and cold flashes, you'll have gorgeous dreams, you'll yearn again, you'll yearn for life. Of course if you're a boy in Brazil you'll have a perpetual half-master, you'll be semi-choked up all the time, you'll regain your emotions.

I discovered that the Black Pope Tancred reconfirmed my feeling about the word seven. It's the only number there is, it's the magic number. To eat vividly I have a tendency to work in multiples of seven. If I'm stir-frying a little pork loin and fresh asparagus I have a tendency to put seven hot peppers and seven cloves of garlic in it. It just makes it a much more vivid little dish. Another vivid food that is much maligned in our country, but makes the most nutritionally sound meals, is black beans and rice (it's a given you can eat a salad with it) or you can make pinto beans and rice. In Mexico the athletic kids are so much stronger than the junk food puffballs that we are breeding up here. Beans and rice are vivid food. You can tell when you go into Cuban bars in Florida or Mexican bars or by listening to my favorite current rock group Los Lobos. That is beans and rice music. That is incredible music of the streets.

Some of the more odious seem to prefer the English rock. Give me a break. When England lost India and her superior diet, she went downhill in a handbasket. You can eat well in London of course but it is generally where there is Italian food. I had a foreign visitor who started to get depressed at being in New York a week with the expense account bungfodder that we eat in Gotham, so I made him a simple dish of fresh pasta with a sauce made out of a cacciatore of rabbit and pheasant and sausage. His energy was immediately restored. The repellent fact of life to anyone who likes to cook is that the domestic duck is full of fat because it is raised on Long Island along with other banalities and absurdities. That duck is appropriate for East Hampton, South Hampton, Sag Harbor. Once you get interested in a vivid diet, I don't mean these kind of yuppie nightmare foods, you get the farmer down the road and con him into raising you some Muscovy ducks if you don't want to do it yourself. Muscovy duck is a very lean, gorgeous duck that I roast just short of twenty-five minutes at a super heat in my forced-air oven. They are delicious when their flesh is a deep pink. A superb duck. Buy Muscovy.

Many of you stickball queens would be a lot better off if you put aside this stickball and bought yourself a shotgun and went into the forest every fall and shot yourself some healthy, meaty fowl. Buy a fishing pole, even now as I am dictating this in my auto I am heading back to my hidden cabin in the forest in the Upper Peninsula of Michigan, and my car is loaded with fishing tackle. I even like the less desirable species pike; I like perch, Lake Superior whitefish, lake trout, the small pinkish ones. There is no industry within a hundred fifty miles of my cabin but there is some acid rain up here but of course Reagan refuses to do anything about it because he thinks of it as some kind of a Grecian Formula. Somebody told him acid rain keeps you from growing gray hair. When I started writing the Dead Food Scrolls I didn't know where it would take me but I'm not able to eat meat as much as I used to. I like it but it makes me weird and vindictive for some reason. If you look deep into the eye of a rib eye steak you fully don't realize it's dead, but just leave it out in the sun for a hot afternoon. Then take a whiff.

Unfortunately some vivid food is sometimes expensive. Don't waste your time on the mediocre French restaurants in New York. Another revelation just hit me with the force of a breeze: why is it that waitresses are more sexually vivid than actresses or models? Easy, they work with food.

Another good number is thirty-three. Make a low cal béchamel into which you add thirty-three cloves of poached and pureed garlic, make mashed potatoes, fresh not instant, Bob. Stir this garlic béchamel into the potatoes, take a little barnyard chicken and stuff it with these potatoes, massage the chicken with Clancy's Fancy or your favorite hot pepper concoction and put it in a greased pan. I like to roast leeks, carrots, and little turnips with my chicken. I braise it on a rack, then you make a sauce with vastly reduced chicken stock to baste with. Roast it forty-nine minutes. You've got yourself a nice little breakfast or lunch. Dinner should be more ample. This will serve one mature adult or two semi-matured adults. Some of you may have noticed that my food columns have lightened up a bit—that's because I don't want to leave behind the legacy of gluttony. Now surely you have the good sense, as I only infrequently do, to eat rather lightly and naturally most of the time. I know it's boring but we don't have a choice. I missed the greatest party of the year where we roasted a pig and a half steer and some barons of beef, I missed it because I was in bed with a vastly red and inflated toe—gout had struck—I had earned that gout but I was ashamed of it and what's more I couldn't go to the party because I couldn't walk. I tried to get there by taking a few Percodan but that didn't touch this pain. The rule of thumb is "moderate to excess." My favorite way of frying potatoes is in goose fat but let's face it, you can't do that all the time. At the dinner table my dad used to tell all us kids that all around the pig's ass is pork. I'm still not sure what that meant but it owns a certain poignancy and urgency to me now.

Let me tell you a little story, almost a Paul Harvey anecdote about how cooking saved seven lives, from when I first started touring with my band Vince Van No Go and His Poor but Proud Crowd. We started out the way every great band did. We played Tastee-Freeze openings, special used car sale days, commemorations at rural airports where they only have one airplane, 4-H club dances in Kansas; we had an elaborate camper and we were so broke that to keep these guys from snorting potato chips I started cooking for them along the road. Sometimes we'd stop to buy a pig or a lamb from a farmer. We'd stop by slaughterhouses. We'd take along a bushel of garlic and the only wine we could afford was Gallo. Those guys were a sorry bunch of tropical dropouts. I put them on this elaborate vitamin-mineral program and vivid food. They all had an average forty-to-fifty-pound weight gain and they all live very happily married and divorced today. They all regained their sexual vigor. They became husky, brawling lads. I don't like to see them anymore because like all musicians on the skids their sole profession is to try and borrow money. They'd all be out there with Hendrix and Joplin if they hadn't started *Eat to Win*.

I recognize of course that President Reagan should eat my menudo in order to regain the foreign affairs advantage. At the very least he could go back to his Musso & Frank's Diet of 1948 where he wasn't scared of a few harmless nitrates. Where he wasn't afraid of some good solid corn fat in his beef, where the oysters were plentiful and garlic abounded. I'm waiting for the leader of a prominent country to have the guts to wear a necklace of garlic bulbs like Don Ho wears his flowery lei. That leader will show the potentiality of being the true king of the world. If you figure that you like all other human beings spend most of your time rehearsing your irritations then what a pleasure it is to spend a couple hours a day eating vivid foods. My next installment will deal with a critical problem, we'll leap into a more interesting cosmos—that is the food of sexuality. The first chapter will be called The Oysters of the Gods. Where to find them and how to prepare them and their direct effect on the genitalia, male or female. This is not what they call sexist. Male and female alike need fundaments fine-tuned by good nutrition.

The rule of thumb is "moderate to excess."

Even while I dictate this to the daughter (a veggie) of a Jersey meat packer, I pour a tankard of Bardolino and tend the fresh rainbow trout grilling over a wood fire. The trout is stuffed with wild leeks, basted with vermouth and butter. Wild leeks provide the creatures of the forest, Mother Westwind's children, with the spirit of garlic. As a grade school tyke I was sent home from school for eating wild leeks at recess and stinking up the classrooms.

FATHER-IN-LAW

Throughout literature (and lower forms of entertainment) the Father of the Bride is an object of just ridicule, a ditherer with a hopefully ample wallet sweating on the sidelines while people actually competent in such matters orchestrate the wedding.

I recently proved to be no exception whatsoever during the marriage of my younger daughter, Anna, in Livingston, Montana. I had no part in any of the central decisions that made the several-day party implacably smooth except in the area of food and wine, and even in the matter of food I deferred somewhat to my older daughter, Jamie, now a novelist, but formerly an employee of

Whenever life begins to crush me I know I can rely on Bandol, garlic, and Mozart. This pleasure in geologic time is no more evanescent than life herself.

Dean & DeLuca in New York City. I was mostly the not very tiny voice yelling "more" and more we had including crab and shrimp from Charles Morgan's company in Destin, Florida, bread and cheeses from Zingerman's in Ann Arbor, Michigan, including Grafton cheddar, Comté, Papillon Roquefort, triple crème l'Explorateur, Vermont mountain cheese, Stilton, also roasted Italian olives. I almost forgot Dunn's Irish salmon, and patés including splendid wild mushroom loaf. I also almost forgot the oysters and the actually *prime* Delmonico roasts, the Norwegian poached salmon, the two hundred pieces of duck confit made by the chef Mark Glass. There were about a hundred in for dinner and another fifty came along later.

Somehow they drank nineteen cases of wine, not to speak of eating all the food. Years ago while cooking beef ribs at his house Jack Nicholson told me that "only in the Midwest is overeating still considered an act of heroism." We'll have to throw in Montana, too. Of course drinking a lot is *de rigueur* at weddings except in the dourest confines of yuppiedom.

Since it was my sole delegated responsibility I gave the wine my full, somewhat manic, attention, testing twenty or so Côtes du Rhône over a year's time in case lots, before settling on a Sablet blanc and Bandol for the red. I'm very good at this sort of testing compared to my miserable college years; my pratfalls are in the arenas of the novel and moviemaking. The Sablet is quite wonderful though I drink very little white wine. The Bandol decision was easy as I had been drinking and serving it for years. I rather like this sturdy, suggestive red with everything, and often with nothing at all. It invariably has made me happy, recalling as it does the primal flavors of sun and earth, rather than lightbulbs and supermarkets. It is also affordable if you can withstand the usual nagging of your accountant. Whenever life begins to crush me I know I can rely on Bandol, garlic, and Mozart. It will also be served in vast quantities at my funeral. This opinion was obviously shared by those at the wedding, the legion of the hollow legged. I salute the Domaine Tempier. This pleasure in geologic time is no more evanescent than life herself.

WINE NOTES

Much about wine is problematic and open to nearly infinite con-jecture. For instance, what is the sex of wine, and are we falling into a sump when we consider the question, a trap of silliness that professional wine tasters so easily fall into? Wine tasting is susceptible to parody, but so are other professions of great intrinsic value, from mad scientists to virtuous strippers to pure-hearted politicians.

But then it is always good to question the terminology of our enthusiasms. We can say that wine is essentially female because it comes from the earth and we don't say "father earth." The best things are female, including females, and allowing this characterization energizes our imaginations in ways not possible to other terminology. Blatant, loudmouthed, bad wines are, of course, male.

There's a lot of tannin in the river beside my cabin, emerging as it does from a swamp. I've also visited a friend while he was, unfortunately, tanning the hide of an otter. I taste tannin in many vintages, especially American, but it's no big deal if it is slight. Wines that have never seen an oak barrel are occasionally called "oaky" but why quarrel about this? From my childhood onward up in the country I have picked wild raspberries, blackberries, blueberries, and other berries, but I must say I do not find these unique flavors in wine, though many apparently do. My perhaps naive honesty prevents me from using these terms that would lie to my taste.

Our sensual memories are so vast, why shouldn't we use the entire reservoir when we describe our affection or dislike for a wine? Sometimes our American tasters seem to be ascetically as serious as Cotton Mather when he "barbecued" Indians. There is black and white and the multifoliate variances of gray but an alarming lack of color, reminding me of the cartoons in French publications poking fun at American wine snobs. But how often have I tasted wines in France with a fine platter of charcuterie on a table or perched on a barrel before us, with joyous badinage, laughter, with no sense that we were deciding the fate of nations.

There is a definite possibility, and I say this with my usual modesty, that what I am saying is totally wrongheaded. My notes on Corsican wines that I tasted could not be published without being bowdlerized. Maybe a wine shouldn't be allowed to remind me of "the thighs of a rich girl depleted by lassitude," one of the tamer descriptions. Conversely we can say jug wines tend to be loutish, abrupt, faintly soiled, evoking memories of the locker room after a football game on a warm September evening. That sort of thing. Bad properly evokes bad.

I recently meditated over a mixed case of three Gigondas, a difficult assignment for a peculiar reason. I have drunk more Gigondas than any French wine except Domaine Tempier Bandol. This kind of familiarity often makes us poor critics of wives, lovers, or longtime friends. A poet friend, Ted Kooser, described the end of his first marriage beginning with the line, "Neither of us would clean the aquarium."

With wine we are back in college wondering if our professor corrected our brilliant essay before or after dinner, before or after he got laid, before or after his usual fantasy about Ava Gardner in the pool house. My main objection to numerical rating of wine is that it presumes the falsest of sciences.

I've spent a goodly amount of time with Jeanne Moreau, the French actress, and the Cayron reminds me of Moreau at age twenty-eight, mildly irritated at you for forgetting flowers, but surpassingly agreeable when you share a bottle of Cayron.

That said, I thought a bottle of Château du Trignon 1999 was soft but a little weak, a boy who would never do a chin-up because he was lazy. The second bottle, however, was drunk with a snack, a freshly sautéed wild brown trout on a bed of sliced tomatoes from my daughter's garden. This made the Trignon quite acceptable in a not very compromised way. Fine with bold food, not alone.

With Domaine de Cayron 1999 we enter another arena. I have drunk a hundred bottles of Cayron Gigondas. It is a nostrum for blues and fatigue in Paris or anywhere. I've spent a goodly amount of time with Jeanne Moreau, the French actress, and the Cayron reminds me of Moreau at age twenty-eight, mildly irritated at you for forgetting flowers, but surpassingly agreeable when you share a bottle of Cayron. If you drank it before the usual obnoxious meeting you wouldn't hate anyone. Last week I drank it at my cabin with two roasted woodcock for lunch and they married pleasantly. The flavor penetrated my rib cage.

The Domaine Les Pallières 1999 threw me off a bit as I had learned to expect more from past experience. There was a sense of the androgynous rather than a decisive move in either direction, and it was rather flattish compared to the Cayron. Of course why tell a reasonably good poet that he's not Lorca or Auden, for that matter? At a dinner two of the company preferred the Pallières to the Cayron. There are no gods to direct us in this matter, but we must do our best without pretending we are Solomon, much less Moses.

Is Winemaking an Art?

Is winemaking an art? Is writing an art for that matter? It can be but rarely is. A discipline or craft is closer to the work in 99.99 percent of the practice and practitioners in either wine or writing. Nothing is more evanescent than the ancient aesthetic tests of range, durability, resonance, the stark requisites of beauty.

Some of us are waiting for a future puff piece called "The Hundred Best Wines of South Dakota," but then how can you blame a mid-range geezer with discretionary capital who may have exhausted his interest in golf, adultery, or fishing and hunting for waking up one spring morning and saying to his wife, "Ethel, I think I'll plant some grapes." (He may even think you plant ripe grapes at this stage.) It's an ancient urge. On a more basic level in many rural areas I've lived in or visited I've been asked to taste some bumpkin's apple, strawberry, cherry, or rhubarb wine. This is frankly not a pleasant experience. You're standing in the parlor and there's no place to spit. At least when you move up the economic food chain you are dealing with varieties of grapes.

In America there's always been a touching effort to democratize the arts. As humans we are seemingly genetically immodest. We are always trying to discover our hidden and miraculous potential. A young lout like I once was reads a Shakespeare or Keats poem and says, "I'm going to write me a poem just like that." A mogul with an especially fat wallet tastes a Cheval Blanc, a Clos de la Roche, a Romanée-Conti, or even a Côte-Rôtie, or Heitz Martha's Vineyard, and says to himself, "I can do this."

Only he can't. He'll probably forever bear the same relationship to fine wine as a publisher does to fine writing. If he produces a passable wine, assuming he owns good earth, he'll attend award ceremonies but everyone there will know that someone less well tailored on the back row has put the "juice" together, as it were. There is nothing so irascibly difficult as making a truly fine wine, given a thousand unpredictable variables. Just watching the weather would be like three months of labor pains.

There's also the question of why anyone who knows publishing, or the art, food, or wine world for that matter, would wish to be an "artist." At best it's a calling that happens when you're young. And so often in winemaking the calling is hereditary. You might during a pleasant evening tasting the ten best wines of the world wish to call the man most directly responsible for each an "artist," but if I were him I'd rather be called a "fine winemaker." In an age when every third athlete is called "great" what do we have left for the Sistine Chapel or Dostoevsky? There is no more uneven ground than the field of the arts.

There are marvelous semi-comic aspects to the problem. Wine magazines and the wine press in general offer tip sheets like those you buy when entering the grounds of Aqueduct, Churchill Downs, or Santa Anita. Many of us stay removed other than at a nominal level from wine pundits because we wish to make our own discoveries, draw our own conclusions. The furthest thing from my own aesthetic

judgments is the world of numbers, let alone price. I am admittedly
an outsider, a mere consumer, but wine simply can't be graded like
a teacher grades term papers. In writing, Ezra Pound advised against
giving credence to someone who hadn't produced a notable work. If
there was a system that directly involved the hundred best winemak-
ers in the world I would subscribe, but these men are far too busy.
Meanwhile I see hot new California wines highly touted that remind
me of Rose Bowl floats that are garish and silly and doomed to last
no longer than their plucked roses.

Is winemaking an art? Maybe for a few, and their identities are
somewhat concealed except to a few. The apprenticeship requires the
entire life. You often have to wait twenty years or more beyond the
publication or release date to have any idea if art has been "committed" despite the immediate reviews. Ultimately you are working in a
medium that is rarely understood beyond the immediate sensation
of pleasure. Like a fine chef's your work reaches fruition only when
it disappears into someone's mouth.

My Problems with
White Wine

May we politicize wine? I will if I wish. This is a free country though
it is quickly becoming less so. I have noted, for instance, that the Bay
Area has become fatally infected with the disease of sincerity. Early last
December in San Francisco I naively looked for a bar where I might
enjoy a glass of wine and a cigarette. Instead I sat in the park across from
the Huntington Hotel without wine, smoking an American Spirit and
welcoming the frowns of a passel of dweebs doing tai chi. They birdlike
lifted their legs as if afflicted with farting fits. When I lived briefly in
San Francisco in 1958 it was an active seaport full of jubilance, music,
merriment, and heartiness. The morning I left town on my recent trip
I heard of the local campaign against the evils of butter.

All of which is to say that you can't talk about wine without
the context in which it exists, like life herself. Even in non-Marxian

economic terms it is far more difficult to find a favorable white wine
at a decent price than a red. Is it partly because the aforementioned
sincere people who drink only white wine have driven the price up
or because they are dumb enough to drink any swill if it doesn't own
life's most vital color, the color of our blood?

We certainly don't celebrate the Eucharist with white wine.
Christ couldn't have spent forty days in the wilderness alone fueled
by white blood. The great north from which I emerge demands a
sanguine liquid. White snow calls out for red wine, not the white
spritzers of lisping socialites, the same people who shun chicken
thighs in favor of characterless breasts and ban smoking in taverns.
In these woeful days it is easy indeed to become fatigued with white
people, white houses, white rental cars.

This said, let's be fair. The heart still cries out for a truly drinkable white under twenty bucks. I've tried dozens and dozens. I need
white wine when I eat fish and shellfish. Of late several have been
acceptable if not noteworthy: Château de Lascaux, Reuilly, a Les
Carrons Pouilly Fuissé, and an Ermitage du Pic St. Loup kept me
alive until I could get at my main course and a restorative red.

Whenever I have wine or food problems I consult Mario Batali
in New York, or Gérard Oberlé in Burgundy, France, but my most
reliable trump card is Peter Lewis in Seattle, whom I consider to have
the most wide-ranging and educated palate in North America. In
recent correspondence Lewis said common "white wines tend to the
flaccid. The 'international style' in which they're made these days
emphasizes the exotic: the overly floral, tropical phenolic profile
coupled to heavy-handed oak treatment strips the fruit of its delicacy;
whereas the truly exotic, as in Viognier from Chateau Grillet or Lys
de Volan, combines true power with all the femininity of peach fuzz
and honeysuckle (the seductive quality of the minute hairs on the
back of a woman's thigh in high summer)." There!

But isn't life a struggle to gather the funds to cover one's vices? For
thirty years since I first had a glass I've had an affection for Meursault,
even lesser vintages than those of Henri Boillot. I've drunk Meursault
when the weather was a tad chilly, say in the early spring with a simple

sauté of sweetbreads, fresh morels, and a few wild leeks. To be sure my single eye flickers to the red sitting on the sideboard in readiness for the substantial main course. I wouldn't drink the Meursault alone unless it was over ninety degrees and I was sitting with a French vixen in a shaded courtyard in Beaune and she demanded the wine. Any fool except maybe a congressman loves Chassagne-Montrachet. I could drink three bottles of Didier Dagueneau's Sauvignon Blanc with a gross of oysters in Cancale if there were an available bed three feet away for my nap. The bed would be on a pier and the great French singer Esther Lammandier would croon a medieval ditty.

I see that women and food rather than government can help me abolish my prejudices, also an extremely fat wallet. Once before giving a poetry reading I was handed a glass of cheapish Californian Chardonnay and I said, "This might be good on pancakes if you were in the wilderness." I actually chewed on the tip of a cigar to cleanse my mouth.

I admit I love Domaine Tempier rosé, which is about twenty-five dollars, and find Château La Roque rosé at twelve dollars a more acceptable deal in this twilit world of color and flavor compromise. I drink the latter because my wife and daughters drink it so it's right there within reach, an important qualification. I just recalled that on a warmish day last year I also like Côtes du Rhône blanc from Sang des Cailloux with barbecued rabbit (a basting sauce of butter, garlic, lemon, tarragon, and dry vermouth).

White wine is Apollonian, the wine of polite and dulcet discourse, frippish gossip, banal phone calls, Aunt Ethel's quiche, a wine for those busy discussing closure, healing, the role of the caretaker, the evils of butter, the wine of the sincerity monoethic. It occasionally, of course, rises to greatness, and you may have some if you've been economically diligent or are an heir of some sort. I'm sure that even the cheaper varieties have brought thousands of soccer moms sanity-healing sex fantasies.

We drink wine with our entire beings, not just our mouths and gullets. Temperaments vary. My mother used to torture me with the question, "What if everyone were like you?" I have it on good authority that both Dionysus and Beethoven drank only red wine while Bill Gates and a hundred thousand proctologists stick to the white. Peter Lewis added in a letter that we're not crazy about white wine because we don't get crazy after drinking it, because we tend not to break into song or quote García Lorca after drinking it, because white wine doesn't make us laugh loudly, because it fatigues us and doesn't promote unbridled lust, because it pairs less well with the beloved roasted game birds whose organs we love to suck and whose bones we love to gnaw.

Yes, we're fortunate that everyone isn't like me. I recall Faulkner saying, "Between scotch and nothing I'll take scotch." Meursault isn't the color of blood but it's the color of sunlight, a large item in itself.

EAT OR DIE

I have been enraged of late. At first I thought of it as only the slowly rising fetor of the holidays, preceded by a longish book tour of two months that began in France and ended in Mississippi. Book tours promote a ghastly self-absorption, a set of emotions inimical to art. Also an excess of deference, so that you're startled when you finally return home and your dogs, cats, and wife exhibit a graceful disinterest in you.

And maybe the rage is because I wrote many poems in the summer, and when I boarded the first flight of the tour the muse fled on another flight with her usual suitcase of sexual aids. Since October I've only managed a simple tercet:

> *The old couple coughed and coughed.*
> *The old couple coughed and coughed,*
> *Then hit each other with wrinkled fists.*

Catchy, isn't it? And maybe the rage comes from the fact that our body politic in the United States has been fed by Chef Bush a fresh skunk hacked up with an ax and served with no sauce except the creature's own verminish exudates. The social services departments in nearly every county in every state in this country offer courses in anger management, often obligatory for certain louts given to public mayhem. It's been suggested I enroll. I have too few teeth left to gamble on any more fistfights. I recall that my grandfather Arthur had his last major fistfight at my current age, sixty-five, and then avoided further fights by dying. Memory can be a warning. He was also a good cook.

Actually, a few days before Christmas I received my first clue on how to deal with my current brain disease. The clue came in the form of three fresh truffles brought along by a friend, David Sanfield, who is a chef and caterer in Los Angeles. He also packed along the usual banal beluga, some French cheeses, and two capons that had admirably fulfilled their destiny by having been de-nutted.

David arrived in the evening and we ate the caviar before a simple green chile stew, a good restorative for a traveler. The combination of pork, hot chilis, and a head of garlic illustrates once again that peasant food can return errant fops to earth.

Before bedtime and after several bottles of Domaine Tempier Bandol, we shaved a goodly portion of truffle into a bowl with nine beaten eggs for breakfast. This makes for good scrambled eggs, after which a walk is in order, and then suddenly lunch looms and perhaps a thimble of wine.

Courage is needed to prepare the coming dinner, *poularde demi-deuil*, wherein dozens of paper-thin slices of black truffle are slid under the skins of the fowl (thus the bird is in half-mourning). This is my favorite peasant food. The more truffle, the better the dish, right up until the fowl has an ebony hue.

*　　*　　*

My late mother, a Swede of iron temperament, liked to tell me to count my blessings when none were apparent. Do little things really mean a lot, as the song insists? I had obviously been living too high in my mind, which Jung suggested was a source of anger and depression. I needed to lower my sights to the nose level of the refrigerator. Gifts had arrived, including guanciale, pancetta, and salami sent by my friend Mario Batali in New York City; also a cooler of triggerfish, grouper, and shrimp from Charles Morgan in Destin, Florida; and cases of wine from Kermit Lynch in Berkeley, California.

Guanciale, which is made from the inner, meatier part of pork jowls, will bring you back to earth. My son-in-law, with a little help from me, made some last fall, but ours wasn't of the sublimity of Mario's. You cover these cheeks in salt and herbs for two weeks, then hang them in a cool place to cure. As with pancetta, you chop or julienne a goodly portion to begin certain hearty pasta sauces. The earthen flavor lifts the heart and mind well above the bad taste left by current politics and publishing, the sheer noise of pundit logorrhea, the deluge of rhinestones presented as crown jewels. Pork products are not hothouse flowers. Years ago in France, Gérard Oberlé, the famed Burgundian gourmand, made me a fifteenth-century recipe that required fifty pig noses, which, of course, had to be special-ordered. How else would I have been short-listed for the Prix de Gros Ventres in France?

I recall that my grandfather Arthur had his last major fist fight at my current age, sixty-five, and then avoided further fights by dying. Memory can be a warning. He was also a good cook.

Most artists understand the weeks just before the winter solstice are a dangerous time, rife with alcohol, suicide, and brooding until the elbows virtually grow into the worktable. Wise artists learn that the darkness that surrounds us can be dispelled by body pleasures. I eat well to avoid suicide, and now in mid-January my anger is largely dispelled, though Bush is still bushy and I'll never get a solstice parade in New York. Anger can still make momentary visits. Last night, after a fine dinner of oxtail cannelloni at the Cafe Sonoita, I discovered we had locked ourselves out of the house and our hidden key had slipped down the crack between two timbers. My wife went out front and sat in the moonlight and listened to the creek while I picked up an ax and freed the key, though not with the ax Bush used to kill the skunk he's feeding us.

Now I'm serene as Gandhi after he had one of his magnums of Lynch-Bages. It occurred to me I might help others with emotional problems in my new position as food editor of *Brick*. Serious suggestions are welcome—and I don't mean curing lust by soaking your parts in ice-cold pineapple juice, an old Hawaiian nostrum. When the Chinese have fatigued tendons, they eat stewed tendons. Is it really that simple? In Wawa, Ontario, I once had a fried pork liver and onion sandwich that did nothing in particular, which illustrates that there are dead ends in this matter.

PARIS REBELLION

During these times, many of us would have been far happier as trout making occasional little jumps up above the water's surface for the view of the carnage. Has my country become a pack of wild hogs bent on eating the world? Tune in to the end of this column. Certain members of my family, in the midst of the usual Nordic emotional squalor, used to say, "It's always darkest before it gets darker."

I recently drove from Montana to my cabin in the Upper Peninsula of Michigan on Route 2. The road is so pleasant I returned the same way. During the entirety of the five days of driving, I was able to get CBC on the radio and became quite concerned with what our media calls "our northern neighbor"—our media, those desperate schoolmarms of banality. CBC is a great deal more pungent than our own National Public Radio. It was fun to be transformed into an "alarmed citizen" of another country. I became angry at Canada's

own lust for conquest when I heard of MP Peter Goldring's plan to
annex the Turks and Caicos. CBC then segued to the difficulties in
the beef industry, the embargo being an obvious vengeance move
by the Bush cronies for Canada's refusal to join the party in Iraq.
Having recently read *Slaughterhouse Blues: The Meat and Poultry
Industry in North America* by Stull, Schlosser, and Broadway, I found
it hard to warm to the problems of the cattle raisers, though in truth
the middlemen—processors and retailers—are the central malefac-
tors. Ranchers are much like writers who are told to feel fortunate
when they receive 10 percent of the gross for their efforts. All in
all, though, I wondered if I should have joined in the singing of "O
Canada" at a garden party at Margot Kidder's on Canada Day evening
in Livingston, Montana. I actually mouthed the words, not having
a singing voice, rather owning one that resembles shoveling coal.
Rosie Schuster seemed to have forgotten her own national anthem,
doubtless an alcohol-related glitch or a politically related stance.

   It is understandable indeed to drink the wine of forgetfulness.
I'm somewhat of an expert in this area. How can one combat the
feeling of helplessness in being mere photons within the berserk fate
of nations? Some of us were not willing to accept that the French,
Germans, and Canadians were collectively less intelligent than Tex-
ans. Often my rebellious nature is reduced to smoking in nonsmoking
motel rooms, but recent events fueled my rage, which is that of a
forest fire—and they are always described as "raging."

   So in May I took myself and my wallet to France in protest
over being told by the media and government that I shouldn't drink
French wine. I wanted to encounter these "cheese-eating surrender
monkeys" at close hand, though in truth I've made at least twenty
trips to France and this one had the unpleasantness of a book tour.

   But France! How I love even its occasionally caustic nastiness.
At de Gaulle I wilt in relief to be temporarily out of the Holy Roman
Empire (even Jesus has lately become an oil guy), though some of
the wilting might be ascribed to the nice wines I drank en route on
Air France. Due to the acutest claustrophobia, I have to sit up front.
Many years ago when I sat in back, the sweat of my animal fears

soaked through my new clothes. It is hellish to be a sensitive poet with partly canine genes.

To keep my rebellion aggressively fresh, I walked over to the lavish Bon Marché food court, luckily a scant block from my hotel, where I bought a smallish picnic brunch of several cheeses, a slab of foie gras, bread, and a couple of bottles of Gigondas, nothing fancy, though at the checkout line I trotted back for several varieties of herring to be safe. These picnics are a habit, and I have to eat everything because my room has no refrigerator. The wine will keep a couple of hours but not much longer. Because forests and greenswards are in short supply in Paris, I have my picnics in my room overlooking the garden of the Hôtel Matignon, where I watch birds cavort and also politicians doing extremely low-impact exercises. Michel Braudeau, the editor of *La Nouvelle Revue Française*, once told me that "it is unthinkable not to have a decent lunch," but then I'm booked for seventeen dinners in a row, and I can no longer be absolutely free with my tummy twice a day. For a change I only drank one of the bottles of Gigondas before my après-flight nap. I very much wanted to say, "Give me freedom or give me death" while I drank the wine, but I'm superstitious enough not to taunt the gods who manage such things.

An attractive aspect of Paris is the freedom of the press. I've been told the press isn't as free as it seems, but if you consider the many cities in America that have been reduced to a single newspaper that may not wish to quote you exactly, it is wonderful to shoot off your mouth without regard for propriety. For instance, years ago in Chicago I was asked for my feelings about the recent death of Nixon and I said that a wooden stake should be driven through his heart to make sure. The newspaper refused to quote this! In Paris, however, when I said that as a gourmand, I couldn't be a politician because they regularly shit out of their mouths and that would taint my dining experiences, the newspaper quoted me in full.

You safe souls in a neutral country might wonder what it's like to lead this life of foreign intrigue, fraught with danger and the tension of walking into the Select or Montparnasse and boldly ordering "un verre de Brouilly." To work up an appetite, I walk relentlessly, picking out a pert bottom to follow though these young ladies walk so fast it's a real workout. Soon enough, though, my thoughts naturally turn to *jambon persillé*.

Frequently in Paris I dine at L'Assiette on rue du Château. Alain Senderens of Lucas Carton is often there, and Catherine Deneuve, unlike her American counterparts, may be eating heartily in a corner. Years ago I took an actress-model to dinner in New York City, and she ate only a single oyster and a single shrimp on a paltry bed of arugula. Her meal cost me forty-two bucks, an unlucky number, and she put ice in her Meursault. On this current imperiled trip, I had fresh hand-caught turbot two evenings in a row with a group of wine-drinking French leftists. I always have a secret side dish of potatoes Parmentier in which is hidden a large artisanal *boudin noir*. As a chain-smoking heavy wine drinker, I am not concerned with such trifles as *vache folle* (mad cow disease). In Burgundy, for instance, my breakfasts always include five different kinds of *fromage de tête* from the butcher shop of M. Dussert in Arleuf. A glass or two of Collioure or Domaine Tempier Bandol defends my body from viral intruders.

Two and a half weeks in France went swiftly, with my third eye ever alert (I actually have only one) and trained from my time as a private detective in Key West. I admit most of those who followed me merely wanted a book autograph, but then there seemed to me an uncommon number of men in their thirties in butch haircuts and wearing Haspel drip-dry suits, a virtual CIA uniform.

Unlike life herself the best came last. After an exhausting time at the Palace Hotel in Lausanne (Bush himself was at a meeting at the far end of Lac Léman but chances are he wasn't following me) where I had a wonderful goat stew (*cabri*) with hot peppers, I went to Burgundy for a few days of restful serious eating. In Burgundy I stay with my friends Gérard Oberlé and Gilles Brézol, who are renowned left-wing trenchermen. They also have twenty-five thousand books in their manoir so that I have something to read. More important, they are close friends of Marc Meneau, who owns L'Espérance in Vézelay, my favorite restaurant in France. Marc had planned a special lunch to help us recover from the collective brutality of life in our time.

Such a meal requires a lengthy period at the table and this one took six hours during which all world problems were gracefully resolved. My French is poor, which enabled me to eat more than the others. Marc had butchered a little *cul noir*, a local black-assed piglet, which set a theme for the lunch. We began with some *amusettes: choux au boudin noir jus de pomme, melon en gelée à l'anis, oreille de porc braisée aux fèves.* Everyone seems to understand that eating pigs' ears restores morale. We drank a Bourgogne Vézelay La Vigne Blanche bottled by Meneau, also a Sancerre Le Chêne Marchand 1990 by Lucien Crochet.

Now it was time to get serious. Next came *gelée d'homard aux filets de sole en chaud froid et petits pois,* after which there was *tête de porc cul noir à la broche vol-au-vent aux pieds de porc et herbes du jardin.* I began to flag a bit but Didier Dagueneau's Pouilly-Fumé Silex restored me, along with a Château Montrose Grand Cru Classé de Saint-Estèphe 1986. Marc knew I was missing morel mushroom season back home, so was kind enough to prepare a *paume de ris de veau rôtie aux morilles galette de pomme de terre au jus de morille.* I ruined an eight-dollar shirt when I punctured the faux potato, and morel juice squirted out with enormous force. I slowed down with the many desserts and cheeses, taking a thirty-yard walk in the garden. I recall that there was a three-year-old cantal made from the milk of cows with lyre-shaped horns (poetry!), two more wines, and a goblet of ancient Calvados. When we got back to the manoir in the twilight, we decided against preparing any supper.

I promised at the outset of this column to tell you what the United States is going to do. It turns out it's too expensive for us to eat the whole world. The total check for the Iraq war and restoration will be six hundred billion dollars. If only this much money had been spent on French wines for our entire populace, there never would have been a war, only well-oiled diplomacy.

ODIOUS COMPARISONS

While deeply embedded in Paris I awoke from a strenuous post-lunch nap and wondered if we humans had a more than nominal connection to the universe. It was as if the gods had decided to burn a giant question mark on my mental lawn. "Wherefore art thou, Jimmy?" I asked myself. Modern man is always at the crossroads when he should be doing something sensible like floating in a boat on a river. The Seine just down the street didn't present an immediate possibility so I had a hasty cup of coffee and turned to the alternative that God has always led me to in a lifetime of bitter conundrums. Wine. Yes, gentle reader, wine. When troubled, just have a glass of wine. The truest thing Ernest Hemingway ever said was "Good is what you feel good after."

However, a large step away from the delicious world of sensation is the world of criticism. Whether you are drinking wine or reading a book, quizzical man who has no particular idea why he is alive will ask himself if the wine he is drinking or the book he is reading is any good. Here I must present my trump card rather than waiting for the questionable timing of conclusions. I recently read a fine book by Lawrence Osborne, *The Accidental Connoisseur: An Irreverent Journey Through the Wine World*, wherein he quotes the *garagiste* Pierre Siri as saying, "You can't really describe wine, you can only remember it," to which I would add, you can't really describe literature, you can only experience it.

Now we are within the desperately familiar arena of human limitations. I recall that one night in Key West I read Knut Hamsun's novella *Victoria* in a single sitting and actually sobbed when I put the slender volume down. The first glass of a truly great wine can be as vivid and palpable as sex and, in truth, quite as indescribable unless you wish to resort to "We fell back on great waves of nothingness."

The existence of much wine and literary criticism seems to presume a stringent orthodoxy, the possibility that there is a perfect scorecard on which one may rate literature or wine, or weigh them on one of those precise gram scales so favored by cocaine dealers in the distant past. This bespeaks the immodesty of the critic, or the reductive capabilities of anyone who shrinks the world to fit into the briefcase of his wobbly ego.

Of course, one occasionally reads a literary or wine critic whose taste or palate is generally admirable. As I've often said, Ezra Pound limited his trust to anyone who had created a notable work. Perhaps this is a tad mean-minded. In literature in our time we've had Edmund Wilson, Randall Jarrell, and more recently George Steiner who sense an unnerving level of pomposity. I'm just the farmer, not the middleman or retailer. As the author of twenty-five books or so I've had hundreds of reviews, essays, even books, written on my work to which I pay minimal attention. The goose trying to lay golden eggs shouldn't be using a mirror to look at its butt.

The human mind loves to posit absurdities. You can also easily bite off your own fingers, such is the dark power of the human mouth. But this is not to say that wine and literary criticism is without a specific value. This would be to doubt the necessity of plane or train schedules or those teachers who, however unpleasant, made us aware of the range of human mental activity. I recall my excitement on first reading Brillat-Savarin, Lichine and Parker, Edmund Wilson and George Steiner. It would be dumb of me not to check in with Gerald Asher, Frank Prial, Hugh Johnson, or Sven Birkerts. We just shouldn't confuse educated comment with primary experience.

Meanwhile in Paris I missed the eclipse of the moon because I was inside *Assiette Lulu* drinking a St. Estèphe, a wine that causes moon dreams. I'm headed for an actual thirty-seven-course lunch in Burgundy with, naturally, at least fifteen wines. I wonder idly if a doctor will be in attendance. Life would be impossible without wine, fishing, and dogs.

To rate either wine or literature as if we were scientists is frivolous.

On our long circular journey to this lunch which in the future should be an Olympic event we traveled south of Dijon and Beaune passing my beloved Clos de la Roche though I've never owned a bottle, only sponged on those whom God has given fat wallets. We stayed at the exquisite Villa Louise in Aloxe-Corton and dined at a roadhouse named *La Regalade*, a lovely simple supper of pâté, frogs' legs, and sweetbreads drinking a Nuit-St.-Georges and a Vosne-Romanée. At dawn or a few hours thereafter we sped toward Marseille in order to have the excellent bouillabaisse at Michel's. Next day Lulu Peyraud gave us an exquisite lunch at Domaine Tempier (urchins, a broth of *coquillage*, lamb leg done in the fireplace, *pied paquets* done Provençal style).

This little travelogue is offered for a single purpose. With good food and company the numerical absurdities become more so, a "90" wine becoming a "95" because wine doesn't exist in the vacuum of charts but at the center of our lives. The professor who marked your essay 78 after a bad dinner may have given it a 91 after a good lunch. A book that is thought a classic in the western states is utterly ignored in Gotham's verminish cement canyons. To rate either wine or literature as if we were scientists is frivolous. Both are in the humanities, not the sciences. More later.

WINE CRITICISM AND
LITERARY CRITICISM (PART II)

In my first installment on wine and literary criticism, "Odious Comparisons," I became a bit strident in these contentious arenas, and a small portion of the feedback was aggrieved. The reaction brought to mind the children's story of "The Emperor's New Clothes." Depending on your religion only Jesus, Muhammad, and the Buddha are faultless. All other mortals betimes lack certain articles of clothing. Once when I was a child fishing with my father he told me to my consternation that the Queen of England had to go to the toilet the same as the rest of us. There is evidence that Einstein was on occasion an unfaithful husband and I recall an article that said, "Picasso was insensitive to the needs of women." Even so awesome a creature as the president of the United States is occasionally wrongheaded. Earlier in my career my collection of novellas called *Legends of the Fall* was maliciously attacked in the London press by the renowned C. P. Snow. I yawned and wandered down to the bank to make yet another deposit. We fear the negative but without it there's no positive.

My main point in both wine and literature was to insist on the primacy of creation over comment. I take as bedrock Benjamin Franklin's statement, "Good wine is a constant reminder that God loves us and wants us to be happy." We must remember that we're not dealing with proud death or the fate of nations, or the dozens of fatal asteroids whirling in our direction. Tastes in wine and literature are as personal as dogs. I can't quite imagine my response if someone referred to my beloved English setter Rose as a "nitwit fleabag." If guests don't like the Domaine Tempier Bandol I serve them they're no longer welcome in my home. Two years ago I broke off a nascent friendship when the gentleman, a Yale graduate, attacked the work of my adoptive uncle, Henry Miller.

Wine and literature affections are not a science but a matter of taste and emotion. I revere Emile Peynaud, Gerald Asher, Clive Coates, Jancis Robinson, Simon Loftus, and yes, Robert Parker himself in the major books, and Kermit Lynch has also established himself in this austere group of ultra-worthies. I also have five personal friends, Peter Lewis, Guy de la Valdène, Will Hearst, Gérard Oberlé, and Michael Butler, whose personal taste in wine I consider more exacting and elevated than my own. I'm what you call an Ace Consumer in the area of food and wine and a producer in the literary field. This is a disclaimer of expertise in wine but not intelligence.

Both book and wine reviewing, however, bring to mind my memories of the wonderful old comedian Pigmeat Markham and his routine "here come da judge." Among us mortals even the most profound spiritual experiences are freely marketed. Witness the television evangelists. On a lesser level you can buy a star and name it after yourself. In wine and literary reviewing and criticism we have the questionable relationship with the wine industry and the book industry. The rich, squeaky wheels tend to get all of the grease and one's credibility feels tampered with. How often in literature have

I noted that fine works are basically ignored if not published by the mainstream companies. The lesser, off-brand publishers do not contribute to the advertising revenue of the large reviewing media and cynicism becomes freely nurtured in the savagery of the marketplace. The concept of a level playing field is as laughable as peace in our time.

I'm fairly sure that the numerical system of rating wines was not devised as a marketing tool but that's what it has become. The truly great Russian writer Dostoevsky insisted, "Two plus two is the beginning of death." Aesthetic values are decidedly non-digital and can no more fairly be applied to wines than to a thousand or so "top" books a year. I could rather freely trust Parker in most areas but I would prefer a comment to a number. After Parker, however, the food chain descends toward the Proterozoic. Since this isn't a science, how does a judge become qualified? In my years in Hollywood I watched hundreds of cads pass themselves off as "producers" to young starlets. Both in the press and on television news there are hundreds of pundits who assume that talking is thinking. Evidently pundits are pundits because they say they are, and the same with many creatures in the wine press.

In a Paris restaurant last November I had a mildly irritating but comic experience. I was seated near an American couple in their mid-thirties and the man was driving the sommelier batshit by looking up the numbered ratings in a book for the wines on the "carte." By the time the customer finished, his wife looked like she wanted to run for it and the sommelier was searching for a club or at least a riding crop. I've seen versions of this before but not to an extent that became so transcendently silly. I could imagine this dweeb going in a bookstore and wondering why the stock didn't have spine stickers with ratings. French magazines run cartoons about such American "wine lovers."

While driving through France with Peter Lewis and Guy de la Valdène I sensed a number of times from the backseat that I was driving them crazy with some of my peculiar wine questions but they willingly answered because the option was to have me start singing songs like "Shrimp Boats Are Coming" or my Wilson Pickett or

Sons of the Pioneers medleys. Peter, who is expert in both wine and literature, made the point that it would be helpful if there was a way to contextualize the judgments of wine critics. Good literary critics like Edmund Wilson, George Steiner, or F. K. Lewis clearly establish where they stand. It would be useful indeed to have a specific idea of the tastes of wine reviewers and critics. You would then know what particular direction they were coming from in their virtually thousands of judgments.

Science does offer us a detailed consolation in the matter of taste, but it won't fit into any ballpark. In January there was an item in the *New York Times* Science section that at the same time clarified and clouded the issue. The fact is that taste buds in the human mouth can be quantified. "About 25 percent of the population are supertasters, blessed or cursed with a heightened sensitivity because the concentration of their taste buds can be a hundred times as great as the concentration in nontasters, who also make up about 25 percent of the world. Regular tasters, about half of all people, fall somewhere in between."

These facts raised some troubling considerations. Should all of those who judge wine be forced to troop off to Mayo Clinic in Minnesota to have their taste buds counted? Minnesota is a good idea as a California clinic couldn't very well be trusted in this matter. Literary reviewers could be given a simple diagnostic test of world literature and many would flunk outright. Imagine giving members of Congress a test on American or world history! But in the arena of wine this is explicit evidence that there are a large number of possible supertasters. In our population at large that means there are about seventy million people with this potential.

Last night I awoke at four a.m. brooding about these matters. The old saying "You shouldn't lose sleep over it" came immediately to mind as I stared at the waning moon, the same moon on which one of our astronauts had swung a blasphemous golf club. We Americans are extraordinarily proud of our pragmatism though this xenophobic pride often borders on the fungoid. I said in my memoirs that we seem better at everything than the French except how to live life, which includes food and wine. I have met French oenophiles who are scornfully amused by our numerical systems but these same people are irrationally attached to their Michelin Guides.

My mother, of 100 percent Swedish derivation, once said to me, "what if everyone was like you?" I admit that might be a sad situation. Why resist a system that so many find helpful? Maybe I have a numbers phobia? By general agreement I'm not allowed a checking account because I've never been able to fill out a stub. I have no talent at dates and can recapture most incidents of my life only by remembering what dogs I owned at the time.

So if I can't accept pragmatism in wine or literature perhaps it's my own problem. I fear the banality of the uniform. Will the wines of the future all adhere to the style of the wines judged to be in the high nineties by certain people? Once in New York City I studied the Racing Form all morning, went out to Aqueduct, and lost every bet. I've read about touted wines that on tasting I thought unworthy of a Missouri truck stop, but then how many well-reviewed books have I read that carried the scent of Limburger cheese? In literature our pragmatism can be perversely wrongheaded if you look at the hundred or so MFA programs at universities that hope for a uniform approach in teaching people how to write poetry and fiction. It becomes California Cabernet fiction and poetry with only a couple out of a thousand worthy of our attention. Some of these schools yearly outproduce the English Romantic movement.

I'm cooking guanciale in a pasta sauce this evening. I trust that there will be no overtones or hints of bacon, brisket, shrimp, or tongue. Before dinner I'll give my dog a chunk of the sharp cheddar she loves, pour a twelve-ounce goblet of humble Rasteau or Bandol, and listen to some Brazilian guitar music. In critical terms I won't try to figure out if this predinner experience is commensal or symbiotic or etiolated. This is an after-work hour of humility where I'm free to ponder, if I wish, the memories of the thousand or so bottles of great wine I've drunk in my life. I won't wonder if the Rasteau is an eighty-three or an eighty-five, or if my new novel is a forty-seven or a ninety-one, or if the girl I saw at the coffee shop is a ninety-nine point eight, the same as my body temperature and the evening air in Bahia.

FOOD, SEX, AND DEATH

In all of the ten years or so that I spent as a member of the criminal underground in Buenos Aires, I never saw anything so callous
as the present Bush junta's looting of democracy. What began as
merely obnoxious has become sinister. As the current chairman
of the Christian Environmen-
talists, I also talk to God, but
not on the cellular. At least I
go outside and sit on a stump
or rock. The Gospels teach us
there's a difference between
talking to God and playing
God. Bush's theocratic junta
is busy demonizing Islam and
is as daffy as our ancestors who

My heart and words are pure,
or relatively so, at least for
a member of the tribe of
writers, that peculiar race of
junkies, alkies, cads, whiners,
amateur gynecologists, and
desolation angels.

launched the original Crusades. I'm tempted to refer to Bush et al. as the spawn of Satan, but I don't want to fall into their malicious pit of discourse with its foghorn drone of murder.

That said, I'd like to confront more important subjects: to wit, food, sex, and death, which have all been desperately trivialized by our culture. In moments, perhaps hours, of despondency, I wonder if I have any clarity to offer. Yup, as we say in the northern Midwest. Having kept myself remote from suffocating or drowning in the holding tank, the septic tank of our culture, I can say my heart and words are pure, or relatively so, at least for a member of the tribe of writers, that peculiar race of junkies, alkies, cads, whiners, amateur gynecologists, and desolation angels. They'll do anything to get your attention, like starting a story with "I can never forgive her for killing our beloved dog with a butcher knife."

Occasionally, my self-righteousness makes me a tad nervous. Maybe I'm a victim of a genetic glitch in my family? Maybe I suffer a number of mental and bodily diseases for which there are no apparent symptoms? I can't forget my great-uncle Floyd, who was the most unsuccessful knife thrower in the history of the American circus. An émigré from Sweden near the Arctic Circle, Floyd had an uncommon flash and sense of showmanship but ended up wounding a total of eleven women, none fatally, before the Barnum and Dailey authorities convinced him to retire. Curiously, despite his public record, Floyd had no problem finding women to stand there and take their chances. A cousin told me that when Floyd died at age eighty-eight in Wisconsin on May 18, 1957, he said on his deathbed, "I could have been a famous knife thrower, but I just couldn't throw knives."

I also admit that I reached full sexual maturity at age seven, about the same time that many began to caution me about my gluttony. One afternoon, I caught and ate ten nice trout and felt a bit ill—but not too ill to climb a dozen trees that evening to peek in the windows at the members of the high school cheerleading squad whose high-kicking antics drove me into a batty sexual froth. More than once, I was caught by a puzzled father.

"Jimmy, why are you up in that tree?"

"I'm picking walnuts for my mom."

"But that's a pine tree."

"Nobody told me."

That sort of thing. I want to make my own record clear, as so many in America are doing this election year, when we all feel a little like toilet seats with so many big political asses aimed at us. It's certainly time to head to the woods or mountains with a load of groceries and French wine. In our own case, we are in the mountains near the Mexican border, purposely without a television so we don't have to actually watch those zoo monkeys throwing shit at each other.

Recently, due to the deaths of my brother in December and one of our dearest friends only three weeks before him, I've been trying to pitch my vaunted negative capability out of this moving window and come to some conclusions. For instance, I've noted that a large number of otherwise intelligent Americans believe that a particular combination of food and vitamins will produce miracles. Is living until eighty-one instead of seventy-eight a miracle? I have at odd times tried tofu and think of it as a gustatory self-laceration, well below boiled pig liver on my list of preferences.

Many of my male friends have, of late, been on strange diets so that younger women won't regard them as biological outcasts. If they are successful, younger women will think of them as thin old men. Of course, it is natural to wonder how you got so old, but then you're ignoring the obvious answer that it happened behind your back in moment-by-moment increments. I've never been the man I used to be. If we keep descending into reality, we discover that we are as likely to be attractive again as our boyhood dog is to arrive at the back door with that softball he couldn't find fifty years ago. I suspect that time, our singular most fatal disease, has to keep itself largely behind our backs because that's where the culture wishes it to be.

It is wonderful how early in life we begin tinkering and toying with our genitals—and then move on to the genitals of others. This is the lovely way that species further themselves. In the outer reaches of the universe, even stars continue to calve. How disturbed should we be that everywhere we look, banality has metastasized and sexuality is a trillion-dollar industry? Not much.

In these times of personal mental duress, I found myself making soup, a far reach from November, when I sat down in France with a dozen others to a thirty-seven-course lunch. The lunch was basically scholarly in nature—in short, we were searching for truth of the kind that university professors are said to look for, though I know only a few of these rascals feeding at the public trough.

I suspect that, in making soups, I was looking for bedrock. Of course, none is to be found, but it is consoling to reduce confusion by making a primitive soup of shinbones and short ribs, turnips, rutabaga, cabbage, a head of garlic, and some fresh sage. One can ignore the fetish of chicken soup and simply make a good one. I also cooked a posole, a Mexican slaked hominy stew, with an antelope neck a friend had kindly sent—along with venison and elk—from Montana. The renowned Andrei Codrescu had told me that big peasant women in Romania and Albania will, in the middle of winter, hack meat off a frozen carcass with an ax and stuff it down in their capacious undies for a day or so, the better to brown it for the soup. I wanted this simplicity, having fantasized as a boy that I might run into a group of half-naked savage women deep in the forest who would welcome me to join in the feast of a whole deer they were roasting. This precious meat would naturally give me energy for the sexual bacchanalia to follow. This spectacular event hasn't happened yet, but maybe it's more likely in Canada.

Part of this simplifying process was to watch thirty or so foreign films in the evenings, mostly Mexican, Spanish, and Italian. I was early on put off by a French film where an otherwise attractive woman said, "I feel like a piece of lost luggage." It was one of those French films where the only story solution is collective suicide.

I realized during this despondent period that, in terms of food and sex, people will do about anything to get excited and stay excited. There are food magazines published now that are frankly the equivalent of *Penthouse* or *Hustler*, full of froufrou recipes by young chefs who couldn't roast a proper chicken at gunpoint.

Doubtless, this food is eaten at wife-swapping parties starring the most daring young Republicans. They eat rare turkey breast sausage with jicama salsa.

Further along on the path to the primitive and restorative, I've been cooking with guanciale, treated pork cheeks sent by my friend Mario Batali along with a fine chunk of lardo, the neck fat of a pig fed a special diet of cream and fruit in the last month of its life. Lardo is brined, then seasoned for six months in salt, garlic, and herbs. You slice it thin and let it melt into warm bread or spread it lavishly on plain pizza. All the great cardiologists admire this dish. One told me that, though the Buddha died after eating bad pork, he probably would have died sooner if he had left pork out of his diet.

By this point, many of you are probably wondering at the subtlety with which I've woven food, sex, and death together with the dense beauty of a Berber rug. The other evening, two lovely women walked into the dining room attached to the grocery store in my mountain retreat, also used by Vladimir Nabokov, who thrived on sticking pins in local butterflies. One of the women ignored me while I struggled with a tough pork chop, but the other's eyes flickered at a point above my hairline. I scented her plume of pheromones and would have dropped my fork for a peek up her skirt, but she was, sadly, wearing hiking trousers. I loitered, pretending to read Merrill Gilfillan's fabulous *Rivers and Birds*, but didn't get past a single pork-stained page, which happened to be sixty-six, my age. When her order of fried chicken arrived, she first ate all of the skin with a fair amount of salt. What did this mean? Doubtless something perverse, I thought as she cleansed her lips with a vaguely oversize tongue, a tongue that didn't jibe with her Botticelli face. Perhaps it was the rough tongue of a lioness that can easily lick the skin off a human body. I'd love to take the chance.

I fear that, in my despair, I'm losing weight too precipitously. Whole ounces of flesh are floating off into the void, which, among other things, is a fat trap for all of the world's silly diets and famines. Does this mean that my novels and poems will become thin and sallow? Can the death of my brother and our dear friend possibly mean I'm going to die someday? Will I be able to smoke cigarettes and drink wine in the afterlife? I conclude with a recent poem, which you must paste on your bathroom mirror.

Time

Nothing quite so wrenches
the universe like time.
It clings obnoxiously
to every atom, not to speak
of the moon, which it weighs
down with invisible wet dust.
I used to think the problem
was space, the million miles
between me and the pretty waitress
across the diner counter stretching
to fill the coffee machine with water,
but now I know it's time
which withers me moment by moment
with her own galactic smile.

A Really Big Lunch

On our frequent American road trips, my friend Guy de la Valdène has invariably said at lunch, "These French fries are filthy," but he always eats them anyway, and some of mine, too. Another friend, the painter Russell Chatham, likes to remind me that we pioneered the idea of ordering multiple entrées in restaurants back in the seventies—the theory being that if you order several entrées you can then avoid the terrible disappointment of having ordered the wrong thing while others at the table have inevitably ordered the right thing. The results can't have been all that bad, since both of us are still more or less alive, though neither of us owns any spandex.

Is there an interior logic to overeating, or does gluttony, like sex, wander around in a messy void, utterly resistant to our attempts to make sense of it? Not very deep within us, the hungry heart howls, "Supersize me." When I was a boy, in northern Michigan, feeding my grandfather's pigs, I was amazed at their capacity. Before I was caught in the act and chided by my elders, I had empirically determined that the appetite of pigs was limitless. As I dawdled in the barnyard, the animals gazed at me as fondly as many of us do at great chefs. Life is brutishly short and we wish to eat well, and for this we must generally travel to large cities, or, better yet, to France.

Never before have the American people had their noses so deeply in one another's business. If I announce that I and eleven other diners shared a thirty-seven-course lunch that likely cost as much as a new Volvo station wagon, those of a critical nature will let their minds run in tiny, aghast circles of condemnation. My response to them is that none of us twelve disciples of gourmandise wanted a new Volvo. We wanted only lunch and since lunch lasted approximately eleven hours we saved money by not having to buy dinner. The defense rests.

Some would also think it excessive to travel all the way from Montana to Marc Meneau's L'Espérance, in Burgundy, for lunch, but I don't. Although there are signs of a culinary revolution in the United States, this much-bandied renaissance is for people in cities such as New York, San Francisco, Seattle, and Chicago. When traveling across America over the past forty years, I've repeatedly sought extreme unction of a sort while in the midst of digestive death in the parking lots of restaurants. I've found it best, in these situations, to get some distance—to drive for a while, pull over, take a walk, fall to my knees, and pray for better food in the future.

> *If I announce that I and eleven other diners shared a thirty-seven-course lunch that likely cost as much as a new Volvo station wagon, those of a critical nature will let their minds run in tiny, aghast circles of condemnation. My response to them is that none of us twelve disciples of gourmandise wanted a new Volvo. We wanted only lunch.*

I suspect that it's inappropriate to strand myself on a high horse when it comes to what people eat. We have proved ourselves inept fools on so many mortal fronts—from our utter disregard of the natural world to our notions of ethnic virtue to the hellish marriage of politics and war—that perhaps we should be allowed to pick at garbage like happy crows. When I was growing up in the Calvinist Midwest, the assumption that we eat to live, not live to eat, was part of the Gospels. (With the exception, of course, of holiday feasts. Certain women were famous for their pie-making abilities, while certain men, like my father, were admired for being able to barbecue two hundred chickens at once for a church picnic.) I recall that working in the fields for ten hours a day required an ample breakfast and three big sandwiches for lunch. At the time, I don't think I believed I was all that different from the other farm animals.

It's a long road from a childhood in rural Michigan to being the sort of man who gets invited to a thirty-seven-course lunch. But, above all, a gourmand is one who is able to keep eating when no longer hungry, and a gourmand without a rich sense of the comic is a pathetic piggy, indeed. Once, at Taillevent, in Paris (a restaurant that is always referred to as a "temple of gastronomy"), I had the uncomfortable sense that I was in a funeral parlor. I heard no laughter except from my own table. And when I wanted a taste of Calvados as an entremets the waiter actually told me that I'd have to be patient until after the cheese course, an hour distant. Luckily, an intemperate French count who was at my table told the waiter to bring my Calvados immediately or he would slap his face; at those prices, you don't want to be schooled. Haute cuisine has rules for those who love rules. Those rules have, for the most part, driven me into the arms of bistros. If I were given the dreary six months to live, I'd head at once to Lyon and make my way from bistro to bistro in a big stroller pushed by a vegetarian.

The thirty-seven-course lunch, which was held on November 17 of last year, was based on recipes by the great cooks and food writers of the past (among them *le maréchal* de Richelieu, Nicolas de

Bonnefons, Pierre de Lune, Massialot, La Varenne, Marin, Grimod de la Reynière, Brillat-Savarin, Mercier, La Chapelle, Menon, and Carême), and drawn from seventeen cookbooks published between 1654 and 1823. It was food with a precise and determinable history. My host for the lunch was Gérard Oberlé, a man of unquestionable genius, whom I had met a decade earlier at a wine-and-book festival near Saumur, on the Loire. I don't recall seeing any books at the three-day party, where I was a wine judge, along with Alain Robbe-Grillet and Gérard Depardieu. (None of us was particularly startled when we were told that the wines had been "prejudged" and were there for decoration only.) Early one morning, I discovered Oberlé eating a sturdy platter of charcuterie on the patio of the château where we were staying. It took me a number of years to uncover all the aspects of his character—as if I were peeling the laminae from a giant Bermuda onion (which Gérard somewhat physically resembles; but then so does the Buddha). Gérard is a book collector and a dealer in illuminated manuscripts, a musicologist with a weekly program on Radio France, a novelist and an essayist, an "expert of experts" dealing with insurance fraud (assessing the actual value of private libraries destroyed by fire), a countertenor who once sang Purcell's "Come Ye Sons of Art" while hunting woodcock in Michigan's Upper Peninsula, a student of the history of French food who has produced a couple of what he calls "two-kilo" bibliographies on the subject, a wine and salami scholar, a former officer in a society for the protection of the integrity of *fromages de tête* (headcheese), a culinary eccentric, and a grand cook. Once, in Cancale, on the Brittany coast, where we were eating the rare and enormous seventy-year-old oysters known as *pieds de cheval* (horse's feet), he remarked, "These would be difficult to eat in a car."

Soon after I met Gérard, I visited his manor, in Burgundy, where he prepared a particularly interesting dish of ancient origin—a torte of fifty baby pigs' noses. "Really a simple dish," he said. As he explained it, you soak the pigs' noses overnight in clear water, then simmer them for about two hours in red wine, herbs, and garlic. Later, you add potatoes and bake the dish with the upturned noses forming a delightful mosaic on the surface. Such dishes are usually only for the extremely curious or those with an agricultural background. I recall both of my grandmothers boiling pigs' heads with herbs and onions to make a headcheese, for which the especially toothsome cheek, tongue, and neck meat was extracted, covered with the cooking liquid, and gelatinized in a glass dish.

By the time I met Gérard, I had already been exposed to excesses of every sort, including those of the film industry, and I had known a number of big eaters, myself included. But I had never met a truly refined big eater. Not long afterward, Gérard threw a dinner with fifty courses. Why? Because it was his fiftieth birthday. Why else? When I first read the menu, it seemed incomprehensible to me, though there was an interior logic—the meal was designed after one described in Petronius's *Satyricon*.

This is not to say that Gérard concentrates on the arcane and the frivolous. In my dozen or so visits to his home, I've experienced many French standards, in versions better than any I'd had before. You know you are not in a restaurant when you enter Gérard's kitchen and notice a wooden bowl with a kilo of black truffles waiting to be added to your all-time favorite dish, *poularde demi-deuil*, or "chicken in half-mourning." The dead fowl has been honored by so many truffle slices, slid under its skin, that it appears to be wearing black (not to mention the large truffle stuffed in the bird's cavity, to comfort its inner chicken). When I said, "Gérard, you shouldn't have," he replied, "I'm a bachelor. I have no heirs."

Over the years, on my visits to France, Guy de la Valdène, Gérard, and I had discussed the possibilities for a "theme" meal, and we had read the menus of several that Gérard had already given. At a certain point, it began to seem entirely reasonable to plan a lunch that began with twenty-four courses and then urged itself upward. And no restaurant was more logical a location than L'Espérance, in the village of Saint-Père-sous-Vézelay, a scant hour and a half from Gérard's home, in the Morvan. Of all the great chefs in France, Marc Meneau, a very tall man who looms above his employees as did de Gaulle above his citizenry, is one of the least aggressive, apparently devoid of any interest in becoming a public figure. His restaurant, long a required destination for gourmands, is pure country French, elegantly set in a grand garden, with nothing whatsoever in its decor to intimidate the customer. (And it would soon regain the third Michelin star that it had lost in 1999.)

Gérard had known Meneau for years, and with Guy and me safely at home in the United States he proceeded to plan the feast, using his improbable library as the source. Having once sat in on an after-lunch confab on the "*vrai ancien coq au vin*" (reduce seven liters of Merlot down to one, whisk in the rooster blood, etc.), I can only imagine the countless hours of discussion that ensued between Gérard and Meneau.

When the morning of the event finally arrived, I wasn't particularly hungry. This didn't alarm me—many professional athletes before a big game feel that they would prefer to spend the day with their Tinkertoys or in the arms of Lucrezia Borgia. I had already been off my diet for two weeks, touring the French countryside with Guy and Peter Lewis, a Seattle restaurateur. Everywhere we went, we ate the best food available, with the excuse, not totally accurate, that we'd worked hard, saved our pennies, and had it coming. (The novelist Tom McGuane once noted that in the course of thirty-five years of correspondence between us I had lost a total of eighteen hundred pounds—so I was really "getting down there.")

The day dawned cool and misty. There was a certain anxiety in the air at the manor, with Gérard watching to make sure that I didn't partake of the breakfast that I thought I needed. All I wanted was a simple slab of the game pâté from the evening before, but when I tried to sneak into the kitchen from the outside pantry door he was there in front of the fridge like a three-hundred-pound albino cat.

I've always felt that there is no lovelier village in France than Vézelay, and no lovelier religious building than its cathedral on the hill, the Madeleine of Vézelay. I'm not Catholic, but I've lit candles in that church in prayer for troubled friends, and it has always worked.

At least, they're all still showing vital signs. But I had no time to run up the steep hill and light a candle for my own digestion. The twelve of us sat down at noon. To my left was the vintner Didier Dagueneau, whose exquisite Pouilly-Fumé we had been drinking since our initial Krug Grande Cuvée. The first time I met Didier, I was startled by his appearance, which is that of a Minnesotan pulp cutter. During the winter downtime at his vineyard, in Pouilly, he travels far north, toward the Arctic, to run the dozens of sled dogs that he owns and whose racket irritates his neighbors. To my right was Gilles Brézol, Gérard's business partner and a man of sophisticated intelligence, who taught French for a year in Alabama and Nevada during the civil rights upheaval. I've had dozens of meals with Gilles, who eats as much as I do but remains irritatingly slender. In fact, in this group of mostly book collectors and journalists sworn to secrecy no one was technically obese. Although the lunch had originally been planned for eleven, a twelfth guest, a beautifully tailored, elderly French gentleman, unknown to all of us, had been invited by Meneau, in accordance with the superstitious notion that any large group should include a stranger, who might very well be an angel in disguise.

Meneau came out of the kitchen; his only advice was "*Courage*" (or "coo-rahj," as my phrase book likes to say). We began with a girlish delicacy—a clear soup made from poultry, diced vegetables, and crayfish—followed by tartines of foie gras, truffles, and lard. The next soup was a velvety cream of squab with cucumbers, served with cock-crest fritters. Then there was a soothing crayfish bisque, and I began to wonder how long we would be pursuing the soup motif.

But, oddly, I felt squeamish about the first of the hors d'oeuvres— oysters and cream of Camembert on toast, which proved to be the only course I couldn't eat. (We all have our own food phobias, and a mixture of pungent cheese and oysters makes my little tummy recoil.) Next came a chilled jellied loaf of poultry on sorrel cream, followed by a private joke on me—fresh Baltic herring with mayonnaise. (According to my late mother, I was wild about herring from the age of two. Her family was Swedish, and the fish was a staple.) I loved the tart of calf's brains with shelled peas but was not terribly fond of the omelet with sea urchin, a dish that Louis XV liked to prepare for himself—though it was certainly better than the cottage cheese with ketchup that Richard Nixon favored as a snack. (There is a well-founded rumor that George W. Bush nibbles on bologna with marshmallow bonbons.) A fillet of sole with champagne sauce accompanied by monkfish livers was wonderful, as was the roasted pike spiked with parsley. I did pause to consider whether all of these hors d'oeuvres might dampen my appetite for the main courses. The wine steward noted my unrest, and a quick goblet of Montrachet tickled my enthusiasm upward. There were only two pure-blood Americans at the table, Peter Lewis and I, and we had agreed not to shame our own holy empire.

We headed into the "second service" without an appropriate break—say, a five-mile march through the mountains and an eight-hour nap. The courses, naturally, became more substantial. First came an oven-glazed brill served with fennel cream, anchovies, and roasted currants, then a stew of suckling pig that had been slow-cooked in a red wine sauce thickened with its own blood, onions, and bacon. I leaped forward from this into a warm terrine of hare with preserved plums, and a poached eel with chicken wing tips and testicles in a pool of tarragon butter. But I only picked at my glazed partridge breasts, which were followed by a savory of eggs poached in Chimay ale, and then a mille-feuille of puff pastry sandwiched with sardines and leeks.

Now it was halftime, though there were no prancing cheerleaders. The menu advised us to "languish" in the salon and nibble on ravioli with carrots and cumin and thick slices of "Noirs eggs of puff pastry with squab hearts." Instead, I went outside, where the grass was wet and my feet seemed to sink in even farther than usual. In the walled herb garden, I began to reflect that this kind of eating might not be a wise choice in the late autumn of my life. Perhaps I should fax the menu to my cardiologist in the States before proceeding? I soon realized that this was one of the ten million insincere impulses I've had in my life. I began to walk faster for a dozen yards and almost jumped a creek, but then thought better of it.

The "third service" loaded even bigger guns, or so it seemed, with its concentration on denser, heavier specialties that tried the patience of my long-fled appetite. From Massialot, we were offered a "light" stew of veal breast in a puree of ham and oysters in a pastry-covered casserole, and a not-so-light gratin of beef cheeks. La Varenne's gray squab was boned, stuffed with sweetbreads, squab livers, and scallions, and spit-roasted. It was the Prince des Dombes who said, "Nothing arouses me but taste" (*"Je ne me pique que de goût"*). He would have been a disappointing match for a vigorous girl. You can imagine her hanging a rope ladder from her tower bedroom for knights-errant—or, better yet, woodchoppers and stable hands—to climb, while the prince aroused himself in the kitchen. From his files, we had wild duck with black olives and orange zest, a *buisson* (bush) of crayfish with little slabs of grilled goose liver, a terrine of the tips of calves' ears, hare cooked in port wine inside a calf's bladder, crispy breaded asparagus, a sponge cake with fruit preserves, and cucumbers stewed in wine.

It was consoling to begin winding down with a swirl of turnips in sweetened wine, radishes preserved in vinegar, a warm salad with almonds, cream of grilled pistachios, meringues, macaroons, and chocolate cigarettes. These were simple warm-ups to the medley of desserts served to us in the salon: a rosette of almond milk with almonds; a soft cheese of fresh cream with quince jelly; rice whipped with sweetened egg whites and lemon peel; a grand ring-shaped cake, a savarin, flamed with Old Havana rum and served with preserved pineapple; little molds of various ice creams; and a "towering structure of every fruit imaginable in every manner imaginable."

Sad to say, my notes from the meal are blurred and smeared by the cooked exudates of flora and fauna and the wines that rained down on us as if from the world's best garden sprinkler. Reading through the veil of grease, I see that my favorites among the wines served were Chablis Les Clos, Montrachet 1989, Volnay-Champans 1969, Château Latour 1989, and Côte-Rôtie. Of course, any fool would love these great wines as he felt his wallet vaporize.

There. Time to do dishes. As Diderot said of a lunch at the fabulously wealthy Baron of Holbach's home, "After lunch, one takes a little walk, or one digests, if it's even possible." Night had long since fallen, and I reflected that lunch had taken the same amount of time as a Varig flight from New York to São Paulo.

In the salon, my fellow-diners were yawning rather than gasping or sobbing. Was this another example of the banality of evil: a griev-ous sin committed—in this case, gluttony—and no one squirming with guilt? I have noticed that Frenchmen are far less susceptible to heart disease, in part because they don't seem to experience the stress of self-doubt or regret. My mother, a Swedish Lutheran, liked to ask her five children, "What have you accomplished today?" If I'd told her, "I have eaten thirty-seven courses and drunk thirteen wines," I would have been cast into outer darkness. But then this was the Iron Mom who also said, with a tiny smile, in reference to my life's work, "You've made quite a living out of your fibs."

At midnight, while sipping a paltry brandy from the nineteen-twenties and smoking a Havana Churchill, I reflected that this was not the time to ponder eternal values. I was sitting next to Gérard, who was cherubically discussing the historical subtleties of certain courses. In a way, we were forensic anthropologists, doing arduous historical fieldwork. How could we possibly understand the present without knowing what certain of our ancestors had consumed? Marc Meneau, his lovely wife, Françoise, and thirty-nine members of his staff had led us on a somber and all-consuming journey into the past.

At dawn or a few hours thereafter, I felt relieved, on stepping out of the bathtub, that I hadn't fallen on a hard surface and broken open like an overly mature muskmelon.

* * *

No question looms larger on a daily basis for many of us than "What's for lunch?" and, when that has been resolved, "What's for dinner?" There have been mutterings that the whole food thing has gone too far in America, but I think not. Good food is a benign weapon against the sodden way we live.

As with sex, bathing, sleeping, and drinking, the effects of food don't last.

By the time I reached Paris the next afternoon and took a three-hour stroll, I was feeling a little peckish. I'd heard that certain quarrels had already arisen over our lunch, and I felt lucky that my capacity for the French language was limited to understanding only the gist of conversations—sort of the way the average American comprehends our government. On the phone, the natives were restless to the point of "scandal," and from the tornado of rumors (everyone knows that men, not women, are the masters of gossip) I learned that many had found both the food and the service disappointing, the lack of "theater" sad. (As for myself, I couldn't make a judgment. I once helped to cook a whole steer and a barrel of corn for a picnic in Michigan and have eaten many ten-course dinners, but our French lunch had left those occasions in the numbered dust.) The most interesting rumor I heard was that the tab for the lunch had been picked up by a Louisiana billionaire, who couldn't attend because a pelican had been sucked into an engine of his Gulfstream. This detail was so extraordinary that it seemed likely to be true.

That last evening in Paris, before my flight and the tonic Chicago-style hot dog that awaited me at O'Hare, Peter and I dined at Thoumieux, my old standby restaurant, near the Invalides. We had a simple Gigondas, and I ordered two vegetable courses, then relented at the last moment and added a duck confit. Long flights are physically exhausting, and good nutrition lays the foundation of life. On Air France, I was sunk in profound thought, or so I felt at the time. As with sex, bathing, sleeping, and drinking, the effects of food don't last. The patterns are repeated but finite. Life is a near-death experience, and our devious minds will do anything to make it interesting.

CARTE

The Hosts

Luncheon

Monday Seventeenth November

of the Third Year

of the Twenty-First Century

The great authors and great cooks

who have inspired us in the realization of this menu

Le Maréchal de Richelieu

Nicolas de Bonnefons

Pierre de Lune

Massialot

La Varenne (Le Cuisinier Français)

Marin (Dons de Comus)

Grimod de la Reynière (Almanach des Gourmands)

Brillat-Savarin (Physiologie du Goût)

Mercier (Tableau de Paris)

La Chapelle (La Cuisine Moderne)

Menon

Carême

The Principal Works

1654	Les Délices de la Campagne	Bonnefons
1674	L'art de Bien Traiter	Le Sieur Robert
1662	Le Nouveau et Parfait Maître d'Hotel	Pierre de Lune, écuyer de cuisine du duc de Rohan
1663		
1691	L'école Parfaite des Officiers de Bouche	Anonyme
1691	Le Cuisinier Royal et Bourgeois	Massialot
1651	Le Cuisinier Français	La Varenne, écuyer du Marquis d'Uxelles
1733	Le Cuisinier Moderne (Major work)	Vincent La Chapelle
1782	Tableau de Paris	Louis-Sébastien Mercier
1739	Dons de Comus ou les Delices de la Table	François Marin
1742	Nouveau Traité de la Cuisine	Menon
1745	La Cuisinière Bourgeoise	Menon
1755	Les Soupers de la Cour	Menon
1740	Le Cuisinier Gascon	Louis Auguste de Bourbon, Prince de Dombes
1808	Manuel des Amphitryons	Grimod de la Reynière
1823	La Physiologie du Goût	Brillat-Savarin

∞

Marc Meneau and Françoise Meneau

Vincent David	et	Pierre Rouvier
		Christophe Baillon
Julien Viollet		Laure Trèche
Stephane Barre		Régis Baillot
Jean-Baptiste Marin		Virginie Rota
Estelle Bachelet		Jonathan Ganirenq
David Sarrazin		Delphine Paoli
Jeremy Barnard		Thomas Grino
Martial Facchinetti		Vanessa Lagano
Damien B.		Tristan Ringenbach
Pierre Voisine		Cécile Annet
Ryoji Usukie		Emeric Chambon
Adeline Bouvier		Bruno Leroux
Jean-Charles Boulmier		
Brahim Kanouté		
Christophe Chalon		Ludivine Maes
Stephane Romeu		Katia Chevalier
Ludovic Piganiol		Noémie Alves
Brice Bechard		
Jean Claude Royer		
Marie-Lyne Boivin		
Evelyne Michel		
Gheorghe Varga		Jacqueline Mestre

have put all of their passion into preparing this meal for you.

∞

A Cook:

This is a man capable of inventing that

which you've never eaten anywhere else.

Not any man can be all together at once

Great at the oven

Great on the stove

And great at the spit.

Grimod de la Reynière

1st Service

Oils

(Nicolas de Bonnefons)   Clear soup of poultry
                                (rice–diced vegetables–crayfish)

(Marc Meneau)   Sauté of leeks and potatoes
                                (tartines of foie gras–truffles–lard)

Soups

(La Chapelle)   Velvety cream of squab with cucumbers
                            (cucumbers–cock crest fritters)

(Menon)   Crayfish bisque in *feuilletage*

In Les Delices de la Campagne, *the Soup of Health is a conventional
affair well supplemented with decent meat and reduced with a little
broth. One made of cabbage would provide the essence of cabbage.*
                                                Nicolas de Bonnefons

Hors d'Oeuvres

(Menon)   Oysters on Camembert toast
                        (only the cream of Camembert is considered)

(Marin)   Chilled jellied loaf of poultry on sorrel cream
                        (chicken meat and livers poached in clear broth)

(Massialot)   Fresh Baltic herring with mayonnaise
                            (potatoes dressed in mayonnaise and
                                marinated fillets of fresh herring)

∝∾

(Marin)   Tarte of calf's brains with shelled peas
                               (morsels of brain breaded with parsley
                                        and sautéed)

                               Louis XV's omelet with sea urchin
                               (Louis XV very much loved to cook and
                               would make certain dishes of his own,
                                    this omelet amongst them.)

(Marin)   Fillets of sole. Champagne sauce
                               (accompanied by monkfish livers)

                        Pike spiked with parsley and oven-roasted

*In the last century considerable amounts of meat were served in
pyramids. Small plates which cost ten times as much as a large one were
not yet known. You couldn't eat delicately for another half century.*
                                   Mercier, *Tableau de Paris*, 1786

∞

2nd Service

(*La Chapelle*)
Brill served warm in a fennel stock
(oven-glazed brill–fennel cream with
anchovies–roasted currants)

Stew of suckling pig
(slow-cooked in red wine, thickened
with its blood–onions–bacon)

Warm terrine of hare with preserved plums
(served in its own cooking juices)

Poached eel
(with chicken wing tips, testicles,
tarragon butter)

Glazed partridge breasts

Savory of eggs poached with Chimay ale

Thin layers (*mille-feuille*) of puff pastry
sandwiched with sardines and leeks

The guy who works in the "new" style
Is preferable to the one who is completely out-of-date.
                                        Menon

Between the second and third services,

a moment of rest in the salon,

where you may languish and sample your choice

of raviolis with carrots and cumin,

of thick slices of Noirs eggs,

of puff pastry with squab hearts.

A magnificent cider will refresh your palates

and disperse the first "fog."

∽

3rd Service

(Massialot)

Casserole of round slices of veal in the
manner of Maxarine
(light stew of veal breast and cooked puree of
ham with oysters covered in the casserole
with pastry decorated as bay leaves)

Gratin of beef cheeks thinly sliced

(La Varenne)

Gray squab roasted with strands of parsley
(boned, stuffed with sweetbreads, squab
liver–scallions–wrapped with sprigs
of parsley, spit-roasted)

(Prince des Dombes)

Wild duck with black olives and
orange zest

Bush of crayfish and little slabs of
grilled goose liver

Terrine of the tips of calf's ear

(Prince des Dombes)

Hare "in a bag" (*en Musette*)
and Port wine
(hare cooked in a calf's bladder
with Port)

Crispy breaded asparagus
(asparagus partly dipped in batter
and fried–sauce)

Light sponge cake with fruit preserve

Cucumber stewed in wine

Cordon Bleu: Term destined in culinary literature reserved for a simplified cuisine, placed within reach of all by the labors of the mother or father of the family. The Cordon Bleu was the insignia of the Knights of the Sacred Spirit. By what "miracle" does this word slip toward very skilled male and female cooks?

J. F. Revel

It is the moment of transition
from the salty to the sweet,
or from cooks to the pastry chef.

Swirl of turnip preserved in sweetened wine
radish preserved in vinegar
Warm salad with almonds
Cream of grilled pistachios
Stuffed cakes–Meringues–Macaroons–Chocolate "cigarettes"

Nothing arouses me but Taste.
Prince des Dombes

4th Service

Rosette of almond milk with almonds

Soft cheese of fresh cream with quince jelly

Rice whipped with sweetened egg whites and lemon peel

Ring-shaped cake (Savarin) flamed with rum

and served with preserved pineapple

Little molds of ice cream

Towering structure of every fruit imaginable in every manner imaginable

Diderot recounted to Sophie Volland
a meal he had made in the countryside
at the house of the fabulously wealthy Baron of Holbach.
"After lunch," he said, "one takes a little walk
or one digests, if it's even possible."

Champagne Krug Grande Cuvée in Magnum

Pouilly Fumé 1999 Pur Sang (Didier Dagueneau)

Chablis Les Close 1999 in Magnum (Jean Marie Raveneau)

Montrachet 1989 (Château de Beaune)

Morgon 2001 (Marcel Lapierre)

Volnay Champans 1969 (Hubert de Montille)

Cider l'Argelette 1997 (Eric Bordelet)

Musigny 1990 in Magnum (Jacques Priour)

Château Latour 1989 in Magnum

Côte-Rotie 2000 (Jamet)

Wattwiller 2003 in half bottle

Vin de Constance 1998

Condrieu 2002 Les Ayguets (Yves Cuilleron)

Tokajis Aszu 6 Puttonyos 1983 (Château de Sárospatak)

TONGUE

At one time I was a champ but now I'm wondering if I've become a chump? Or only a chimp with car keys? By the age of thirty, I had climbed all of the major mountain peaks of the Midwest. One of them, in particular, near Kingsley, Michigan, intrigued me and challenged me. Known locally only as "the Big Hill," it was a very big hill indeed. There were no trails, no available mapped routes, and there was the sensation of climbing an enormous virgin, perhaps like the tiniest of ants might feel climbing the leg of a Sapphic giantess after she had bathed in a forest spring. I was also burdened by an onion sack of morels because it was mid-May in the Great North. On my descent, while sobbing with exhaustion and cold, I was met by a dense fog of mosquitoes but luckily caught a brown trout of about three pounds on the Manistee. I roasted the trout and sautéed the morels with wild leeks for my little family.

To be frank, we were fraught with worry. We lived in a shabby house rented for thirty-five bucks a month. It was a questionable deal because many nights in the winter the temperature couldn't be raised to fifty and my little daughter wore her snowsuit to bed. My abs (abdominal muscles) rippled from manual labor at two dollars an hour. My head was swollen with the pride of having published my first book of poems with W. W. Norton. I refused to teach, thinking it unworthy of a Thief of Fire. In short, I was the same sort of flaming asshole that most young poets are with the inevitability of winter ice on Hudson Bay. At the time, a visiting rich friend said, "This is so Dickensian."

Soon enough, however, my career wildly burgeoned with readings throughout our great nation for the National Endowment for the Arts for a hundred dollars a performance. The experience was so absolutely gruesome that over thirty-five years later, I claw at my face when thinking about it. In Detroit, I lost my plane tickets in a strip club. In Minneapolis, it was thirty below in January and I fell down a snowy bank of the Mississippi River. If it hadn't been for a solid lid of ice, I would have perished. On an Indian reservation in Arizona, a huge girl lunged at me with her pet rattlesnake. She was thrilled to frighten me.

Oddly, this kind of thing is still happening, though at a slightly higher fee. When we jump ahead from then to now through the vast shitstorm clouds of public appearances, however, I feel obliged to help others. Along with murder and thieving it is the Christian thing to do. It's always improper to whine, or so my mother said, but then she mostly traveled to the rural mailbox and the grocery store. How can I help other poets? Easy. By advising them to get a job and not to do readings. I remember the day in my mid-thirties when I received a letter announcing I had been chosen for the "Texas Tour," which was nineteen readings in thirty days. While composing a "no" letter, I wondered idly what such activities had to do with the writing of poetry. There are many who think that all of the social activities surrounding literature are part of literature. They aren't. Nothing matters but the work itself.

How did I liberate myself from this squalid world: the garrulity that is a central manifestation of mediocrities; the bus, train, and

plane travel; the colleges that were green lumps of ivy on suburban
hills; the ten thousand professors who, like realtors and editors, tell
you that they don't have time to read?

I did so by becoming, briefly, a chef in a women's prison, and
then an international white trash sports fop, and then the lowliest
of functionaries in Hollywood, the "writer"—a word that is uttered
with sardonic amusement out there, raising images of a nerd who
drives an old Honda.

Cooking at a women's prison—really a low-security home for
wayward girls, though a number of prisoners were murderers—was
hard work but not unpleasant. Before I began, my heart soared because
I've always enjoyed cooking for crowds. Even as a child, I'd make
hundreds of mud pies for friends. Unfortunately, state institutions had
rigid guidelines for prisoner food, including heavy use of government
surplus. I've never been one to be intimidated by government regulations, with the exception of several raids by the IRS on my person.
The problem at the women's prison was that the menus were preset
by the state and there was no budget whatsoever for fresh garlic and
red wine. Perhaps the prohibition against red wine is understandable
for criminals, but then they always seem to be gobbling drugs with
impunity and the availability of red wine would be a health measure.
(Drug use in state and federal prisons runs consistently over 80 percent and it's puzzling how governments expect to control drug use in
the free world when they can't do so in their prisons.)

Sad to say, my chef job lasted a scant month. My staff was a
mélange of ethnic and racial backgrounds and uniformly ungifted as
sous chefs. Sample dialogue:

"Girls, we need to peel two bushels of russet potatoes," I'd say.

"Eat shit, white boy," said Vera, a large black heroin dealer from
the Cass Corridor of Detroit.

"*Chinga su madre*," said Rosa, a heroin mule from Sonora.

And so it went.

I had to buy fresh garlic and herbs out of my own pocket until
one day a half dozen of these monster vixens wrestled me into submis-
sion on a pile of dirty laundry. Big rumps broke my nose and loosened

two teeth. When I cried out and we were discovered by a guard, I was judged the guilty party and fired. I do remember fondly certain of the malcontents—Carrie, Judy, Mara, Evelyn, Meredith—our late-night Crisco fights over the tubs of tuna with Judy sitting happily in the big bowl of mayo. Amid the squalor of newspapers, television news, bad jobs, bad government, it was exhilarating that there is a durable spiritual aspect of food and sex, that even in a prison kitchen, tuna and tarts can be a form of prayer.

I'll hastily move through my career as an international white trash sports fop and a Hollywood shill. In the former, I was self-indulgent in Africa, Russia, and Central and South America in a single year. I caught fish and shot game birds and wrote about it, a somewhat limited genre. In Hollywood, I wrote brilliant screenplays that were turned into mediocre movies. I quit in disgust seven years ago and gave myself over totally to literature. Since quitting, I have done fourteen book tours in the United States and France, which are every bit as nasty as Hollywood pig poop. Publishing and Hollywood are busy cloning each other and contain the same mushy innards one discovers when cleaning squid. Naturally I love good books and good movies but they are as rare as honest Republicans.

Many people ask me, "Jim, how do you survive the mudbath you've organized as a life?" The answer is easy. Food and wine. Just this moment, in Grand Marais, Michigan, on the eve of a book tour to France, where I'll be winning certain prizes that, like those I've won in America, I've never heard of, I've opened a Sangre de Toro, an ordinary Spanish red, with its secret ingredient, the blood of a bull. Of course bulls are rather unreliable as role models so I should have opened a Vacqueyras Sang des Cailloux (the blood of the rock), but this wine is unavailable in the Upper Peninsula. When the blood is thin, drink blood. Even faux blood will suffice. Our strength comes from metaphor not reality.

This key to vigorous survival was found in a mere ten minutes of reading in Chinese medicine. I admit that this scarcely represents mastery of the subject but who cares? The world is full of nitwit authorities. Chew a leaf a few minutes and you know the tree.

Everyone should understand that the hardest thing is still melody which presumes harmony. The dimensions and the nature of the universe make all human pretensions and inventions not much more than silly. The DNA of a flea is more intricate than Mozart, though admittedly, I'd rather listen to Mozart than a dead flea.

Life must go on after my failed attempt to become an Olympic synchronized swimmer, and after that, to write an opera based on women's TV exercise programs. The women frequently die after wrapping themselves into these Rube Goldberg machines, all to make themselves attractive to louts.

On a recent book tour that covered nineteen cities in thirty-five days, I used the Chinese one-on-one concept and it saved my heart and brain from exploding. When my stomach was sore I ate tripe in the form of menudo at Mexican restaurants. When my mouth was tired from babbling I ate Jewish corned tongue and guanciale, Italian treated pork cheeks. For sore feet it was pig hocks, and tired legs demanded beef shanks and lamb legs. When my gizzard was on the fritz I was lucky enough to find *confit de gésiers* at Vincent's in Minneapolis. In the same city toward the end of my tour I acquired a Russian peasant heartiness by eating borscht and Russian sausage and drinking Russian wheat beer at Kramarczuk's. My fatigued tendons recuperated by eating stewed tendons at the Family Noodle Shop in New York City. In Seattle, Armandino Batali cooked me a giant beef tail for general strength, and in New York City, his son Mario and I tested forty dishes at his restaurants to cover all the possibly neglected basics. One giant lacuna in America is finding a restaurant that serves both brains and testicles, though both are frequently served in Montana in the vicinity of my home.

Well, you see the drift. I admit I spent more money than usual on digestive nostrums. Now I'm on the eve of a French book tour where it will be easy to find brains and tongue, also skate wings *au beurre noir*, which will help me fly through the cultural sewer of book publication, the photo ops and endless babbling. I have been diverted by an item on television news that described a punishment fad among American parents called "hot saucing," wherein they dab the tongues of their naughty children with hot sauce. I've always considered Tabasco a sacrament so this new practice strikes me as another gesture of the Antichrist, or at least the advent of torture into child raising.

This is my last day in the Great North. After preparing my simple Spanish chicken dinner dish I'm setting off for a long wilderness hike with the ghost of my dog Rose, who died this summer as a result of my inattention as I convalesced from my book tour. In one of the grand vagaries of the human mind and imagination, I can occasionally see Rose on my hikes. She crisscrosses the landscape, a white setter against the greenery, looking for ghost birds.

DUCKS

Duck Scaloppine with Dried Cherries and Grappa
Scaloppine d'Anatra alle Ciliegie e Grappa
Recipe by Mario Batali

> Duck breast is not typically served this way in Italy, but I find the deep red meat with the fat still attached delicious, as well as easy to prepare. Cold duck fat gets ugly, so serve this immediately, with braised red cabbage.

> MAKES **4** SERVINGS

> 1 whole MAGRET DUCK BREAST (about 1½ lb), split
> ½ cup ALL-PURPOSE FLOUR
> SALT and freshly ground BLACK PEPPER

¼ cup EXTRA-VIRGIN OLIVE OIL
¼ cup DRIED CHERRIES
½ cup GRAPPA
½ cup DRY RED WINE
½ cup CHICKEN STOCK
2 tbsp UNSALTED BUTTER
1 bunch SCALLIONS, thinly sliced on the diagonal

1. Leaving the fat on, slice each duck breast across the grain into 6 equal pieces. Using a meat mallet, pound the pieces into "scaloppine" ⅛ inch thick and about 4 inches long. Season the flour with salt and pepper, and dredge the scaloppine in the seasoned flour.

2. In a 10- to 12-inch sauté pan, heat the olive oil over high heat until smoking. Add the duck pieces and cook, *without* turning, until deep golden brown on the first side. Add the cherries, grappa, wine, stock, and butter and bring to a boil. Cook until the liquid is reduced by half, 6 to 7 minutes, then turn the duck pieces over. Cook for 30 more seconds.

3. Transfer the duck to warmed serving plates, sprinkle with scallions, and serve immediately.

Ducks

We tend to eat the avian species who sing less well. No one to my mind has produced a CD called "Summer Duck Songs," and the wild forms of these species—the mallards, pintails, ringbills, bluebills, wood ducks, and teal I shot for the table long ago—were equally unmelodious. In ancient times, among many primitive peoples ducks were sacred creatures—albeit readily eaten, which makes them even more sacred. Doubtless part of our current crisis of values in America is that so few of us raise any of a dozen types of delicious ducks for the table. This is not a fashionable time to compare us unfavorably with the French, but driving through the Burgundy countryside I've counted tens of thousands of ducks. Perhaps they should be raised on the wide-open spaces surrounding monuments in Washington, D.C.?

My friend Mario Batali is a high priest of ducks, an intercessor for the less gifted. I will cook everything he writes down, because it makes life far less brutal.

WINE STRATEGIES

I'm trying to devise new strategies to counter my postelection melancholy, the sudden lump of emotions settling in the gizzard that on that late evening could be purged only by a good bottle of French wine, a Les Bécasses Côte-Rôtie, if I remember correctly, drunk in full, somewhat sullen gulps. When dawn came it became clear to me on the sofa that national politics were beyond my control.

Added to this was my recent diagnosis of diabetes so that I could no longer gulp a bottle (or two) of wine a day with my Adam's apple leaping in victory at each swallow. Medical authorities, such as they are, have promised me that I can return on a more modest scale once this dread disease is under control. The glory days, however, are gone. Hara-kiri was an unsuitable option, but splitting a single bottle between Saturday and Sunday wrenched my heart. After Raymond

Chandler had to quit drinking to avoid certain death, he remarked that life had lost its Technicolor.

Can a gulper become a sipper? That remains to be conclusively seen. Part of the diabetic regimen is to shrink the body, throwing away the precious pounds so lovingly added in France, the best restaurants in America, and my own home kitchen where moderation was given only minimal thought. Despite medical evidence there is the primitive idea that we should not throw away our weight when winter is coming. I've never needed those wine stopper gizmos because I thought it a sacrilege to let a partial bottle diminish in a long, lonely night.

Normal people don't think they have a spare hour a day for walking. They are, of course, free to be as normal as they choose, but for an abnormal wine lover this hour is piffle compared to possibly having a half bottle a day by mid-April, when I expect to look like a male model with my abs rippling in the sunlight. Maybe I couldn't walk an hour a day for my country, but I can for wine. Down here in Patagonia, Arizona, near the Mexican border, I can see the bottles shimmering at the end of the narrow country road where I huff along diverted by nature but also knowing that fermentation is a central fact of nature.

I'm currently saving money by not drinking wine, and I don't want to. The numbers are insultingly obvious when you go from ten bottles a week to one. I've always been left-wing and socially aware, and I hate to cut into the income of the vintners of Côtes du Rhône. Even if I make my mid-April deadline for upping the ration to a half bottle a day, I'm a nothing muffin compared to, say, my September book tour in France where when I did a signing at any of a number of bookstores fine bottles would be opened on the spot. This grand French tradition does not exist in the United States, where in a recent thirty-five-day tour I was left with my own slender wallet. Ten years ago in San Francisco I was given a rich, thickish California Cabernet which was delicious poured on my hotel waffles. On one long tour in France I ended up with five cases of individual wines that I was tempted to roll on naked but thought it might be painful. I store these wines in Paris and Burgundy to avoid paying duty. To give my government any more money than the max tax I've been paying for twenty-six years is to encourage further bad behavior. I admit that this election I wrote-in Bill Clinton as a protest because one evening during his second term he ate two French dinners, one at six and one at ten. It is wisdom to double up on wine and food when you start too early. I think I read this somewhere in the Bible though not near the chapter on foreign policy.

Lucky for me, two days after I was diagnosed with diabetes my friend the New York chef Mario Batali arrived to join me and another friend, the renowned wine tutor Guy de la Valdène, for a visit. This four-day event for some hunting and fishing was my inadvertent swan song to a glorious life of excess to which my cowardly body had had a simple-minded reaction. Sad to say the Montana weather turned awful, the worst four days of the late autumn, and we bitterly resigned ourselves to eating and drinking with a small crowd. Mario had sent ahead three cases that included magnums of 1990 Le Pergole Torte by Monte Vertine, 1990 Brunello Riserva by Talenti, 1985 Gaja Darmagi, and 1997 Sori Tilden. We also had an ample supply of Joe Bastianich's excellent Clerico in addition to a number of bottles from my diminished cellar including a 1970 Lafite-Rothschild, a 1960 Heitz Martha's Vineyard, and a 1973 magnum of Mount Eden. (I admit I'm prejudiced against most California wines, which can be used to paint a house dark purple, but there are exceptions.) In early October we drank a couple of fine cases from the Rhône Rangers at Edmunds St. John.

Naturally you can't drink this quantity without proper food. The first evening we cooked a simple carton of two-pound Kobe rib steaks, and in the ensuing evenings we had a white truffle extravaganza with homemade pasta and a wild piglet Mario braised with garlic and citrus. Fortunately for our health my wife Linda's garden was still full of autumn vegetables. The four days constituted my at least temporary swan song to gluttony and drinking wine in proper volume. Back to intelligent strategies for the infirm. When my body and the doctors whisper to me, "Jimmy, you're ready," I intend to have on hand a quantity of bottles that I will drink at an austere speed.

These, of course, will not include the grand bottles of the past that are mostly drunk by unworthy stockbrokers. Far in the past, remoter than Reagan, I see those magnums of 1949 Latour, 1953 Margaux, Clos de la Roche, and ordinary bottles of Pétrus and Cheval Blanc. Bill Gates could take his company to the top if only he began swilling these wines in quantity.

My own modest list will include wines that I can count on to restore my spirit, including Domaine Tempier Bandol (especially Tourtine and Migoua), Châteauneuf-du-Pape Vieux Télégraphe, Tour Vieille's Collioure, Vacqueyras from Sang des Cailloux (writing novels is like drawing blood from rocks), Hermitage, the Nuits-Saint-Georges I had at lunch at the Confurons' vineyard, and some Grands Echézeaux I'll earn by climbing the Eiffel Tower naked in winter. I'm not a white wine enthusiast, but I'll include Silex, Montrachet, and Meursault for warmish days.

Now I'm in the realm of the possible. Throughout this long winter I'll be scaling mountains, or at least foothills, here on the Mexican border with our dogs Mary and Zilpha, who don't need anything like wine to look forward to. Drinking a fine glass on the sofa while petting the dogs is a pleasure not afforded to us by politics much less by writing novels. Drinking a fine glass while petting Lucrezia Borgia might be even better, but I haven't seen her in recent years. Not that long ago I said in a poem that our bodies were beautiful women who were never meant to be faithful to us.

RESUMING THE PLEASURE

Has anyone ever said, "Let's fly to London and taste some fine teas"? Flights across the ocean are far too perilous to gamble on anything but extreme pleasure. In all of my years as a commercial pilot flying the biggest birds created by man I was always mindful that death was my true copilot. That's why when I hit the ground, as it were, I was off and running to a wine bar to hoist down a mag or two. In Paris that meant Juveniles and Le Rubis.

Of course in actuality I'm only a novelist and poet and have been so since I received my essential calling at age fourteen while reading John Keats. I immediately set about learning the territory which I quickly surmised included women, nature, and wine, a triumvirate virtually forming the spine of literature, not to speak of a vigorous life.

Returning to earth I recall myself as an eighteen-year-old listening to Berlioz's *Requiem* with my sister with a seventy-cent fifth of Gallo and a burning red candle, a metaphor of the hotness of our souls on the verge of real life, which seemed somewhat distant from the rural Midwest. My wine drinking, mixed with other forms of alcohol, began and continued in a rather disorderly fashion until this early winter when I came down with type 2 diabetes. My valves were blown according to the body mechanics, the doctors, my threads stripped bare from purported overuse. For the time being no more wine, pasta, potatoes fried in duck or goose fat, or pomegranate soufflés, and as for alcohol a mere two ounces of vodka a day, the kind of paltry drink a publisher has when bent on cheating a writer. I also had to drop thirty pounds, which meant throwing away the hundreds of thousands of dollars I had spent on my ample tummy that many women in the world considered an *objet d'art*. But most of all it was the absence of good wine that brought me to tears and occasional sobs. Literary writers aren't gunslingers or poker players. Our gifts demand fragility and extreme vulnerability to life. I didn't want to be manly, I wanted wine and her shy handmaiden, fine food, with the intensity that a man marooned on a glacier for four months might desire a Big Ten cheerleader.

I do value the experience when Peter speculates aloud why I like a particular wine so much. It's really not adequate at times for me to merely say "yummy" or "mother dawg."

After four nasty months of improbable physical exertion which included pushing back from the table before I was ready, and pondering the mysteries of yogurt which even my dogs scorned, I was ready to return to earth. I invented a project to visit Collioure in France and search for the missing manuscripts of Antonio Machado, one of my favorite poets, who had lost a valise of poems while escaping Franco's Spain with his family in 1939. Machado was a great poet, and there was an ineffable melancholy about the matter that had troubled me for a long time. Another reason to go to Collioure is that I had seen an extraordinary film about the vineyard of Christine Campadieu and her husband, Vincent Cantié, Domaine La Tour Vieille.

Fortunately my friend and wine maven, Peter Lewis, had French intentions for writing a wine bar piece, so we decided to travel together as we had done before on what we euphemistically call our "wine and food tours." Peter has amazed a number of my French friends with his knowledge about their wines. These are not the most agreeable people, as we all know, habitually greeting the most splendid meal with a sardonic *pas mal*. Peter is a modest fellow and burgeoning novelist, agreeing with my contention that wine criticism bears the same relationship to wine as fustian theology does to God. As a novelist and poet I value the judgment of those who have created notable works. If I were a vintner and Mr. Brunier of the fabled Vieux Télégraphe in Châteauneuf-du-Pape told me he liked a bottle I had created, I would be thrilled, less so by a positive review in a wine magazine.

I do, however, value the experience when Peter speculates aloud why I like a particular wine so much. It's really not adequate at times for me to merely say "yummy" or "mother dawg." It's fun to talk about wine without saying, "There's a chiaroscuro of flavors here reminiscent of the colors of a fledgling finch, or perhaps the saddle of Lucrezia Borgia." After a few hasty days in Paris, the high points being the seafood at La Cagouille and everything possible at Lulu's Assiette over on rue Château, we had two mediocre days in Lyon until Thierry Frémaux who runs the esteemed Institut Lumière and also runs the Cannes Film Festival took us out for an extraordinary meal at Le Passage.

Our intentions, however, were elsewhere. As we drove south-west toward Collioure, the only problem was my feet. I'm a country boy who only rarely walks at length on cement and the formula the doctor concocted of walking two to three hours for every bottle of wine was mildly punishing though it is fun to feel like a faux marine.

In this remote corner of France it is easy to slide into the realm of the senses where we quite comfortably belong. I felt quite at home in Collioure and I was in my hotel room for an entire ten minutes before I sipped a glass of La Tour Vieille. From the balcony I could see the rooming house where my hero Antonio had perished, and I had a splendid sense of freedom from the Roman Empire that the United States has become. An hour later we were at the house of Vincent and Christine eating Christine's wonderful home-cured anchovies (Collioure was the center of the French anchovy fleet) and then some rice and tiny squid in their own ink covered with a layer of the best langoustines I had ever had. As we drank a number of vintages of La Tour Vieille I reflected that the wine felt as if it emerged from the local earth in the same manner that Domaine Tempier belonged to Bandol. For several days we wandered the area, including the nearly vertical vineyards which explained why Vincent and Christine are both handsomely slender. Another evening Christine fixed a stewed rabbit and a bowl of fresh favas with blood sausage, the splendid food of the earth from which the wine had sprung. The third night we visited Le Cabaret, a restaurant owned by Antoine Delmas, an old friend of Cantié's, and were served, among other things, a four-kilo *loup de mer en gros sel*, one of the most pleasurable fish dishes of my life.

In a curious way the true nature of our trip only became apparent a month later when in a complete slump I made a round trip between Montana and Michigan and on the way home on a route through northern Wisconsin I saw a sign for Redwine Road in a remote rural area. Under this blessed road sign I semi-dozed and relived my trip, the gorgeous eel stew at the home of Jean and Nicole Meurice near a salt marsh (frankly I've had food in a number of French homes that exceeded in quality anything at a half dozen three-star restaurants), the bottles of Château La Roque of Pic St.-Loup I drank in the Montpellier region in keeping with the theme of *terroir*. I find Montpellier an engaging city and we were lucky to discover a relatively new restaurant manned only by Chef Jean-Christophe Blanc and his wife Whitney. The food here is simple and direct but utterly elegant. One day at lunch we raised our glasses of Pic St.-Loup to a woman having her hundredth birthday party. She smiled at us and drank deeply from her glass of red.

We had a fine dose of the natural during a day in the Camargue, then made our way to Anne Igou's Nord-Pinus in Arles, my favorite hotel in the world, bar none. Arles is a splendid walking town and has a marvelous market with a tinge of the proletarian absent in high-rent areas such as Avignon. There's a dearth of Texas women in five-hundred-dollar sunglasses carrying their dogs that are cross-bred from monkeys and rats. In Arles I'm close enough to the territory to confine my wine drinking to Domaine Tempier's Bandol. In fact, Lulu Peyraud's vineyard was our last stop before we returned to Paris. This completely private restaurant is my favorite place to eat in France along with Gérard Oberlé's fabled kitchen in Burgundy. My obnoxious, self-administered blood test in the morning revealed that I had passed again, having failed only one day in twenty when I missed my three hours of walking, certainly a small chore compared to the pleasure of wine.

How can humble grapes produce something so delicious with the cooperation of human alchemy? Drinking wine is beyond the vagaries of language and numbers and finds its essence, like sex, totally within the realm of the senses. Would you rather read *The Joy of Sex* or play Parcheesi with Penélope Cruz in Collioure?

SNAKE-EATING

Everyone knows that if Adam and Eve had eaten the snake rather than the apple, the world would be a better place, but then, intelligent Canadians will query, better than what? The parallel world bandied about by the ancients where our land is sea, and our sea land? Jealous Christian men are forever worried that small dogs, male cats, and snakes are looking up their wives' skirts, forgetting the hundreds of species of insects that have vivid sexual lives. They have also forgotten the message of the Gnostic Gospels that as members of the mammalian

Everyone knows that modern criticism is a gated community and that the literary ethos of our time is contraction, an etiolated minimalism where the corpse is sat on to expel the last breath of living air.

species, we must eat our fears. When my old English setter Tess was startled during her nap in the yard by an emerging gopher, she quickly killed and ate this Republican beast who undermines the foundation of our existence, the ground.

The girl drove into the countryside on a warm August morning turning into the driveway of an abandoned farmstead feeling edgy because for the first time she was steering a car in her night clothes and without panties.

This is a complicated essay that demands a little sexual content to keep the attention of the readers, especially the millions of distraught hockey fans who now drink beer while staring into broom closets. On a recent trip to Toronto, a prominent Canadian critic, who doesn't wish to be outed on the matter, quipped that the novels of Updike, Roth, and DeLillo could be much improved if skin pictures were interspersed in the pages. He was drinking a large glass of anisette without ice and I let the suggestion, obviously a good idea, pass without comment. I'm not going to go out on a limb that has no tree attached. Everyone knows that modern criticism is a gated community and that the literary ethos of our time is contraction, an etiolated minimalism where the corpse is sat on to expel the last breath of living air.

Back to snakes. The first rattlesnake I ate was cooked by a retired surgeon at streamside while we were taking a lunch break during trout fishing. We were in a canyon in Montana where the crotalids abounded. I thought my surgeon friend did a rather clumsy job of skinning the snake and said so, at which point he admitted his surgeon's degree had come mail order from Phoenix, Arizona. Sure, he had lost a lot of patients, but he and his family had had a nice life and that's what's important in California. When he flopped the whole rattler on the hot coals it contracted in an alarming imitation of life, with the snake's departing soul seeming to hang there in the rancid smoke. The meat was fairly good with a lot of salt, pepper, and Tabasco, reminding me of the muskrat of my youth that we ate on our little farm near the Big Swamp in northern Michigan.

She deftly shed her blue peignoir and climbed the apple tree with the grace of a gibbon.

Bite after bite we chew our food with the kind of quiet heroism that is unacknowledged by sporting journalists. In a culture in a state of severe decay, the peripheral always subsumes the primary; thus my exploits as a bold eater and mountain climber have been given short shrift in a world of skating and pucks. How proud I was on that zero-degree morning that I gave up being a hockey goalie for the warm, albeit musty, halls of the arts, and for scaling peaks unknown to others in the mountain-climbing fraternity. True mountains are not to be measured in numbers, any more than saying that a beautiful girl is five feet eight inches tall describes her qualitative aspects, say the back of her knees, which are as soft as a mole's tummy.

Life seems to be taking my breath away. Last year at age sixty-six, I climbed a nineteen-thousand-foot mountain in Mexico called Orizaba and still had to do the cooking at base camp at eleven thousand feet because other members of the expedition were the typical fruit-and-granola ninnies. Naturally at this height soufflés are out of the question. I made a stew of a smallish but overripe boa constrictor with habanero peppers and squash. This snake tastes a bit like the chow dog I had been served and had unwittingly eaten in northern Mongolia. I admit that the boa constrictor put me off snake-eating in the year that followed, though there were definite aphrodisiac qualities. I made love to three Mexican women after we danced to internal music on a ledge with a mile-high drop. At dawn I cooked us a middling omelet from the eggs of the local monkey-eating eagle, averting my eyes from the pink embryos, which are improbably nutritious. I had to carry Michael (he pronounces it Michel), the expedition poet, down the mountain because he had stubbed his toe on a book he had been forbidden to carry. We all know certain dweebs who can't go to the toilet or make love without a book or laptop in their company. Halfway to Veracruz, we had to wait three hours at a thatched-roof restaurant for our tacos while a twelve-year-old girl poached what I thought was a boa's head but turned out to be a beef tongue. Like fish, snakes are better cooked fresh and no refrigeration was available, while well-salted beef tongue can last for weeks even on the equator. While I slept in the dirt with the dogs, Michael tried to seduce the girl. She stabbed him in his stubbed toe with an ice pick, which stymied his sexual impulses. When we reached Veracruz, I swam a few miles out in the harbor to inspect the propeller of the Greek freighter, pushing away at the last possible moment when the vindictive captain started the twelve-thousandhorsepower engine and put the ship in gear. When I swam back to the Emporio, I thought of owning twelve thousand horses, but then, my Montana ranchette is only ten acres.

This year my breath is too short for me to make the Orizaba climb. We killed seventy-three rattlers last summer on my Montana property, but I haven't the gusto to eat the few that I saved in the freezer. It's a little like a teenager who gets drunk on gin, pukes, and then is intolerant of this liquor, and may very well puke again while showering with juniper or pine-scented soap. Our fragile minds fill up with taboos as our lives pass. A Venezuelan Indian tribe, no matter how close to starvation, will not eat an anaconda that has devoured one of their children.

Curiously, our godlike intelligences, rarely used, can differentiate between similar species. Who can resist a hot bowl of anguillas, "baby eels," in their bath of olive oil and garlic? If we didn't eat these babies, they would end up swimming as many as seven thousand miles to the Sargasso Sea to mate before returning to their homeland estuarine waters. Try to imagine, if you will, spending your entire life underwater.

The girl hung by her knees from an apple tree limb giving a blue jay
a peculiar view of her parts. The bird shrieked in alarm.

Perhaps the very last snake I will ever eat was during the Athens Olympics last summer. I had stupidly gotten involved with an ex-ballerina in New York City who had become a performance artist, a category of the arts that I find difficult to hold clearly in mind. It was a pathetic case of geezer lust and my little sack of Viagras were crumbling in the humidity so that I dried the damp blue powder with her hair dryer and snorted it like cocaine in the days of yore. I also had undiagnosed diabetes, so I was either asleep or furious and missed the prime event, women's synchronized swimming. I was dozing in a nightclub when my ditzy performance artist was doing her food-chain routine by trying to throw spaghetti marinara to a litter of unweaned piglets. No one from New York knows, but certainly country folk are aware that unweaned piglets are interested in only mother's milk. The crowd booed, she was inconsolable and ran out the back door into the Athens night. The nightclub owner, a faux Zorba type, wanted to cook one of the piglets. I find false heartiness repellent and wandered over to the Thai compound to see a friend and there was served a viper stew, the snake supposedly killed fresh that morning in the mountains of Thessalonika. Food is as much a crapshoot as literature, and I wondered later if venom in the stew had entered a wound where I bit my lip after ingesting too much Viagra.

Take it from me, seven jalapeños is one too many in a Thai pork dish. Sometimes I wonder if my wisdom is in decline. When I hear the expression "the wisdom of the body," I am puzzled.

Where we winter in Patagonia, Arizona, is the only area in the United States with seven types of rattlesnakes, but I'm no longer tempted. The javelinas that eat the snakes are much more interesting on the plate, though when butchering a javelina you must be careful to carve out the rank scent glands, which are reminiscent of a Republican wife after an inaugural ball. On warm moonlit evenings, we watch the rattlers do their horizontal dances in the yard.

The girl dropped from the apple tree and ran through the orchard grass so loose-limbed that she was kicking her own pale butt.

Tomorrow I have to endure a medical procedure in Tucson that involves a twenty-four-hour fast. This is new territory for me and I suspect that I'll feel not a little like my old hero Gandhi. Without being unpleasantly specific, I will reveal that the surgeon, who apparently has a valid license, will visit my innards from two directions to discover which of my fifteen thousand meals caused the cherry bomb explosion a few weeks ago. Take it from me, seven jalapeños is one too many in a Thai pork dish. Sometimes I wonder if my wisdom is in decline. When I hear the expression "the wisdom of the body," I am puzzled. Perhaps I have eaten too much of the world? An elephant's anus cooked in a hole of hot rocks by the Kikuyu in Africa could have done the wrong job, or was it the thousand-year-old sea cucumber in Shanghai? Maybe it was mom's super-dry pot roast or Labrador's fermented caribou. My DNA has troubled Tucson medical authorities to the extent that Menninger's had been suggested rather than Mayo. Last winter in the Yucatán, a very old legless Mayan chieftain asked me seriously if I was part dog after his vicious guard dogs tried to climb on my lap in instant friendship. I wonder. Maybe it's time to be someone else? After a month of eating mostly yogurt and rice, I have dreamed that I'm camping on a glacier as white as my food. O, how I crave a braised pork jowl swimming in its fat, a Szechuan chicken cooked in a couple of pounds of bird peppers, or even a simple white truffle the size of a baseball grated on a bowl of pasta.

Back in the car she sat nudely on the hot mammalian leather of the seat.

BEAR POSOLE

I had this dish years ago in the Sierra Madre and have made it several times myself to avoid letting gift meat go to waste.

1. Cut bear meat into inch cubes.
2. Simmer with slaked hominy, nixtamal. Canned hominy is no good.
3. Add cumin, chile, garlic.
4. Simmer until meat is tender, usually 2 hours. Mexicans improve this dish with a cleaned calf's foot but pig's feet work to improve broth.

FOOD, FITNESS, AND DEATH

In the past year or so I've lost my brother, my dog, my cabin, and my health. These things happen to people. Permit me to mix some husky metaphors. A novelist is a cartographer of an imaginary country that he willy-nilly populates and in which he constructs a landscape. He strip-mines his soul. His mental incontinence leaks all over the place. (Yes, I have wept when I've killed off one of my characters.) Emotions tend to fly around in his brain like birds wired on crystal meth.

That said, let's go on to matters that might interest the average Jill and Joe. How feebly the arts compete with the idea of what we are going to eat next. How vainly have I struggled to create a poem as interesting as a recipe, or as a naughty photo for that matter. The dark power of food haunts us. Naturally, I remember my deceased Mom but deep in the North American night I'm more likely to ponder a caribou roast I had last year at Sarah MacLachlan's house in

Toronto, or the tagliatelle Mario Batali suffocated in white truffles at our home last fall. Historians have said that pork fueled the westward movement of empire in the United States. Apparently in Canada it was beaver jerky or something else on that order. Even as we speak, a faux gasoline known as ethanol is being

How feebly the arts compete with the idea of what we are going to eat next.

made out of field corn. Cows and cars feed at the same trough in this bifurcated world.

All living creatures live by the credo "Eat or die." United Nations nutritionists recently pointed out that of all species, humans, pigs, dung beetles, and Labrador dogs are the most susceptible to overeating. In my own case overeating plus the confused substitution of wine for water caused type 2 diabetes, plus duodenitis and esophagitis, as well as gastritis, which tagged along when I decided I could be my own doctor (which is somewhat like a mass murderer deciding that he doesn't need a lawyer).

I'm telling you all of this to help you de-banalize your lives. I want to help and all I'm asking in return is that you put all of your stray pennies into an old sock that has no twin and send them to this magazine so that it, too, can survive.

It is deceptively easy to think we're normal when we're not. I know a vaunted Canadian writer who misplaced his car for several weeks. Normal people don't lose their cars. When I wrote for *The New Yorker* about a lovely thirteen-hour, thirty-seven-course lunch I had eaten in France, I was startled by the number of readers who questioned my sanity. To my hero Balzac this meal would have been piffle. Rather than having a new wine with each course we strictly limited ourselves to nineteen wines, though in retrospect a glass of each did add up. I can see clearly now that such behavior may have contributed to my eventual infirmity.

I said recently in a poem called "Jimmy Lite," "There's nothing so silly as wisdom I can't apply when I get on a plane. The rest is the sediment of despair, the ice cream cone dropped on the sidewalk in 1948." And I won't bore you with all of my recovery nostrums and routines: the endless wilderness night-walking, the injections of coyote blood; the sexual marathons in Veracruz; the failure to meet Penélope Cruz in Spain; the very cold swim with a pod of killer whales off the Queen Charlotte Islands; the doomed attempt to reforest Haiti; the orgies of rice, yogurt, and oatmeal, that torpid Irish exudate.

In May, after denying myself all of life's pleasures, losing thirty-five pounds, and becoming the world's most boring person, I went to France to test myself against the Enemy (gluttony and alcohol). Since my life had already migrated to another country I had the feeling at Charles de Gaulle that I was possibly carrying a Paraguayan passport. Curiously, I had no doubts about my strength to win this battle. As the world well knows, Americans have a touching belief that they are always doing the right thing whether it's banning consensual sex between Native adults or invading Iraq. Especially of late mine is a nation fraught with acute mental dysentery.

The ostensible reason for the trip to France was to find the lost poems of Antonio Machado. Since Machado is one of my top ten poets in the history of civilization it's unthinkable, however true, that a valise of his poems was lost when he ended up carrying his mother from Spain to France to escape the craven Franco. Naturally, you remember your mother when you're carrying her. This was in 1939, within a month of my own birth, a thoroughly irrelevant detail. I couldn't accept that the probable grand poems were permanently lost. In the arena of natural history it was similar to the moment that the last auk died. Like Dante, Machado early in his life had fallen in love with a thirteen-year-old girl. He waited until she was a proper sixteen to marry her, but then she died at eighteen of TB. In the girl's last months the poet would push her in her wheelchair through the umber hills of Castile. Machado died in Collioure and I hoped to locate his manuscripts in an attic or woodshed. Machado was one of the very few poets who could fill in the missing lines of the ancient manuscript of Earth. Of course my mission was as unlikely as walking to the moon. Simply enough I was obligated. Machado discovered me in my illness last winter and gave me courage to survive. I didn't discover him, he tripped over my cot in a spare, cold room and told me in my profound discomfort to at least take the dogs for a walk in the morning. Life is the small pieces.

So there I was driving south from Lyon, having recovered from a few days in Paris by eating a Lyonnaise specialty called "Saint Cochon," which is an attractive pile of offal, blood sausage, ears, cheeks, tongues, that sort of haute cuisine, followed a few hours later by a classic *tête de veau* in order to achieve a balance between pork and beef. I climbed the three thousand steps to the cathedral on the hill to burn up the wine needed to cut through the animal fats that had collected in my tummy's sink trap. I had figured out with my doctor in Tucson, Carol Howe (who recently quit the medical profession for moral reasons to become a librarian), that it takes about two hours of walking to burn off a bottle of wine. One day in Paris thus required five hours of walking but there was the added boon in the menagerie of the Jardin des Plantes of seeing an infant kangaroo crawling out of his mom's pouch. All poets of worth remember Apollinaire's line "fermez la poche du kangourou." My traveling companion, the noted writer and gourmand Peter Lewis, joined me on those strenuous walks because with cholesterol over four hundred he had recently received a heart stent to help flush his torso.

The search for Machado's poems was, of course, exhausting partly because this country in the extremest southwest France is mountainous with only goat trails rather than roads. I rifled through the rooms of a twelfth-century nunnery where I sensed masturbatory practices though the Germans had naturally bombed the place. My Armani suit was filthy and my fingers were bloody from lifting stone slabs and lowering myself into cisterns with rope, kicking away vipers in my handmade Calabrian brogans, yet no valise of poems.

Luckily, to keep up my strength the Collioure area has French food with a punch. This is the anchovy capital of France and these tiny fish eaten in a state of decay in sufficient quantities offer optimal energy though they also give me gout. The splendid wines of the area made by Domaine La Tour Vieille killed the pain of gout and assuaged the heartsickness of not finding the valise of Machado's poems. I actually knelt by his grave in the cold rain and told him I was doing my best. The grave was laden with fresh flowers and poems with the rain blurring the ink so that the poems sank into the ground in a liquid state, perhaps reaching the bones of the poet buried beneath. Kneeling there and shivering in the twilight I naturally thought of dinner and wine, the food Christine Campadieu had so brilliantly cooked, the tiny squid with the poetic ink staining the rice, the langoustines, the fresh favas with blood sausage, the rabbits browned with pork fat in a tomato sauce, and the food just over the bruised lip of the future, the four-kilo *loup de mer* buried in *gros sel*, the eel stew, all a marriage of the Basque and Catalan and not to be found elsewhere.

At this very moment in Montana, having just dispatched a Republican rattlesnake with a scythe, I have decided to offer a ten-thousand-euro reward for the return of the verified poems of Machado. It's time for others to take up the search and earn a weekend in Paris or Paraguay. I don't have the money at present but I can always sell my renowned sexual favors to an actress for that amount. Life herself resists meaningful decisions but this reward idea is brilliant.

I don't want to die as another grumpy, exhausted old writer. It's time to plunge on leading with the heart and chin, the feet, consuming the necessary wine. The human sensorium is geared to safety but this lacks appropriate boldness for poets, those thieves of fire, but mostly academic Bic lighters. Yesterday while I was standing in a turbulent river trout-fishing it occurred to me that there's good and bad exhaustion. Whether men or women, we're publishers' boy toys. Have I ever had a publisher in my minimalist career who didn't push steroids in my direction? They want stronger, bigger, and faster novels, but then publishers have always been corporate nymphos craving new meat.

The idea of course is not to survive but to prevail and rice and yogurt don't do the job. The Gandhi diet is for bliss-ninnies, or the body-Nazis who take their garlic in capsules. I recently read the book *Pig Perfect*—it is a compass pointing to the correct route for a poet's diet. In this book there's a recipe for a *cocido* Extremadura-style that includes a ham bone, pig's knuckles, veal neck, back ribs, pig's jowl, a pork loin, chorizo and morcilla sausage, and veal and pork meatballs. What poet could ask for more?

Next March I will return to Collioure to try again. Everything has got to be somewhere. I frankly can imagine Americans discarding a valise of poems but not the French. There's the option of organizing ten thousand volunteers but this is a project that requires purity of heart and body. A possible clue came in a recent dream where I saw the valise of poems deep in a mountain cave guarded by giant red-eyed goats with sharp teeth. We'll see in March if this is true.

THE FISHERMAN GOURMAND

I've always liked to present the image of a hearty fellow who wears rough-hewn clothes and drives a dirty SUV, hunts birds, and prefers fishing to all other activities. However, I've never cared for what is called camp food in the outdoor community. I recall an expedition to the borders of Yellowstone Park in the early 1970s with my friend Guy de la Valdène and a number of Livingston sportsmen. While the others were out for early-season elk, Guy and I fly-fished Suce Creek. It was visually interesting fishing because the others, who were on horseback, were trying to drive a herd of elk out of the park so they could be shot legally. This was a fresh insight into western life. However, dinner was something called Bob's Campfire Chili, a wretched potage of hamburger, chunks of tomato big as a baby fish, literally pounds of chopped celery, kidney beans, and scarcely any seasoning. We did fake eating like they do in the movies, pretended whiskey was food, and took over the cooking chores the next day.

A nutritional scholar studying northern Plains foodways would come up with a slender volume indeed. Fine cuisine assumes a certain amount of leisure and money. I'm not on a high horse; everyone gets to eat what he wants. In the Sandhills of Nebraska, I didn't shrink back from the Nuts and Gizzards $3.95 special of deep-fried calf testicles and chicken gizzards, which were fine when covered by a pink sheen of Tabasco. This proves I'm a normal guy. In addition to having your own garden, the miracle of Montana food is offered by Federal Express and United Parcel Service. The world's food supplies are available on an overnight basis. Only moments ago, I opened a cooler containing three fresh abalone and some loins of albacore tuna sent by a predatory friend in California.

I'm lucky enough to work hard the rest of the year and fish for fifty to sixty days in the warmer months with my friend and guide Danny Lahren. We float the Big Hole, the Missouri, but mostly the Yellowstone. As others have noted, a life outdoors encourages the appetite. For coronary reasons I avoid the classic Montana breakfast of side pork or chicken-fried steak with eggs, potatoes, and cream gravy, though I admit to loving it. I trade the rowing chores with Danny because I'm the usual neurotic writer and like the soothing, somewhat autistic rhythm of rowing. Also, you get to eat more with impunity.

Junk food is junk, and you can't let down your guard when fishing.

But what to eat? When fishing the Big Hole or the Missouri, we detour to the Front Street Market in Butte, a very good delicatessen, and curiously the closest at hand. The owner, Jim Yakawich, prepares us a huge sandwich on ciabatta bread that includes provolone, mortadella, and salami. We add Italian vinaigrette, onion, and roasted peppers in the boat just before eating to avoid the sandwich becoming soggy—few sportsmen are hearty enough to eat a wet sandwich. If the weather is cool enough, we pack along a Côtes du Rhône for the late afternoon. Frankly, alcohol in more than scant amounts is contraindicated in fly-fishing. Leaders become tangled and fish are misstruck, so the wine is usually saved for the last half hour of the day's fishing.

For our Yellowstone floats I order supplies from Zingerman's in Ann Arbor, Michigan, arguably the best all-around delicatessen in America, with a grand array of the world's cheeses, especially French and English. Equally important are gift packages from Mario Batali in New York City and his father, Armandino, in Seattle. From this father and son pair I receive a dozen different artisanal salamis, lamb and duck prosciutto, as well as the sacred guanciale for the evening pasta course. There are also chunks of lardo taken from the neck fat of pigs fed only on milk and cream and fruit in the glorious last months of their lives, not less glorious than our own in my opinion.

Frankly, though, food is rarely on my mind during the hours of actual fishing, and my purge from the cultural detritus (a euphemism) that my profession often buries me in and that drives me to all the comparative solitude I can muster. Fishing requires a magnum level of attention that is curiously restorative rather than exhausting. We carry the new Sibley bird book and binoculars, and identifying birds is the only break in our concentration. We can chat about food, wine, or women but not about politics.

When our more exotic food supplies run short, we pick up fried chicken and coleslaw from Albertsons. Until lately, I'd scorned this fried chicken, but to my surprise I have found it quite good. One must order the dark meat assortment, as wise heads have determined that the ubiquitous "skinless, boneless, chicken breasts" have sapped the moral vigor of America. Generally speaking, both the mammalian and the avian species are careful about what they eat. Junk food is junk, and you can't let down your guard when fishing.

FOOD AND MOOD

Existence is grounds for dismissal. It has only recently occurred to me that I might not be allowed to eat after I die. This is discouraging. "Make hay while the sun shines," they used to say back on our ancestral farm, a tiny splotch of poor land in northern Michigan that ensured our continuing poverty—that is, except at the table, because if you have cows, pigs, chickens, and a big garden, you eat bountifully if not well. Even in the Great Depression when the gut of urban America was scoured clean, country people hunched at a full trough and thus it is that I come from a long peasant tradition of three square meals a day. We ate a lot even when we weren't hungry because it was the way of my people.

Perhaps I should have called this little essay "Food and Religion" because, after all, religion is a mood, albeit an occasionally substantial mood. Toss aside your simpleminded incredulity for a while and think of me as Baba Ram Jimmy, a round, brown old man who has lifelong sought spirituality through food and drink. Right now in America it is hard to see the stars and moon through a blood-smeared windshield. In such difficult times we must turn to the sacral elements at hand, to specific rituals of worship, even if our private God is a twenty-ton Olmec stone head so neutral that it makes the Buddha look like a fraternity glad-hander. Needless to say the obvious rites at hand are breakfast, lunch, and dinner, by which we connect ourselves to holiness while still recognizing we are but animals in human clothing.

I am currently in physical and mental training for another assault on the mountains near Collioure, France, to look for the lost valise of poems by Antonio Machado, and much in my recent life has warred against this noble mission. After a glorious trip to northern Italy in late October to parse the mysteries of the white truffle, the inept folk at Lufthansa held me captive in Frankfurt, Germany, for a full day during which I caught a near-fatal virus. When I reached home in Montana, I fainted and tripped on a throw rug (non–alcohol-related household accident). The fall turned my face into a purple grapefruit (photo available). Instead of a visionary experience, this fall produced nothing; a discouraging view, this pure nothing. The trauma did induce a temporary exchange of personalities with Paolo Ranucci, a cobbler I met in Modena, Italy, but more on that later.

Inevitably this trauma led to a slump I could ill afford, what with a novel due in March for that Walmart of words, American publishing. There is no place in the world for me except where I already am, and luckily this is usually near a kitchen. I began my recovery from the slump by making posole, a Mexican hominy stew, out of a large buffalo heart a worried friend had sent. A hunting acquaintance gave me a package of mountain lion chorizo, having shot a record-size male that had been preying on calves while it was courting a snarling female. How unaware we become of danger during our absurd mating dances. A writer I know in Paris was struck by a taxi when he hurriedly crossed Boulevard Raspail in order to follow a girl with a pert butt. I made puttanesca (whore's sauce) several times, thinking it appropriate for a writer. I ate antelope short ribs and the liver of a virgin elk, followed by Hungarian partridge, quail, and doves. I turned a keg of salt herring into a huge bowl of pickled herring using the recipe of my grandmother Hulda Wahlgren, who lived to be ninety-seven, though she did say to me, "This is going on too long." I came down with gout, which gave my right big toe an aching pulse synchronous with my face. I drank a lot of French red wine even though my type 2 diabetes requires that I walk two hours per bottle. It's far better to walk than to have your feet cut off because of this disease. Armandino Batali, the father of Mario, sent me a large package of lardo and I began to further turn the corner, back to a Technicolor life. To be sure, lardo is pure pork fat but we don't shrink from the high fat content of the very necessary Jewish corned beef tongue. Besides, if you study the behavior of pigs you witness a lust for life that leaves the tribe of whining writers sucking hind teat, a shriveled and unproductive food source indeed.

I knew my recovery was nearly complete when I wrote ten pages of my novel on New Year's Eve. I hadn't written that much in a day since I completed my novella *Legends of the Fall* in nine days in 1978. I certainly won't try it again because the effort ruined a night's sleep. The earth began to whirl too fast. The dead used my brain as a chat room. I sensed there was a bear in the bamboo thicket outside the patio. My dog Zilpha didn't want to sit on my lap, a nightly ritual, until I coaxed her with a piece of herring. Labs seem to be the only breed that enjoys herring.

So I'm now back in training for Machado and for a book to be called "Pilgrimages," wherein I visit the graves of twenty writers I revere and try to reconstruct a bit of their mystery, and also what they ate. Research can also become errant and confusing. For instance, one day I was nonplussed to discover that three different small third world cultures have idioms that refer to the female pudendum as a *grief muffin*. Of necessity, these are cultures where muffins are part of the diet. We are where we live. This becomes evident in the foodways of the rich folk in the United States, who wander to and fro across the land acquiring lifestyles commensurate with their warm feelings about their wealth. They are fond of a neutral cuisine that reminds one of Umberto Eco's ideas on imitation. Women wearing fifty-grand's-worth of turquoise and lace granny dresses serve you Mexican food as remote from Mexican cuisine as a Winnipeg McDonald's. Genuine food tends to emerge from the spirit of place. When I was eating the boned stuffed pig leg, zampone, in Parma, I thought how shameful that this great dish wasn't available in the United States. Couldn't the woebegone Republicans of Iowa be saved from political mischief by being set to work boning the millions of local pig legs, but then these people are repelled by the staff of life, garlic. The spirit of place even enters our sexual behavior. When I was in a little town north of Kathmandu, having failed to climb a peak in sneakers, I met a drunken Tibetan prostitute while I was dining on a bowl of tsampa and rotten yak blood. Through an interpreter this woman offered to sleep with me for a thousand dollars, but I couldn't partake in her *couloir* or *crevasse*. We tend to think of all Tibetans as strict adherents of the Dalai Lama but this is apparently not true.

Back to Paolo Ranucci. I met this cobbler in Modena when I stopped by his dusty shop one morning after a nail in my worn shoe had bloodied my foot and ruined a two-dollar pair of socks. He speculated about why I wore such cheap shoes when he had seen me emerge from an expensive restaurant across the street the evening before. "Instead of the esteemed Sassicaia, drink Antinori plonk a couple of days and then you can afford a good pair of shoes," he said in English. Sensing an anti-American binge in the offing, I countered by asking why Italians are uniformly ignorant of their great poet Gaspara Stampa. This intrigued him and we went to a café for a few glasses of harmless prosecco. It turned out that in the 1970s, Ranucci had attended the writers' school at the University of Iowa for two years but then, for reasons of the bad local food and a shortage he sensed in his own talent, he left. He returned home and continued the family tradition of shoemaking, pointing out that the brogans he wore in the café had been made by his father in 1948. I admitted that my disgusting shoes were less than a year old. We had a light lunch at Giusti of tagliarini laden with white truffles, braised pig cheeks, and veal chops to fill any stray empty stomach corners, plus a couple of bottles of old Barolo. Once again I had spent my shoe money. It's so easy when you're hungry and throwing caution out the always-open window.

Ranucci's point of view was colored by pastel melancholy. He had decided he'd rather be a good cobbler than one of a hundred thousand mediocre poets. "Why bother if I can't be a singular lamp burning in our collective death ward?" he asked. I was stumped while we sipped at our crystal goblets of grappa. He advised me that on my upcoming trip for a week in Florence, after a full day in the Pitti Palace and the Uffizi, I should meditate on the liberally given American degree, the master of fine arts. Isn't it a little cheeky? he wondered aloud.

We spent a couple of hours walking off lunch, when a stretcher would have been more appropriate for me. I fell down in what I thought was the garden of the Finzi-Continis, my face narrowly missing a pile of dog shit that appeared to be a metaphor of our invasion of Iraq. We visited the market, perhaps the finest in Europe, and I bought a large white truffle to eat like a soiled apple with my after-nap coffee. Ranucci cautioned me on my religious habits, saying that I might visit Dante's house in Florence and try to envision a better Beatrice than the possible sin of gluttony.

And so I did. Luckily I had packed a difficult book, *Holy Feast and Holy Fast: The Religious Significance of Food to Medieval Women* by Caroline Walker Bynum. I had never thought of the figure of Beatrice as nearly as interesting as a bowl of steaming tripe, but I had been wrong before, having stridently insisted in the 1980s that this whole computer thing was going nowhere. I took the Bynum book along to a fine meal at Cibreo and several pages became shamefully stuck together with tripe juice. I had spent the afternoon at Dante's house, and that night under a full Florentine moon I dreamed of my own Beatrice, only she was wearing garishly red hot pants. On my dawn ten-kilometer run along the Arno, I questioned whether it wasn't a little too late for Beatrice to become an intimate part of my life, especially when she wouldn't properly dress the part.

Now I'm on the eve of an unpleasant trip to New York City, where I intend to resign from everything. Writing novels is massively discouraging, compared to tercets and strophes. New York City is enshrouded of late with a sickly green bubble, a theme park for the rich with *The New Yorker* and the *New York Times* its possibly blasphemous mouthpieces. A martini costs fifteen dollars and a passable hotel room five hundred. New York City makes the supposed greed of Paris look like a Girl Scout bake sale. Mario Batali's Casa Mono restaurant is next to my little hotel and I have written ahead to see if they will make me oatmeal

I fell down in what I thought was the garden of the Finzi-Continis, my face narrowly missing a pile of dog shit that appeared to be a metaphor of our invasion of Iraq. We visited the market, perhaps the finest in Europe, and I bought a large white truffle to eat like a soiled apple with my after-nap coffee.

crepes filled with an epiphyte flan, those flowers I saw hanging from phone lines in Veracruz that live solely on air and rain.

Of late, I've had the urge to return to Earth for a while before being launched into space as a fatally skinless rocket. I've been noticing tiny black beetles and a number of new species of small brown birds, the soul life of crows, and have been studying Roberto Calasso's *Literature and the Gods*, sensing that these waifish creatures, the gods, can't be approached directly—and certainly not by publishing books. Their names are unavailable to the ambitious.

VIN BLANC

A few decades ago it occurred to me that so much of life for a novelist and poet is flying solo and usually in a remote area above the Mato Grosso. There are no lights in the world below, and should you be lucky enough to crash gently on a canopy of trees you will be met by hordes of anacondas and fer-de-lance after you shinny down a tree trunk. We are isolated stockbrokers of life's essences, and it is always 1929.

The grand thing about wine is that it's something you get to do with other people, along with the noble sports of fishing and hunting. When your "eye is in fine frenzy rolling," as Shakespeare would have it, you forget that you are a tribal creature and need the company of others. There is a grand pleasure in opening a good wine and cooking with friends. In fact, opening fine wine is as near to the sacramental as I get, having abandoned organized religion in my teens after a Baptist minister told me that Mozart's music was "satanic." Everywhere we are witness to the extreme confidence some people have in their stupidities.

As the years have passed you might say that I sought my spirituality through food and wine, a pleasant place to look for spirituality along with the natural world. Just the other day I was floating on the Big Hole River trout fishing with a friend. About a half hour from our destination and the end of a good fishing day we anchored in an eddy and opened a bottle of chilled Bouzeron. The wine

We are isolated stockbrokers of life's essences, and it is always 1929.

seemed as mysteriously delicious as the flowing river. We drank in silence, watching clouds of swallows and bullbats swoop after the late afternoon insects. There isn't a three-star restaurant in France that offers a better location to drink wine. Just before finishing the bottle we suddenly had to move on because a mother moose and her baby plunged through the wild roses on the nearby bank. This is like being rousted by the world's largest bar bouncer, about a thousand pounds to be exact.

This has been a time of reconsiderations for me. Only last year it would have been unthinkable for me to have a bottle of white wine in the drift boat. I connect hunting and fishing with the color of blood. With type 2 diabetes, however, two bottles of red wine a day became inappropriate, a euphemism of course. One bottle a day is possible with a proper morning walk with the dogs, or rowing a drift boat for four hours in a fairly heavy current.

My true, personal revolution came in Parma, Italy, last autumn. I discovered that I could have a glass of Prosecco di Valdobbiadene and then continue on with the hard work of tourism. Naturally I prefer markets to cathedrals. When I have a glass of red I mostly want another glass of red. I spent hours in the splendid market in Modena on a single glass of prosecco. I even discovered that when you drink prosecco while cooking you don't blow the recipe. When I explained my discovery to my friend Mario Batali, he said, "Everybody knows that." He's a big fellow to say the least and regularly drinks prosecco while he cooks. When we got home I ordered a number of cases and my cooking has improved. The red arrives when the game birds are properly roasted, not before.

I find that I often discover things that many people know. It reminds me that when we discovered the Grand Canyon there were already a thousand Havasupai Indians living within it. When I talked to a number of sophisticated friends about how appalled I was after seeing the film *Mondovino*, they lectured me on my innocence as an immature hermit, which is the essential trajectory of the novelist and poet.

Mondovino somewhat bruised my sacramental feelings about wine, but not for all that long. I quickly realized that the wine world shares a specific silliness with the worlds of art, literature, and food, not to speak of religion. At times all of these are a microcosm of the boxing world with a dozen Don Kings at the top. It is the silliness of myopia, the frog at the bottom of the well pit that thinks the well pit is the world. When I'm told that Napa Valley is the new Vatican of the wine world I say that it reminds me more of a fiefdom of Pat Robertson. To be fair and since I know them so well I have to say that for pure shabbiness compared to the worlds of art and literature, which is to say galleries and publishing, wine takes third place.

My bruises from *Mondovino* healed rather quickly when I realized yet again that taste is idiosyncratic. There is no Monoethic Palate to guide us, no numerical Ten Commandments to guide us with a steely embrace. Of course this is a paint by number world. Learning the world for most of us is a permanent elementary school. If you need to know what refrigerator to buy, check out *Consumer Reports*, and any amateur with a chunky wallet can concentrate on the hundred best vintages in the world. It's the next ten thousand vintages that are up for grabs. Around here in Montana there are eco-ninnies who love the natural world with a severely limited and prescriptive guidebook. Everywhere we go we also meet wine-ninnies.

Back to Bouzeron and the spirit of wine and the fact that I didn't discover this affordable wine earlier because I was basically a red wine snot. Of course on occasions I liked Puligny-Montrachet, Meursault, Sancerre, Silex, Domaine Tempier rosé when my wife and daughters would share their well-guarded horde of the latter. My first Bouzeron came with a meal of *poulet estragon* with roasted vegetables. I was a little dumbfounded by how much I liked the wine and immediately consulted my Wine Master in Seattle, Peter Lewis, who explained de Villaine's Aligoté thus: "It is utterly pleasant and unassuming. You don't need to stretch or strain to appreciate it. It is uncomplicated; but that's not to say that it is simple. Just that the experience of it is not cerebral; it's sensual without being hedonistic." After describing certain technicalities Peter goes on to say, "It's a quaffer, lovely to drink; in fact, at times it seems a little too easy to drink. It's one of those wines that seem mysteriously to evaporate from your glass—you weren't aware that you were drinking that much."

When I'm told that Napa Valley is the new Vatican of the wine world I say that it reminds me more of a fiefdom of Pat Robertson.

And there you have it. In any event, Bouzeron reminded me of my discovery of Domaine Tempier Bandol so long ago, a wine still guaranteed to counteract the weariness brought about by the corrosive parsimony of spirit found everywhere in America today. A wine that you love haunts you by ordinary means. I was struck dumb by my last bottle of 1968 Château d'Yquem in my diminished cellar, but when you find a wine you truly love under twenty bucks you should bow down and give thanks to the gods.

I have had reason to be quite embarrassed lately, a rare emotion for me. I have long poked fun at the pathetic attempts professional tasters make to characterize wine in terms of fruit other than grapes. I was caught severely off balance when Kermit Lynch sent me a case of mixed whites to dabble with. I felt immediately trapped by the ineffable mystery of taste. A ripe peach tastes exactly like a ripe peach. A fine porterhouse tastes like nothing else in the world but a fine porterhouse. Brouilly tastes like Brouilly, which I have drunk dozens of times at Café Select on Montparnasse. Good flavors are described in a general atmosphere of pleasure. Bad flavors are easier to describe because of the immense world of shared experience. So this case of varied white wines trapped me both in my own limitations as a writer and in the rather obvious limitations of language itself. I make countless aesthetic decisions when composing a novel but am far less comfortable making critiques of the work of others. With wine it is especially difficult because you must approach the bottle at the level of the vintner's intentions, just as it is pointless to say that Stephen King isn't as good as William Faulkner.

So here I am hoist with my own petard but still refusing to introduce my case of white to the local fruit market. Here are a few favorites, leaving a number of them in silence.

1. *Domaine de la Tour du Bon 2004*: Pretty good but a little sweet for my taste. Acceptable on a warm twilight watching birds from our patio in Patagonia, Arizona. One of the thousands of wildflowers I can't name even though I like them all. Naturally had to open a red for the rather musky buffalo shank stew I had made for dinner.

2. *Philippe Faury Saint Joseph 2004*: My father was an agronomist who with eyes closed could name the weeds and grasses he smelled. Naturally I can detect a herring egg sandwich when I bite into it. In this wine I can taste the stones of the Rhône Valley. The place suits me and so does the wine.

3. *Condrieu 2004—Faury*: This wine was easy because I drank it with a sauté of pike, perch, and bluegill fillet Fed Exed to me as a gift from Minnesota. There was an edge of tartness I revere in expensive wines and it was very friendly with the fish.

4. *Ermitage du Pic St. Loup*: This was also easy because I love the *terroir*, and had pleasant memories of drinking it in a café in the grand square of Montpellier while watching the prettiest woman in France walk by. This wine tastes as soft and pleasant as the back of a girl's knee after she has taken a

dip in the Mediterranean. I drank it with the light-breasted scaled quail I had shot, then downshifted to the mighty Vacqueyras, Sang des Cailloux, for the shoulder of wild pig.

5. *Château la Roque*: I'm served this frequently in France while I'm waiting impatiently for the red. I have learned to like it and turn to it when I find a bistro list flimsy. I love odd menu items like beef snout in vinaigrette (the best is at the wine bar Rubis in Paris) and the la Roque can stand up to it.

I have not betrayed my first love, red wine. I have only tried to balance my unbalanced taste. White wine has offered me a specific equilibrium on my travels and at home where I try to mind my manners. Since I have leavened my wine drinking with white I haven't had a single gout attack which in the past was a regular event. It's hard to be on a book tour in France when you're walking like Joe Cocker. Being an idiosyncratic man with idiosyncratic tastes I still won't drink white wine after dark. The darkness beckons red.

ETERNITY AND FOOD

At my age every word I write may be my last. In my late teens while I was suffering from a nearly fatal disease, the doctors, Bob and Bob Jr., gave me fifty years to live. I've always loathed the notion of "living on borrowed time" even though I'm confident that God wears a watch as big as the moon and with no dials. Unlike nearly all intellectuals I have no problem chatting about God though I've never connected with Him on my cellular like George Bush. I recently spent time with a physicist-inventor who has devised a clock that will last ten thousand years to be installed in a cave at an elevation, not incidentally, of ten thousand feet on a mountain in Nevada.

The big question this morning is, Did I have a prequel? And will I have a postquel? Is there an end to eating? Are we all mere mortals or are there exceptions? Apollinaire said that Jesus held the world's high altitude record. To the contrary of a recent Sony movie Jesus never married Magdalene. Their relationship went kaput when he spent his forty days alone in the wilderness. Women aren't biologically structured to wait forty days according to Kinsey who interviewed ten thousand grocery delivery boys during the Second World War when so many husbands were away fighting for freedom. One can imagine the scene repeated countless times. The boy puts the bags of groceries on the kitchen table, his skin tingling with premonition. He half turns and she leaps on him like a mountain lion jumping a fawn.

Eating is a race against time. This morning I shot yet another crotalid (rattlesnake) near the steps of my study, its writhing body finally slumping into a question mark. No more rodentia lunches for this Republican sucker whose relative killed my beloved English setter, Rose. I pitched the dead snake to the pigs, and the big sow, Mary, ate it with the evident pleasure of a hungry man before a plate of foie gras. She smiled at me as if to say, "Thank you, we're on Earth together. When you eat my big hams I'll be turned loose in heaven in a field of ripe sweet corn and muskmelons."

All of my jobs have required considerable fuel. During the few months I worked as a contortionist for the Cirque du Soleil I astounded kings and presidents, not to speak of hordes of riffraff, by my ability to stand on a forefinger, the finger made improbably muscular by writing longhand so that it looks like a buffalo turkey wing. Big jobs demand immense meals.

Writers need to be a little cynical about their motives and I have noted that certain of my vaunted ancillary projects tend to take me to countries where I wish to eat. I call this activity "eating the country." How can you pretend to understand France or Spain unless province by province you eat what they eat, thus making your empathy a matter of biology. Last fall's zampone (stuffed pig's leg) eaten in Parma and Modena has entered my neurons and increased my sympathy for Cesare Pavese, just as eating dozens of different game birds in quantity made me a better bird-watcher.

Let's get utterly serious, whatever that might mean. We simply have no evidence that we've had a prequel or will have a postquel.

Years ago in a tavern (I'm a student of taverns) in Dannebrog, Nebraska, on the edge of the Sandhills, a group of very old farmers welcomed me home insisting that I had left the area in 1938. Frankly, I don't look like anyone else what with buckteeth and a blind eye. Nothing I could say would dissuade them that I wasn't the local young man who had hit the road just before the Second World War when in fact I was only a few months old. Of course as an artiste I was daffy enough to give the conviction of these geezers some credence. Maybe this was why I felt so comfortable in the Sandhills during all of the months I was researching my novels *Dalva* and *The Road Home*. Of course I was mildly frightened, having occasionally convinced myself of Rimbaud's dictum, "Everything we are taught is false." Luckily food kills fear and I drove north to the Peppermill in Valentine where a three-pound porterhouse and two bottles of red returned me to the accepted earth. This area produces the best beef in the United States and I especially like the well-aged Chianina-Angus cross. Sad to say this much beef at one sitting will give you Arnold Schwarzenegger dreams of being someone like Pelle the Conqueror swinging a bloody ax and mating bulbous-butted women wearing soiled opossum skins. Specific foods cause specific dreams.

A certain small group of basic nitwits knows that to be a literary novelist and "minor regional novelist and poet" (as I have been called) is to spend a lifetime walking across freshly plowed fields. In other words, lumpy. However, I have no complaints because when not actually writing I get to be outdoors doing important things like hunting, fishing, bird-watching, roasting a wild piglet, studying the sources of creeks, or driving ornate mandalas around the entire country. By profession I collect memories. Once in Toronto after eating a stellar tongue sandwich I saw a woman slip on a banana peel and fall to the sidewalk. I turned away, having been taught by Christian parents not to look up a woman's legs unless invited to do so. When I helped her up I thought she might say something sexy like "Buy me a villa," but she looked in shy distaste at my Quasimodo face. I quivered at her dandelion scent. Her blouse was in disarray and when

I caught a split-second glance at her belly button I knew she was a human being rather than an android.

On a recent trip to Europe I had an accidental insight into my postquel. The trip began poorly in cold rainy Paris in March when thousands of malcontents were busy marching to and fro and burning cars, the acrid smell of which is off-putting to the appetite, but not as much as the giant Salon du Livre, what is known euphemistically as a "book fair" but in reality is a giant Walmart packed with book vendors and their largely tawdry wares. Three times I fainted from torpor and tipped over to the floor as old people are wont to do. I might have perished without the best *tête de veau* of my life one evening at Apicius. For mental and physical well-being I recommend eating the head of a calf. One becomes playful and innocent. And the next noon I had the wild-pig rillettes at La Taverne Basque, a regular hangout of mine on Cherche Midi. A woman is lucky indeed to meet a man who has eaten wild pig rillettes in the last twenty-four hours. Her partner will paw the air and snort loudly.

This much beef at one sitting will give you Arnold Schwarzenegger dreams of being someone like Pelle the Conqueror swinging a bloody ax and mating bulbous-butted women wearing soiled opossum skins. Specific foods cause specific dreams.

In Paris I gave a speech to a mass of students advising them to take drugs, drink as much as possible, and stay on strike forever, after which I flew down to Seville on my necromancer's project called "Pilgrimages," the same project that took me to Collioure to visit Antonio Machado's grave and search for his lost poems that likely were eaten by Falangist goats. In Seville I walked daily on the banks of the Guadalquivir with Christine Campadieu, the famed French vintner who keeps me from tipping over in front of cars and also speaks many languages while I'm limited to Michigan English, a perverse gibberish, though in most countries for some reason I'm totally informed in food and wine terminology.

I was in Seville to walk where Federico García Lorca walked. He loved the Guadalquivir. By chance this day in June is his birthday and were he alive he would be one hundred and eight, which is old indeed. Unfortunately in Granada, a few hours after visiting Lorca's execution site at the Barranco de Viznar, I became quite ill so that on the way home I ended up in the emergency ward at the Resurrection Medical Center near O'Hare Airport in Chicago. My tentative consciousness at the time whirled with Spanish dreams as the IVs in both arms attempted to return me to "normal," also a somewhat tentative state. I thought of Lorca, who it is said was shot in the ass repeatedly with a high-powered rifle because he was "gay," a term not used at the time. I had also stayed in a room he favored at a hotel in Granada but there I mostly had thoughts of Miguel Hernandez dying in prison in Madrid.

Frankly the hospital was reassuring because I had been without food and wine for four days and felt like Dondi Gandhi, a comic-strip waif. In the hospital I was back with Machado wheeling his eighteen-year-old wife around the hills of Castile as her TB-ridden body lost its ability to breathe, and also Machado carrying his old mom across the border into Collioure on a cold rainy night. He died a month later and in the hospital it didn't seem like a bad idea but more of an adventure that you wouldn't be able to write about. As a poet I hope for an epiphany every day and this would be a whopper.

Back to the postquel. On the last leg of the return trip to our winter *casita* on the Mexican border I dreamed I'd be reincarnated as a scraggly elm tree out in a pasture against which cows would rub their itchy fly bites. This seemed a grand idea what with the sensuosity of having one's bark rubbed by mammals, skin to skin as it were, and even more important, it meant that there would be eating after death. Trees, of course, eat not with their roots, which are nutritional conduits, but with the millions of infinitesimal root hairs that protrude into the soil from the roots. In short I would continue a form of existence by eating through my hair. What a relief. It was too much to imagine that Manuela the flamenco dancer from Seville would ever visit and rub against the homely elm but as many of us have noted, we can't have everything.

Now I am back rowing a boat down large rivers and trout fishing. This and cooking seem quite enough though occasionally a strophe will land on my head in the form of an undiscovered bird. I have become involved in a perhaps doomed money project I call "The Michelangelo Mode" in order to earn enough to buy expensive food and French wine. The project involves the relatively new nano science, and also a stray dog I met in Florence last October that was obviously related to a dog of Michelangelo's. Five stories under the Uffizi in a subbasement full of skulls the dog led me to a trove of manuscripts unknown to the museum's employees who sit around all of the time drinking prosecco. The manuscripts smelled like white truffles but the odor may have emanated from my fingertips and mustache because I had been eating white truffles twice a day for thirteen days. The number thirteen is a key here and it precipitated a trip to Arlington, Texas, a nasty headquarters for training Homeland Security employees, but then I needed to use some of their high-tech equipment. A young woman who helped me also smelled like white truffles though it was somewhat veiled by the scent of her lunch at Burger King.

My deep thinking has recently driven my wife, children, and friends quite batty. We all began as female and weighing virtually nothing but immediately began gathering volume. Our enclosed nano souls are a millionth the size of a grain of average beach sand tainted by suntan lotion. We began as the Nano People and our souls retain their original size, while our bodies vary, but can reach a thousand pounds in a number of instances (a big guy named Walter ate several chickens and quarts of Pepsi for breakfast). When the young woman in Arlington noted this soul particle through an electron microscope she insisted on naming it a "wiggly squiggly," which lacks resonance.

The use of nanotechnology on Michelangelo's manuscript revealed, among other things, his prediction that God would abandon our galaxy in 1907 in hopes of doing a better job somewhere among the ninety-five billion other galaxies. This is a tad discouraging but not to an elm tree. I can imagine the approach of a friendly Holstein, her udder swaying slightly in a southern breeze that also ripples my leaves. My root hairs suck gently at the soil in an endless meal. The Holstein turns around because the obnoxious fly bite is near her nether parts. She rubs her butt against my bark. What a fabulous memory of my past life.

THE SPIRIT OF WINE

I have long since publicly admitted that I seek spirituality through food and wine. In France, Italy, and Spain, I seem more drawn to markets and cafés than to churches and museums. Too many portraits of bleeding Jesus and His lachrymose Momma make me thirsty. The Lord Himself said on the cross, "I thirst" and since our world itself has become a ubiquitous and prolonged crucifixion it is altogether logical that we are thirsty.

Yesterday afternoon I was far up a canyon near the Mexican border trying to shoot a few doves to roast when I came upon a calf who was willing to be petted, perhaps because she had no previous contact with brutish humans. While scratching her pretty ears I segued to a tangled group of emotions toward wine. Why does Bordeaux make me feel Catholic, crisp, and confident—an illusion indeed—while Burgundy causes an itchy, sexy, somnolent mood? With my day-to-day

Côtes du Rhône I am a working writer with vaguely elevated thoughts of my responsibilities, but also with my mind's eye on a plumpish waitress at a local Mexican restaurant.

Heading back down the canyon with the calf following me, I recalled some splendid wines I had drunk at a private home in Malibu during my manic days in Hollywood. The collector's house red was a 1961 Lafite, a pleasant substitute for a predinner martini. I was in the kitchen one evening preparing dinner and drinking a bottle of Romanée-Conti from the 1950s when a fashion model asked, "How can you drink that shit? It makes me dizzy." She properly mistook me for a servant and asked for a "Jack and Coke," surely an inscrutable drink, but then so is taste in general. On Friday nights in college two of my best friends would drink an entire case of beer apiece and didn't seem to mind the ensuing vomiting. I was the driver and of limited means so my weekend binge meant only a seventy-cent bottle of Gallo Burgundy. Both of these friends, of course, are now dead and I'm still on the lid of earth rather than under, and drinking wine daily.

During a general state of rebellion in my early teens I went to the Baptist church though our family was Congregationalist, a kind of lowercase Episcopalian. I told my dad who was an agriculturalist that the Baptists claimed that in biblical days the wine was simple grape juice. He said, "Bullpoop," adding that they had been making true wine in the Middle East for four thousand years, and that non-drinkers liked to spread lies about alcohol. He said that when Saint Paul maintained, "A little wine for thy stomach's infirmities," he was talking about actual wine, not grape juice. Since then it has occurred to me that if Christianity offered a six-ounce glass of solid French red for Communion, churches would be happier and consequently more spiritual places.

In the early 1970s during a hokum banquet in Ireland I drank several goblets of mead and was ill for a week with ravaged intestines. The physical mischief caused by bad forms of alcohol is infinite. I have posited the idea, perhaps fact, that heavy beer drinkers must find a type of sexual release in their relentless peeing. One warm day in my favorite saloon in a village near my former cabin in the Upper

Peninsula, an old man drank thirty-eight bottles of Pabst Blue Rib-
bon. This is clearly too much, and he just as clearly endangered his
body during his dozens of walks to the toilet. This amount comes to
twenty-eight pounds of liquids which cannot be retained indefinitely
by the human body, thus the walks to the toilet were a necessary
peril. Another friend in the area, a huge mixed-blood Chippewa,
wasn't feeling well drink-
ing two fifths of whiskey   *It has occurred to me that if*
a day and under my wise
counsel reduced it to a   *Christianity offered a six-ounce*
single fifth. Last summer   *glass of solid French red for*
in Montana I advised an   *Communion, churches would be*
unruly friend that after a
hot day of fishing a quin-   *happier and consequently more*
tuple martini might be   *spiritual places.*
unwise as the alcohol will
shoot through the dehydrated body and land on the brainpan like
an ICBM. In the remoter areas of the country my advice is sought
whereas on our two dream coasts everyone is smart, albeit petulant,
and I am considered a bumpkin. Also a slow study. It took me three
years of hard work and unfathomable willpower to make a bottle
of wine last an hour. Sipping seemed quite unnatural to a mouth
disposed toward gulping.

In a lifetime of thousands of visits to country taverns, I have
noticed that beer drinking causes fistfights and wife beating. A
French theologian, Michel Braudeau, has suggested that heavy beer
drinking cleared the moral way for Germany to begin World War
I and World War II. Beer drinking is at the root of the lugubrious
sentimentality that makes murder for an idea logical. Conversely,
drinking nothing at all is equally dangerous. Try to imagine Washington D.C.'s infamous Beltway as a moral Berlin Wall within
which low-rent chiselers concoct wars and other forms of our future
suffering. I recently read that there are sixty lobbyists per member
of Congress. Think if liquor and beer were forbidden within the
Beltway and each day the lobbyists were limited to giving each

member of Congress a good bottle of French wine. Grace would return quickly to our bruised republic. I would also like to remind those teetotaler fundamentalist titans, Pat Robertson and Jerry Falwell, who are so enamored of political power, that the Catholic Church has maintained its political power nearly two thousand years no doubt because the leaders drink wine. I well remember a group of bulbous priests at a Roman trattoria quite literally pouring down wine. I asked the waiter what they were celebrating and he said enviously that they did it every day. They were drinking Antinori Vipera which is scarcely cheap plonk. Come to think of it, I would gladly contribute to any church that replaced its Communion wine with Côtes du Rhône.

At a wonderful local Mexican restaurant called Las Vigas, I often begin a meal with a shot of Herradura tequila, a Pacifico beer, and an ample bowl of chicharrones which, of course, are deep-fried intestines, after which I have a plate of machaca and beans (Mexican reconstituted dried beef laden with chiles). I hosted a feast for twenty-five friends last April in this restaurant which included a whole wild pig spit-roasted, giant Guaymas shrimp (eight to a pound), platters of machaca, and Herradura and Pacifico. Wine simply isn't appropriate for these flavors. We also had a couple of divine mariachi singers who had a dulcet effect on the crowd, singing their melancholy plaints about love and death which neutralized any strident effects of the beer.

Curiously, New York City is the only place on earth where I feel an urgent need for a vodka martini, actually a raving desire. A day of back-to-back insignificant meetings and the sight of thousands of nitwits milling around talking on their cell phones deeply enervates me. My soul becomes splenetic and I need to Taser myself before a predinner nap. A bar next to my hotel on Irving Place is kind enough to serve me a martini for only thirteen dollars, a price at which you can buy four in Montana. In New York City, however, you can hear expensively dressed career people talking about themselves at a speed that will remind you of the old Alvin the Chipmunk phonograph records. You leave the bar in a hurry, thinking that Castro had some good ideas, and take a snooze after planning the evening's wines.

Life is rarely instructive. One of the wisest and best writers I know, Peter Matthiessen, who loves good wine, once said, "I have never learned from experience." Put that in your pipe and smoke it. Anyway, a Hollywood studio had put me up in the Hôtel Plaza Athénée for a significant meeting about the fate of a hundred-million-dollar movie. I was stressed and jet-lagged over the nastiness of the business world which is as morally compromised as the literary world, and went into the hotel bar for a double shot of V.O. Canadian whiskey which was forty-two dollars, a tad stiff price-wise. I'm not comfortable in the Plaza Athénée in Paris or the Ritz in my collection of fifty-dollar sport coats. I've been easygoing about taking friends out for a seven-hundred-dollar meal but it would be unthinkable to spend that much on an article of clothing. I said to the Plaza Athénée barman, "Are you fucking kidding" and he poured me a four-dollar glass of Côtes du Rhône saying that it was the solution to all the problems in life.

I rarely feel spiritual in New York or Paris except when I've stopped at the old church across the side street from Les Deux Magots on St. Germain and lit candles for the liver of my friend, the renowned gourmand Gérard Oberlé, who caught hepatitis in Egypt and couldn't drink wine for two years. His suffering was incalculable and on several occasions I lit five bucks' worth of candles which brought about his recovery.

The other day on a very warm border winter afternoon, I was sitting on the patio with my wife Linda, sharing a bottle of delightful Bouzeron. We were watching a rare pair of hepatic tanagers at the feeder. These birds evidently don't get hepatitis. It was all very pleasant and I recalled again a passage from the journal of a southern artist who had been hospitalized with schizophrenia. He wrote, "Birds are holes in heaven through which man may pass." I had this little epiphany that wine could do the same thing if properly used. We all have learned, sometimes painfully, that more is not necessarily better than less. When Baudelaire wrote in his famed "Enivrez-Vous,"

"Be always drunk on wine or poetry or virtue," he likely didn't mean commode-hugging drunk. Wine can offer oxygen to the spirit, I thought, getting off my deck chair and going into the kitchen to cook some elk steak and dietetic potatoes fried in duck fat, and not incidentally opening a bottle of Domaine Tempier Bandol because I had read a secret bible in France that said to drink red after dark to fight off the night in our souls.

HERE I STAND FOR A
FEW MINUTES

My words are only hot pads for an unacceptable reality. Many intelligent people, Canadians among them, have recently noted that
the world is apparently committing suicide. This fact is having
severe effects on our mental and physical health. The question
is, How can we personally counterattack the horrors of the world
around us without using excessive amounts of alcohol, drugs, and
television watching, the latter being the curse the Indian chief
Seattle put upon us? The answer, of course, is to achieve the ultimate in physical and mental health. We have to become like those
virtual superheroes in comics and movies so beloved by children
and politicians.

To show you what's possible, in the bad old days when I abused
alcohol and drugs I would regularly need nine cups of coffee and nine

cigarettes to get started in the morning and now I'm down to five of each. I did it all with willpower, a much-neglected secret ability within all of us albeit in minimal amounts.

We are taught that knowledge is power but then we are unsure of what power is. If I go to the doctor tomorrow to find out if fifty years of heavy smoking has damaged my lungs, what kind of power will this knowledge give me? During the many years I made a partial living by screenwriting, produc-

My words are only hot pads for an unacceptable reality.

ers would ask me to create characters who become *empowered* but I never really got a fix on this concept, thus my Hollywood career was doomed. I met many people out there who said that they felt empowered but I couldn't determine by their behavior what this might mean except for their giddy aggressiveness while snorting cocaine. Another hot issue at the time (more than ten years ago) was the mind-body connection. Millions were spent trying to make this concept visual. I inappropriately said in a meeting, "Yeah, I get it. On a hot day a dog wakes up and thinks, I'm thirsty, so he walks across the porch and drinks water from a bowl." The important producer said, "We're not making a dog picture." I segued to a more pungent aspect of this high concept. "You're watching Penélope Cruz in *Jamón, Jamón.* Your mind watches her and your body springs a woody, you know, a boner." The producer took a few calls before he said, "Penélope isn't bankable. Give me something where she's teamed with Michelle Pfeiffer." My fertile mind kicked in and I said, "Perhaps Penélope and Michelle are partners in a low-rent feminist detective agency in Encino. They're framed by a Republican senator and put in a women's prison. There's the obligatory riot and twenty-three naked women are shot by guards with AK-47s in a huge stark-white shower room." I got the assignment and wrote the screenplay in ten days aided by a case of vodka, thus continuing to support my vice of writing books of poems and novels.

But I have digressed. Obviously our livelihoods can be discouraging. An old fishing friend attached bumpers at an Oldsmobile factory for twenty years before he moved up to windshields. His brother taught a seminar on Edmund Spenser's *The Faerie Queene* at a prominent university for thirty years. Once when we were camped out trout fishing, the brothers agreed that their jobs were remarkably similar. Everyone involved knows that the arts are a cruel mistress and few of us indeed earn room and board from our strophes and etchings, and if you make a buck or two there is the additional worry that your work is primarily a soiled toy for the elitist children who can afford twenty-five dollars for a novel or a book of poems.

I couldn't help noticing that even in show business good food is the true source of power and health especially at the highest level. I was lucky enough to take meals with Orson Welles, John Huston, and Federico Fellini, and these big boys were not quick to push back from their plates or wineglasses. A legion of the dweebs and snivelers that make up our population of body-Nazis were startled indeed when Huston and Welles achieved their biblical three score and ten, given their reputations as tosspots and trenchermen. One of my few regrets after a dinner conversation with Fellini is that he said, "We must cook together," and I never made it to Rome to do so.

Of late I've been concentrating on wild food. In November in a twenty-four-hour period I ate an antelope liver and heart and the resulting sense of well-being was astonishing except for the goutish big toe of my right foot, which was a signal not to do this every day. Shortly thereafter I set about making some English game pies. I'm not particularly a fan of English food except for the gorgeous cookbook of Fergus Henderson called *The Whole Beast: Nose to Tail Eating.* I realize the signs are now good over there but their grand traditions ceased after the First World War when citizens tired of being servants or cooks and it took nearly a century for these ruddy clowns to learn to cook for themselves and begin to rediscover the grandeur of their food past.

The game pies were labor-intensive because first of all you have to shoot the game, which requires a fair amount of walking in rough country. I used a couple of mallard ducks, a half dozen Hungarian partridge, which abound in Montana, also a chunk of venison from a hindquarter of mule deer. To help bind the contents I used a half dozen pounds of osso buco with their delightful marrow. I am savagely incompetent as a baker so my wife, Linda, made the necessary lard pie crust. Our long marriage would not have survived without our cooking together.

Everyone who shared in these game pies became light of foot and full of wild laughter but you don't necessarily have to hunt in order to eat food that is powerful. The words *wild* and *vivid* are mostly states of mind. When Mario Batali visited in October he made a marvelous paella using rabbit, lobster, and shrimp. He also brought along some four-inch-thick porterhouses from beef especially fed and raised for his restaurants, and our pasta courses every day included white truffles, a delightfully wild flavor as the literary princelings of Toronto well know.

Now in December down here in our tiny *casita* on the Mexican border I have been shooting a fair amount of doves lately. They roast up beautifully on a wood fire. Yesterday we ate tamales made with elk meat for lunch, then doves and pork ribs for dinner. Everyone should be careful not to buy pork raised on factory farms, which has been denatured of its vivid flavors. A free-range pig is a delightful creature and this characteristic makes its flesh toothsome. Of course feral pigs that you have to trap or shoot are even better. When I cook ribs I usually go two different ways to avoid the monochromatic. I'll go half with a piquant Chinese sauce and the other with a baste I call "the sauce of lust and violence," which is full of various chiles and hot sauces and prevents sinusitis, impotence, and any number of biological infections. I have about a gallon of Tabasco in my pantry in preparation for a possible outbreak of avian flu. On airlines, which are a hotbed, a greenhouse for vermin, I spray all my food with Tabasco, even the brown wilted salads and the puddings writhing with invisible maggots.

Ultimately, of course, fruit, nuts, fish, rice, and beans might be better for our bodies than vivid food on a strict health basis but we would quickly become as frail and limp as albino sea worms and totally without personal power. We all recall how our media in Iraq became embedded in the military's collective ass like ingrown hairs.

It is the intent of our consumer culture, which in fact has become our total culture, to trap us anaerobically in its intestinal tract where we are meant only to cooperate in our own devouring.

Of course death is a black door without hinges and opens in only one direction. Death is our ultimate safety net but until that moment our only option is "resist much." A secret brotherhood insists that there is no God but reality, but I have doubts about this when I read that a single teaspoon of a neutron star weighs a billion tons. Who wants to become yet another conscript in someone else's world of limited ideas? This Sunni–Shiite quarrel has been going on since 632 A.D. and the Catholic–Protestant silliness has been behind centuries of bloodshed including ignoring the first signs of the Aryan binge. The Hitler–Stalin Pact was mere pro forma and earlier the more than three hundred thousand who died in ten days at Verdun had no real idea of the bottomless hole they had marched into. The pathetically undereducated members of the Bush administration and the U.S. Congress now say re: Iraq, "It seemed like a good idea at the time." In any of the dozens of countries I visit, people indicate to me the sense that they are being led by low-rent chiselers.

Oh well, what can I offer you but a few personal clues, mindful of my mom's stern admonition, "What if everyone were like you?" I am scarcely what you call a *role model* and there might be a tiny germ of truth in Mom's attitude. All I do is write novels and poems, hunt, fish, smoke, cook, drink, and treat women, children, and dogs kindly. When I voted in November I had the feeling I was peeing in the ocean but then I won, springing the slightly lesser of two evils onto our world. I may now ignore Paracelsus's warning about "the dark and turbid entrails of lustful women" because I am a geezer that women have tossed into the biological dumpster. It's been more than a decade since a ballerina has said to me, "I want to have your baby." I have discovered that my smoking tends to enliven strangers around me. Since it's no longer fashionable to publicly abuse gays, blacks, Jews, Indians, and left-wingers, the culture has aimed its instinctive vitriol against smokers. I have abandoned my intelligence and no longer use words like *iconic* or *semiotics*. I rarely bray out "ontogeny recapitulates phylogeny" in public. I take two one-hour naps a day, which reduces possible mischief. I walk two hours a day in remote areas where I can do no harm to my fellow bipeds. Last summer I destroyed a cell phone by pouring coffee on it, my only recent violent act. I have tried to help others but my abilities in this area are indeed limited.

Just recently I conceived of a helpful project for the four months before May when I'll return to southwest France to further search for the lost poems of Antonio Machado, certainly a more valid obsession than O. J. Simpson looking for his wife's killer on the golf courses of Las Vegas. The mountains around Collioure are jagged country and such pilgrimages must be made barefoot, especially painful when your knapsack is full of Domaine La Tour Vieille, my favorite local wine. At the end of the day you run down the mountain and hurl yourself into the Mediterranean, buoyed up by the empty wine bottles.

Back to the singular figure of Penélope Cruz, who has expressed dismay that viewers are distracted from her acting abilities by her attractiveness. This is certainly not true for me as I've long considered her among my top three favorite actresses in our solar system and at the moment I am reviewing twenty of her films through Netflix for my project. In short, I want to secure a double suite at the Hotel Canal Grande in Modena, Italy, near which there is one of the best markets in Europe. I am a Christian gentleman so the door between the suites will be operable only on her side. I will have a simple kitchen installed in my portion of the rooms and in a mere thirty days I guarantee I can put thirty pounds on her delicate frame thus making her safe from the loutish misunderstanding of movie view-ers. I am already a Quasimodo in a world without bells and these thirty days of hard cooking would help fulfill my calling as an artist. Doubtless Penélope Cruz will read this piece and either pick up the gauntlet or ignore it. She would emerge from the hotel plump but not dumpy. Maybe we would go to Cannes where I refused to be a judge last year and wear his-and-hers skimpy bathing suits and be amused by the way people would avert their eyes. Penélope would startle the press by only saying, "There is no more grotesque misunderstanding of life than to murder people in the name of ideas."

ONE GOOD THING
LEADS TO ANOTHER

I am intensely knowledgeable on all matters nutritional but somewhat ineffective in applying this knowledge to myself. A friend, the
novelist Tom McGuane, once said to me, "You can lecture a group of
us on nutritional health while chain smoking and drinking a couple
of bottles of wine in less than an hour."

Sad but true, but how sad? Ben Franklin said, "Wine is constant
proof that God loves us and wants us to be happy." Despite this many
Americans own a hopeless puritanical streak that makes them beat
on themselves as if they were building a tract house. The other day
I took out a pound of side pork from the refrigerator, exemplary side
pork raised by E.T. Poultry which I favor above all domestic pork.
I put the package on the table and circled it nervously like a nun
tempted to jump over the convent wall and indulge in the lusts of the

body. My intellect warred against this side pork while my heart and taste buds surged. I was again modern man at the banal crossroads where he always finds himself bifurcated like Rumpelstiltskin.

Naturally the side pork won. My art needed it, plus I knew that a simple bottle of Domaine La Tour Vieille would win the battle with pork fat if drunk speedily enough to get down the gullet to disarm the gobbets of side pork. To achieve health one must be able to visualize such things in terms of the inner diorama.

A number of doctors have been amazed that I am still alive, but the explanation is simple: wine. I started out in a deep dark hole being born and raised in northern Michigan which demographically is the center of stomach cancer in the United States. Up home, as it were, they love to fry everything and when short on staples they favor fried fried. To be frank, the French raised me, though I didn't get over there until my thirties due to a thin wallet. Since my mid-teens I loved and read studiously French literature so that at nineteen in Greenwich Village I was scarcely going to drink California plonk while reading Baudelaire, Rimbaud, and Apollinaire. Instead I drank French plonk at less than two bucks a bottle, slightly acrid but it did the job, which was to set my Michigan peasant brain into a literary whirl.

Whiskey is lonely while wine has its lover, food. Last evening here at a remote hunting cabin in Michigan's Upper Peninsula we ate an appetizer of moose liver (excellent and mild), goose, and woodcock with Le Sang des Cailloux Vacqueyras, Domaine Tempier Bandol, and Château La Roque with Joe Bastianich's Vespa Bianco with our cheeses.

Wine leads us to the food that becomes our favorite. It would be unthinkable for a Frenchman to eat his *bécasse* (woodcock) without a fine wine, say a Clos de la Roche, beside his plate, though this fine Burgundy is mostly affordable to moguls who unlike me don't have the time to hunt woodcock, grouse, doves, quail, and Hungarian partridge. Since I love wild food and wine I have been kept active in the sporting life by these addictions. I will shuffle through the outdoors for hours to shoot tonight's dinner though in the case of woodcock they are better after being hung for a few days. If the weather is too warm a forty-two-degree refrigerator works fine, though you keep your eye on how you rotate the birds. I've never had a woodcock turn "high" on me but you must be much more careful with the white-breasted grouse. I have frequently eaten the "trail" of woodcock, the entrails minus the gizzard, on toast, a French tradition that some of my American friends are squeamish about. I insist that the best cooking method for wood-cock is to simply roast the birds over a wood fire making sure the breast interior is pinkish red. Much like doves and mallards an overcooked woodcock is criminal. Last year near our winter *casita* on the Mexican border I shot well over a hundred doves but when I cooked a few of them minutes too long my wife was utterly disgusted. Perhaps I did something truly stupid like answering the phone.

Whiskey is lonely while wine has its lover, food.

So wine fuels my sporting life but the hunting season ends and I become a bird-watcher rather than a hunter partly to keep moving and make sure my appetite is revved. Woodcock don't freeze well but Hungarian partridge and grouse do, plus there are gifts from friends of elk, antelope, moose, and venison, which all cry out rather silently for red wine.

We had a nasty summer in Montana due to a two-month heat wave. I ate sparingly and shed ounces like dandruff, sensing that I was becoming too light on my feet for Montana winds. The heat forced me to drink whites, my favorites being Bouzeron and La Cadette's Bourgogne *blanc*, their Vézelay *blanc*, too, and also a lot of lowly Italian prosecco which was amenable to the weather. My appetite recovered slightly when the garden flourished in August but it wasn't until September that I could again fully embrace my first love, French reds.

The city of Lyon has kindly decided to give me a medal and is flying me over in a few weeks. Only by dint of tromping through forests and fields several hours a day can one be physically ready for Lyon, which makes me the man for the job. After each meal in Lyon I will climb the mountain, glance at the cathedral but not actually go inside, and then trot back down. Bishop Irenaeus of Lyon irritated me when in the second century he proclaimed animals don't go to heaven because they can't contribute monetarily to the church. I adore the classic bistros in Lyon, also a restaurant called Aux Fins Gourmets. These sturdy folks eat sturdily and I will ferret away a collection of *fromage de tête* (head cheese) in my hotel room in case I awake in the night disconsolate.

After Lyon I will positively reconstruct the nature of my blood in Narbonne, Collioure, and Bandol. Most intelligent people recall the established scientific victory of the Mediterranean diet over half a dozen others. The effect of the south is immediate. Once while writing for a week at the splendid Hotel Nord-Pinus in Arles, I became daily less somber and tormented so that what I wrote there was untypically jubilant. Doubtless if I wrote a whole novel in the south of France I would lose my winning reputation for melancholy. Once on the streets of Arles, for instance, I met a very undoglike lassie who was half-French and half-Egyptian. My knees buckled and I had to have two glasses of wine to make my way a mere block to the hotel.

Our last evening at the cabin we had grouse and woodcock again, and a leg of lamb from my neighbor's ranch in Montana. A friend, Rick Baker, brought along some Beychevelles from the 1980s, a Grand Cru Mondot from Saint Emilion, and more Domaine Tempiers. The Mondot was a little muddy, perhaps from shipment.

All in all it was a decidedly non-triumphant summer. In mid-September I made game pies from venison, mallards, doves, Hungarian partridge, ground veal, and pork fat with a lard pie crust. Superb. Unfortunately it was hot again and I had to eat one with a white Cadette. It worked, but in the middle of the snack it occurred to me that weather is God's work while wine is man's. René Char told us not to live on regret like a wounded finch. A few years ago a friend gave me an '82 Pétrus and I swilled it before I learned I could have sold the bottle and bought a ticket to France where I'm closer to the heart of the matter, wine and its lover, food.

DON'T GO OUT OVER
YOUR HEAD

Of late I've determined that I am largely unfit for human consumption.
We can think of ourselves accurately as five billion tiny fish swirling
in a big green pond and I've only had passing contact with one in fifty
thousand which seems more than enough. This idea came to mind
recently when I finished the last stop on the last book tour of my life
which came by happenstance in a foreign country, Canada, a somewhat alien and mysterious country to Americans. The pork sausage at
the Park Hyatt in Toronto was the best in my long experience and I
felt inclined to stay there indefinitely. Doctors recently have come to
highly recommend the diet of pork sausage, room-temperature Swedish
vodka, and the stray pack of airline peanuts found in one's briefcase.
If you crave greens you merely eat the leaves off the fresh flowers in
your room. If they make you ill, stop eating them.

Toronto seemed like a good place to end a public literary career, partly because I felt at home in the many wooded ravines and kept a sharp single eye out for places I might pitch a tent and lay out my sleeping bag. In the United States these marvelous ravines would likely have been bulldozed long ago for no particular reason. One reason to live in a ravine is so you don't have to go to the airport to fly home. Airports and office machinery lead the list of our current humiliations. Another reason to stay in Toronto is that the people are antiquely polite. I could see I wouldn't be turned away at men's clothing stores for being poorly dressed as I have been in New York City.

I've spent most of my life out in the water over my head and I want to come to shore if, indeed, there is a shore. Right after World War II, my father, grandfather, and uncles built us a cabin on a remote lake for nine hundred bucks' worth of materials. The lake was about fifteen miles from our home in the county seat where my father worked as the government agriculturalist advising farmers. My uncles who had recently returned from the war were in poor shape in mind and body and so was I from a rather violent encounter with a little girl that took the sight from my left eye. My response, wonderfully close at hand, was to spend all of my time swimming and fishing and wandering in the woods. Every morning at breakfast my iron mother (of Swedish derivation) would say, "Don't go out over your head."

Consequently I've spent a lifetime doing so. There is a beauty in threat. A rattlesnake is an undeniably beautiful creature as is a pissed-off mountain lion, or a grizzly bear hauling off an elk carcass. The boy loves the icy thrill of taking a dare and running through a graveyard at night. Why not drop ten hits of lysergic acid and go tarpon fishing? Why not hitchhike to California with twenty bucks in your pocket? We can be perplexed and wanton creatures with all of the design of Brownian movement. When I begin a novel I always have the image of jumping off the bank into a river at night. There is no published map for the river and I have no idea where it goes.

Of course deciding to avoid the public doesn't mean I'm going to stop writing my poems and novels, which are my calling. I've looked into the matter and it will be easy to Cryovac my work like those vain bodies suspended in liquid nitrogen and encased in aluminum tubes. They could have been stored in Saddam Hussein's underground palace, but it turned out that our intelligence was in error and he didn't have an underground palace.

Meanwhile, as I try to make my way to shore I have a number of significant projects and questions in mind, especially whether or not dogs have souls. Rather than stray

Every morning at breakfast my iron mother (of Swedish derivation) would say, "Don't go out over your head." Consequently I've spent a lifetime doing so.

off into the filigree of mammalian metaphysics my research into this question, already considerable, is dwelling on diet, with many clues coming from the coordinates in diet between humans, who presumably have souls, and dogs, who don't—or so it was established by the Catholic Church in the ninth century when it declared that animals don't have souls because they couldn't monetarily contribute to the Church.

To start at the beginning we have to posit that reality is an aggregate of the perceptions of all creatures. This broadens the playing field. I was never a member of the French Enlightenment and most of my sodden but extensive education didn't stick. All I recall from my PhD in physics at Oxford is that the peas were overcooked, the sherry was invariably cheapish, and that in the 1960s in England there were thousands of noisy bands with members wearing Prince Valiant hairdos. I survived on chutney and pork fat and the sight of all the miniskirts that rarely descended beneath the hip bones. No, all of my true education has come from the study of six thousand years of imaginative literature. As Andrei Codrescu said, "The only source of reliable information is poetry." In addition I am widely traveled and have lived my life in fairly remote and vaguely wild locations where the natural world teaches its brutally frank lessons and where the collective media has no more power than a meadow mouse fart on a windy night. Prolonged exposure to nature gives one a sort of *grammatica pardo*, a wisdom of the soil.

Just the other day a woman, a rather lumpish friend, said to me over a lunch of squid fritters, "My life is so foreign, I wish it were subtitled like a foreign movie. Just this morning I noted that unlike me songbirds never seem overweight."

"O love muffin," I said, "life properly perceived is alien, foreign, utterly strange. If life seems familiar you're afflicted with lazy brain. Birds don't plump up because they have no sphincter muscle. They let go fecally on impulse. This would work out poorly in human concourse though it would seem appropriate in politics."

A literary scientist must take note of disparate elements. In the very same newspaper the other day I noticed two important items. The world's oldest man, a 113-year-old from Japan, said, "I don't want to die." (He's evidently waiting for an alternative experience.) In the second article a young woman who is an ultramarathoner wasn't feeling well and did thirteen "stop-and-squats" in a hundred-mile race that she won. It seemed a tad narcissistic to count, but more important she appeared to possess a genetic glitch that made her part bird.

Dogs have great powers of discrimination. They are said to have less than a quarter of the number of our taste buds, but this is more than compensated for by their vast scenting powers. Rover can be snoozing way out in the yard, but if you begin to sauté garlic he's suddenly clawing at the door. The intense happiness you see in French dogs is doubtless due to superior leftovers. I noted that in over two decades at my cabin, my bird dogs were Francophile. They loved Basque chicken, the heavy beef stews called daubes, *cuisse de canard* which is a wonderful duck preparation from southwest France, and Bocuse's *bécasse en salmi*, a rather elaborate woodcock recipe. It should be said that during hunting season it is hard to maintain the weight and strength of an English setter or a pointer. If you're walking five miles a setter or pointer might cover thirty-five if it's high-spirited. Compared to Labradors, setters can be finicky eaters. One of mine named Rose learned to refuse Kraft parmesan in favor of Parmigiano-Reggiano.

Labs, however, show their love of nature by eating it. My Scottish Lab, Zilpha, loves to eat the gophers caught by her housemate, an English cocker named Mary. I've tried without success to rescue cheeping gophers from Zilpha's capacious mouth. She loves green apples though they make her intestinally restless. This omnivorous capacity can be a problem as a recent X-ray showed that she was failing to digest some deer hooves. She is an obedient bird dog and we had a grand dove season along the Mexican border, though she pretended she couldn't find the last bird of the year and on opening her jaws I found the feather evidence. Zilpha, however, is not in the league of a previous Sandringham Lab who once made it in a hip cast to the top of the counter and ate a bunch of bananas, a pound of butter, and a dozen eggs (in the shell).

We had a bitch Airedale named Jessie whose favorite snack was snakes, which she would catch and shake into manageable pieces, while another Airedale, Kate, never got beyond voles, popcorn, and pizza crusts in her preferences. A squeamish French Brittany who fishes with us likes Spanish Zamora or eight-year-old Wisconsin cheddar but will not touch fine salami because it is an Italian product. His name is suitably Jacques and he refuses chicken and pork but is frantic for beef in a hot Korean marinade.

But do dogs have souls? Of course they do for reasons I have delayed. Many scientists like myself have wondered at the sheer number of androids that have infiltrated our population. The obvious test is the absence of the belly button but a primary diet of fast food is also a good indicator. You can also add as evidence the reading of fast food–type books—99 percent of all published books here in the United States—and the predominance of television in their lives. The average bitch mutt is an absolute Emily Dickinson of the soul-life compared to the large android portion of our population.

In this slow swim toward shore I have been considerably impeded by my defect of Lab-like eating the world. I mean not just the food but every aspect of life on earth. My esteemed mind doctor of thirty-five years has been helping me banish this nasty habit. As a literary scientist I must remember that our work disappears quickly like a child's money at the county fair. A certain austerity is required if I'm ever to touch the bottom. Never again will I eat a fifteenth-century recipe, a slew of fifty baby pig noses a dear friend in Burgundy prepared for me. It did look peculiar with all of those tiny nostril holes pointing toward the heavens beyond the kitchen ceiling. His Alsatian, Eliot, had scented these noses when they were still in the refrigerator and was frantic for his portion.

Forget your ninny self-profile and become accepting as your dog. You must totally absorb the dimension of stillness to fully meet the otherness of this creature, at which point you'll have at first what you think is a metaphysical experience, and later realize is a birthright because you are nature too.

In order to sense the rather obvious souls of dogs we must first admit that much of life is inconsequential, a matter of frying eggs over and over, moment by moment, or daily playing "The Flight of the Bumblebee" on an accordion at an amateur show. This is because we're seeing life from our own point of view. In order to clearly see a dog's soul you must give up the hopeless baggage that is your personality. Dogs and other creatures are made nervous by our errant personalities that herky-jerkily infest the atmosphere. Forget your ninny self-profile and become accepting as your dog. You must totally absorb the dimension of stillness to fully meet the otherness of this creature, at which point you'll have at first what you think is a metaphysical experience, and later realize is a birthright because you are nature too. Not surprisingly this attitude or state of being is also of great advantage in writing poems or novels, or cooking. Why get in the way of the actual ingredients? I'm not saying this is easy. It took me fifteen years to get a flock of Chihuahuan ravens to take a walk with me down on the Mexican border. Until last April I was properly on probation.

Once within the lucidity of extreme grief I was lucky enough to see the soul of a dog. She was in extreme pain and we rushed her to the vet in the middle of the night. I was holding her big body in my arms as if she were Juliet or Isolde and after the fatal injection I saw her soul shimmer out of her body. Frankly, the vision was a little banal like a science fiction movie but life is like that.

Rage and Appetite

Perhaps I've done as well as could be expected. I remember in my late teens reading the Thomas Mann novella *Disorder and Early Sorrow* and feeling quite at home within the lugubrious pages. The same with *The Sorrows of Young Werther*, which is all rolled up in a little ball of melancholic antimatter. And there was a succession of fictive biographies of Toulouse-Lautrec, Gauguin, and van Gogh. The suffering lives of writers aren't nearly as interesting as those of painters for the simple reason that a painter's calling justifies seeing as many nude women as they wish and wantonly coupling day in and day out. Nothing so little resembles the female body as a typewriter except perhaps a V-8 engine. A paintress friend in Paris admitted to me over a light lunch of seven dozen Belons that she had reveled in the bodies of dozens and dozens of male models. Often she is too exhausted to pick up a brush or mix colors. To get the feeling I once took a ten-dollar sketch pad into my favorite strip club in the Canadian Soo, but I forgot a pencil. Suffice it to say that this place afforded me a level of reverence not to be experienced in the great cathedrals of Europe or at a typewriter. I believe it was the renowned art critic Bernard Berenson who implied that the Sistine Chapel was a poor second to a Montreal girl's *derrière*.

Mental bedsores pursue us day and night as if they had wings. Recently my haunted, cloaked figure has been struck down by gizmo problems. Gizmos are mechanical objects, the comprehension of which escapes me. Before we left Montana for our winter quarters on the Mexican border, our $40,000 two-year-old car shit-canned for the fifth time. It was ten below in Montana and the heater wouldn't work. In a giant snit I had a new car that we could ill afford delivered by mid-afternoon. When we arrived at the *casita* on the Mexican border the freezer was irreparably broken, as was the fax machine, and the water system that cost ten grand to replace, also the television that I use only to watch Netflix movies. The television refused to play R-rated films, which meant no nude bodies to boost my wilting morale. Not incidentally the radio-stereo and the indoor-outdoor thermometer also went on the blink. To hopefully draw this streak to a conclusion I awoke the other night to a truly violent pain in my lower abdomen. I writhed and flopped around the house like a beached fish. An ambulance took me to Nogales ER, and after five hours and three hypos of morphine I gave birth to a concrete block. At dawn it was wrapped in swaddling clothes beside me on the bed. The euphemism for this experience is called "passing a kidney stone."

Oddly enough by the afternoon the world became transcendentally beautiful as I shuffled along the creek and up my favorite canyon. I was in tears at the splendor of certain ordinary rocks and the mesquite and Emory oak trees clinging to the cliff faces near which an old female mountain lion lives. During the extremity of pain the soul barks out fearful clouds of stinking effluvia. When the hours of pain pass you are at least temporarily rid of your ego and the silly content of your personality. There is nothing to interfere with the luminosity of what is always there, nothing to prevent you from talking to the pair of splendid hepatic tanagers who listened attentively to your most recent poem. Since the CAT scan revealed that I have eighteen more kidney stones I am bound to repeat this experience. If you want to try it, find a rusty railroad spike and drive it into your bladder with a sledgehammer. I now regret the thousand mornings I ate oatmeal and yogurt to ensure health, truly a nasty way to begin a day. This morning I had a hearty bowl of the tripe stew called menudo with the delicate feminine texture of soft tripe. It is best made with a calf's foot in the pot. At the table you add chopped cilantro, raw onion, and a few ground wild Sonora chiltepins with soaring heat.

Doubtless the citizens of other countries have noticed that our republic is imperiled. We are everywhere controlled by low-rent chiselers and satanic warmongers, and now they've grown bored with Arabs and are demonizing Mexicans, my favorite ethnic group. I recently tried to write an essay called "The Zen of Waterboarding," but expect I'll have problems publishing it in the New York Times, even with its fashionable title. I once nearly drowned on a vast, turbulent river while trout fishing. My waders filled up and I was swept under by the current. Struggle was fruitless. I had to abandon life and relax in my last few moments. I relaxed and the river carried me into an eddy where I alarmed a flock of mallards. Facedown in the mud I watched some interesting insects and puked up water. The experience was frankly torturous though without the company of any government employees.

In November I fled to France for solace. Actually the city of Lyon paid my fare in order to give me a medal that weighed two pounds and was consequently too ungainly to wear, plus my secret religion forbids any jeweled adornment. I accepted the medal, rare because they are rarely offered, and because I wished to again search for the lost valise of poems of Antonio Machado. He had to abandon this satchel of poetry while fleeing Franco in order to carry his mother across the border from Spain to Collioure in France. My own mother would have been far too heavy to carry, but unluckily for the world of poetry Machado's mom was tiny. It is still my hope to find these lost poems, which are far more important to the world than the United Nations or internal combustion.

Unfortunately flying involves airports, which in the recent decade have come to resemble giant restrooms with a touch of the dog pound added to sweeten the air. Due to the acuteness of my claustrophobia I have to fly first or business class, and my hideously expensive flights from Chicago to Paris and Paris to Chicago were no more pleasant than pissing down your leg for nine hours apiece. The food both ways was shamefully atrocious, and there was no vodka on the return flight. No vodka? Please! After twenty-five years as a faithful customer I'm abandoning Air France unless they offer me the comparatively pleasant alternative of being dragged behind the plane in a gunny sack. It is a moot point anyway because with the current exchange rate France has become improbable. An Absolut vodka at the Lutetia Bar was twenty-four dollars while it's only fifteen in New York City, but in Two Dot, Montana, and the Wagon Wheel in Patagonia, Arizona, the same drink is three bucks. Several nights in France we slept in blankets in roadside woodlots to save money for food and drink, but the mistral that followed us personally was astonishingly cold. Once we tried to sit up all night at a café, but I fell asleep and pitched off a chair further battering my homely old face. Several times on the trip I was mistaken for the dead poet Bukowski, surely the ugliest poet in the history of the art form.

Why, then, was this two-week trip a triumph of the human spirit whatever that might be? It is not altogether clear, but I suspect that it was because the trip was a pilgrimage. It was helpful indeed that my traveling companion and old friend, Peter Lewis, isn't totally covered with the warts (the *comprachicos* of Rimbaud) of neurosis like I am. We have made many trips in search of the genuine in food, wine, and location, and Peter was enthusiastic about my pilgrimage idea wherein I visit the graves of writers who meant a lot to me, not necessarily the best writers on earth but those to whom I had an intense personal response (sad to say I have limitations and can't visit the graves of Hölderlin, Trakl, and Rilke because I don't care for Germanic food and wine).

We entrained for Narbonne at dawn after a difficult evening at Café Select on Montparnasse in which a group of French intellectuals claimed to me that their new leader, Sarkozy, didn't have a belly button and was consequently an android. Like Solomon of old I suggested that he be asked to reveal his midriff on the Arte channel. In Narbonne we had dinner with Michael Redhill, the publisher of this magazine (*Brick*), Alexandre Thiltges, the prominent French critic, and Gene Griego, a chef friend of mine. We ate lavishly at a restaurant called Brasserie Co. Redhill is a man of marvelous humor and intelligence who should be called back to Canada pronto because he is gaining weight at an alarming rate owing to his free rein with French food, doubtless afforded by his embezzling funds from the usual woebegone arts organization. Outside, in the twilight, whirling in the air above the canal, there were twenty-seven thousand starlings from which pies can be made.

Collioure was difficult indeed. I had a profound stateside dream in October that Machado's valise would be found in one of the deep secret passageways beneath the fifteenth-century chapel of l'Ermitage de Consolation, now operated as a bed and breakfast by the vintner Christine Campadieu and her companion, a Normandy oysterman, Cyril Hess. Peter, Christine, and Cyril crowbarred up an ancient flat stone and lowered me down into a hole with sturdy hawsers. I was wearing a weak miner's lamp and actually wept with fear. I found no manuscripts but only the skeletons of hundreds of vipers whose ancient bones turned to dust on touch. When they cranked me out of the deep hole with a boat winch I was a changed man in ways that are yet to be determined. Back on the reassuring surface of earth I babbled, but they couldn't hear me in the seventy-knot mistral that had plagued the area for days. Above us birds flew south toward Africa at an astounding speed, and miles down the canyon the Mediterranean was rumpled and wind racked. Lucky for us Cyril had brought down five hundred oysters and a large sea bass from Normandy. I drank as much of Christine's Domaine la Tour Vieille as possible, remembering Rilke's dictum: "When the wine is bitter become the wine." I could not accept my failure to find the Machado manuscripts, and my stubbornness continued the next day when we climbed steep mountains until our fingers were bloody, looking into caves where we found only empty wine bottles and used condoms. My depression only lifted that evening at Antoine's restaurant, where we had a half dozen types of seafood, some wild ducks, and a dozen bottles of wine.

Not so bright and early, Peter and I headed toward Bandol to spend the night at my friend Lulu Peyraud's Domaine Tempier. We continued our intense four-day discussion on the illusions of control in us humans, in this case especially me. In my best moments I can accept the fact that I'm a mere trajectory, but most of the time I'm trying to control the world from my operational headquarters called Jim's Brain. This is a demeaning way to live. I have begun to believe that the mystery of human existence so aptly described by Wittgenstein can best be examined when we are asleep or eating, twitching, dreaming, chewing, and swallowing like the rest of our fellow mammals who lack the experience of the French Enlightenment wherein we stood up on our tiny back paws and babbled about our uniqueness. I'm convinced that 99 percent of all literary intent is only an especially otiose form of mammalian narcissism similar to the mating dance of the weasel that I witnessed along the river last spring.

After the usual fine food at Lulu's—sea urchins, oysters, lamb, salmon, kidney stew—and some fine years of her splendid wine, in the morning we drove up to Lourmarin where we looked at Camus's lonely grave covered with rosemary bushes. We found out that my early hero René Char was buried in the next town, l'Isle-sur-la-Sorgue. It was a mysterious experience because we couldn't find his grave among the other dirt-nappers, but I watched an old goofy trying to sharpen a rubber knife near the cemetery entrance, also a radiant girl on a three-legged chestnut horse. Unfortunately I forgot the French for "Will you marry me" and also forgot in my hormonal trance how deeply I'm embedded in the biological dumpster. The cold mistral had pursued us, so we repaired to a café bistro called Longchamps that proved to be an old Char hangout. I truly loved this place and ordered *tête de veau*, which is my habit. Peter questioned, finally, why I had *tête de veau* five times in two weeks in France, and the obvious answer was that the gods told me to. This dish of brains, cheeks, neck-meat, and tongue with *sauce gribiche* seems to bring me closer to the playful serenity of the calf. We agreed, though, that I might better seek the spirits of dead writers in their favorite bars. A beautiful girl in the corner was also eating *tête de veau* and I felt a trembling kinship. She managed not to exchange glances with me.

I was feeling a specific dread about the upcoming Lyon ceremony and for courage stopped near Cercy-la-Tour in the Morvan region of western Burgundy, a little-visited, heavily forested area of great beauty, to visit my friend the renowned writer and gourmand Gérard Oberlé, who a few years ago hosted the thirty-seven-course lunch I attended that took twelve hours, though there were only nineteen different wines. Gérard fed us edible courage in the form of pig's feet stuffed with local snails among other subtleties and told me the utterly startling background of his new novel, which kept my mind preoccupied for days. It is a matter of grace in terms of my pilgrimages to think of writing as a guild of sorts with the disparate members through history offering one another consolation.

We easily define our characters by what we don't want to do, and I've become nearly unable to go out in public unless the venue offers a bonus of some sort. In Lyon it's the rivers and the prodigious market, the lack of the bruised spectacle of tourism, and the couple dozen classic old bistros. I have often thought that if I received an early warning that I would pass on sooner than later, I'd get myself to Lyon and eat for a solid month, after which they could tip me from a gurney into the blessed Rhône. Maybe I'd swim all the way downstream to Arles for my last supper. It also occurred to me how much easier it would be to address an auditorium full of dogs and birds rather than people, though indeed the folks in Lyon lack the abrasive edges of New York City and Paris.

Before leaving for home from Paris we made our way to Père-Lachaise to see the graves of Colette and Apollinaire. When I was a teen, reading Colette had suffused me happily in a nondirectional sexuality, and Apollinaire had got me through semistarving periods in New York and Boston in the late 1950s. After Père-Lachaise we had a wonderful lunch at Le Wepler. Fish soup nurtures my confidence like cocaine does the acting profession. That evening my friend Jean-Claude Boulet took us to Apicius, a posh restaurant that offers the ultimate version of *tête de veau*. I swooned while eating it.

Why did I have tête de veau *five times in two weeks in France? The obvious answer was that the gods told me to. A beautiful girl in the corner was also eating* tête de veau *and I felt a trembling kinship. She managed not to exchange glances with me.*

Back home at this moment I am eating a health breakfast of sausage, eggs, corn bread, and a modest slab of *testa*, pig head cheese that Mario Batali sent along after hearing of my near-fatal kidney stone. As the golden morning light rolled down the mountain across the creek, I examined the *testa* closely as if I were reading a Keats poem, confident that I was seeing a luminous aspect of life on earth. Daily I pray for a huge cash bonus for my poetry to enable me to return to Collioure and find the lost poems of Machado. In the likely event that this doesn't happen I will offer my support to Sarkozy if he sends ten thousand of his security forces to do the job. In our *casita* there is a photo of Machado at a table looking out over the tops of an assortment of wineglasses, waiting for his supper like a lunar dog. There is a stable of gold in his lips.

CLOSE TO THE BONE

A number of years ago I found myself sitting on the back steps of a centuries-old church in Aix-en-Provence watching dozens of workers setting up the daily farmers' market. It was shortly after dawn, and I was enduring the usual jet lag, but with pleasure.

There is nothing like the sight of tons of food to divert one from banal complaints. Plus, there was the astounding experience of witnessing a young woman as she deftly climbed into the church's organ loft and began to play Bach at a volume that caused the stone beneath me to hum.

But of particular interest, despite the early hour, was an immense rotisserie loaded with rows of chickens and ducks. Juices from the fowl were gently dripping downward, bathing the lower tiers and the capacious bottom bin filled with sausages as well as roughly chopped leeks, fennel, and peppers. Even with the resonant and somewhat mathematical beauty of Bach surrounding me, I felt the call of the wild. Naturally, I bought a chicken—thinking that duck might be a little heavy for breakfast—and some of everything else. Growing up in the Midwest, I was taught by wise souls that breakfast lays the foundation for the day, and mine, made complete by a bottle of Domaine Tempier Bandol, left me surging with the kind of energy you don't get from the French custom of a baguette and coffee.

The primal urge to cook and consume meat on the bone has been with us since we figured out how to put food to flame two million years ago. Of course, a roast chicken is, in a sense, utterly ordinary, but then, if we're not careful, so are most of our everyday lives—and also what we tend to eat. But there is something about the presence of bones and the flavor they add that's not to be found in the relatively sterile and ubiquitous skinless, boneless chicken breast. With proper cooking, even a plain hen can rise to the level of what theologians like to call "the divine ordinary." The same may be said of porterhouses, all manner of ribs, whole fish, and just about anything else cooked on the bone. You absolutely must pick up the bone that remains and chew on it as your ancient forefathers did around the fire while listening to the trumpeting of mastodons in the distance.

A skinless, boneless chicken breast carved from a hothouse factory chicken is the moral equivalent of Internet sex.

—*from "High on the Hog," introduction to Roger Welsch's* Diggin' In and Piggin' Out

Perhaps my fascination with this topic is partly genetic, as my father regularly masterminded the roasting of a couple of hundred chickens for church picnics. (A good oven is only an enclosed version of an open fire. Either will work admirably.) It may also be due in part to the technique's nearly inexhaustible applications, commonplace and otherwise. Beyond the everyday hen—something so simple as not to require a recipe—I have roasted half a prime Hereford steer (with help), whole lambs pierced with sixty cloves of garlic, small wild piglets of twenty pounds and domestic porkers of 100, a beaver (unsuccessfully), hundreds of grouse and woodcock, an immense pig's head from a recipe I seem to recall reading in one of the early editions of *Joy of Cooking*, and untold whitefish and lake trout in a basket over an oak fire at our cabin. And more, to be sure.

Only a few weeks ago we grilled a *cabrito*, a young goat, over a very hot fire. Both goat and lamb find true companionship in a basting of olive oil, garlic, and thyme. The ten-year-old daughter of a friend chewed on a bone until it was white, which shows that all of us—even elegant little girls—can be primitive sometimes.

FOOD, FINANCE, AND SPIRIT

I have heard that in our current recession the rich are washing and carefully drying their used tissues. Americans have endured another major financial swindle, likely the largest in our history, and as I write we sit around dumb as dogs on hot August afternoons. Of course dogs are smart up to a point and many of my friends who crave a natural state envy the spontaneity of dogs. However our dogs, Mary and Zilpha, love to eat green apples despite the ensuing stomach distress. Zilpha will also swallow deer hooves and live gophers. She hails from northern Scotland, hence is a Celt, a group not known for moderation. It is fair to say that our hunger and greed have brought us to a sad state. The free-market economy is a leashless Labrador who will eat anything.

Out of sheer repulsion for the low-rent chiselers who run the world I have been tempted to become cosmic rather than natural but this also presents problems. I've read that the lightning storms on Saturn are ten thousand times as powerful as our own and that solar winds reach two million miles an hour. You could cook a steak in a split second but the act of eating it would offer discomfort.

As a boy I only wished to reach a point where I always had five dollars in my wallet. This has now proved an insufficient amount. Certain things like fire, air, electricity, water, and money have always proved difficult for me to comprehend. At our rural agricultural high school we peasants were poorly educated. Our science teacher often slept through class, his stinking stockinged feet propped on the desk. We took chemicals from the chemistry cabinet, poured them in the aquarium, and perceived the mystery of death. When the teacher would awake and mumble about the solar system our star quarterback would keep bellowing, "Bullshit." A whole new world opened to me one afternoon when school was out and a friend showed me how to make love to a heifer by standing on a milk stool. Suffice it to say my fellow students voted en masse for George Bush sixty years later, but then the world has long since learned that America can be a brutish place. I predict that within a year you'll be able to couple with a pretty girl by buying her a McDonald's Quarter Pounder.

Those in the financial community with the collective morals of a Mexican drug cartel are devious indeed and can evidently swipe your money with lasers.

Perhaps I've already spoken enough of high economics and politics. Our recent leaders are the same ones who used to blow up cats by stuffing them in rural mailboxes with firecrackers and gang-rape virgins at the swimming hole in the flooded gravel pit. If not politics they went into banking and real estate.

A pure form of economic understanding came in my mid-twenties when I was a hod carrier for two bucks an hour. If we could afford to have protein with our beans or noodles, life was good. If not, not. Later in life economics become more complicated. In my salad days in the 1980s I made a couple of million but now there is no evidence of this money. I have questioned my wife and long-term secretary about the matter and they are also puzzled. The operable principle here is that sheep are shorn and it's impossible to stay ahead of the shearers. Again we have the recurrent metaphor of the artist as boxer. The rough-and-ready heavyweight Mike Tyson made a hundred million and now he's penniless. No one could directly get at this skilled boxer's wallet, but those in the financial community with the collective morals of a Mexican drug cartel are devious indeed and can evidently swipe your money with lasers.

Ultimately finance is no more interesting to some of us than lazy bowel syndrome, and certainly far less intriguing than the godlike intricacies of a toad or the sprightly roach in the pantry. It is far more sensible to send your kid to a cheapish community college than one of our vaunted Ivy League universities that will cost you fifty grand a year that could be better used for food and wine. Ultimately all that is learned at these so-called best institutions is to wear a necktie, which is a characteristic the financial evildoers have in common: they wear neckties. On a trip last year to the gated community of Manhattan I saw a tie in a shop window for sale for three hundred dollars. If you fail to figure out this satanic connection I can't help you.

Yes, our prayers and bestiality can emerge from the same neural cluster. A certain amount of money buys food and shelter, not to speak of the drip-drop leakage of wine into a particular portion of the brain that consequently leads to the world of the spirit and arts. And a tent in the woods is not enough when winter arrives. I recently pointed out that the millions of foreclosures coming from the subprime scandal will lead to suicides far outnumbering the 9/11 death toll. Those in banking and real estate in America are better at filing their teeth than members of al-Qaeda.

I often wonder if my obsession with language strangled me early and I'm speaking through bruised tubes like my recently deceased friend Hunter Thompson. Many years ago I had won a basketball bet for a thousand and Hunter grabbed the cash off the coffee table and bought cocaine. This was the easy camaraderie of artists at the time.

I had wanted to make dinner, for which cocaine is a severe interruption. My failure as a drug addict had its source in my preference for eating over derangement. The real point here is to illustrate how fast your dollars can disappear.

By now I have given you as much economic wisdom as you can readily retain. Abstract wisdom is as evanescent as one of those five-second rainbows. Read a half hour's worth of Kant's *Critique of Pure Reason*, then segue to a chapter of Apollinaire's pornographic novel, *The Debauched Hospodar*, and see which you remember better. We are earthlings indeed, as our vestigial tailbones indicate.

I was so fatigued after a day of economic thinking and another day of cosmic conscious that it was a relief to turn to food when my friend Peter Lewis arrived. Peter is the ex-owner of Seattle's best restaurant, Campagne, and had accompanied me on last November's brutal trip to France in search of Machado's lost poems. Incidentally these lost poems have created such a lacuna in my life I have taken it on myself to re-create them under the name of Jim Machado.

We started our nutritional binge slowly by grilling some wild salmon from British Columbia, where I'd move if I weren't so decrepit. Along with the salmon we had a Sicilian fish salad made of fresh mackerel and a half dozen bottles of simple Friuli because the weather was so hot. A cooling trend allowed us to gather energy for a gauche peasant dish I demand each time Peter visits. He cooks fatty country ribs in a marinara laden with fresh herbs and sixteen cloves of garlic (I counted them) and then poaches meatballs made of beef and pork sausage in the sauce. To balance these somewhat violent flavors we visited my much diminished wine cellar in the basement of my studio, pushing away three rattlesnakes with a broom left there for that purpose. My vision is on the wane but Peter managed to find a 1958 Barolo, which was fine if a little thin, a 1970 Lafite Rothschild, which was more than drinkable, and the prize of the evening, which was a 1994 Domaine Tempier Bandol Migoua. Why drink such great wines with peasant food? Why not?

The next day Peter prepped long and hard for a paella while I continued writing the memoir of a retired werewolf. Such projects allow me to live an imaginary tactility that is largely absent from a writer's life. After my hero at thirteen has his neck chewed on by a wolf pup in Chihuahua and the wound suckled by rare carnivorous hummingbirds, he is able to make love to a white woman fifteen times in a night and eat fifteen pounds of venison.

The paella was splendid, made with shrimp, clams, chicken thighs, and Balboa chorizo. We had a half dozen good Spanish wines the names of which I have forgotten because I partook in all of them plus some fifty-year-old tequila sent to me by my urologist-surgeon, Alfredo Guevara, who is concerned with my health.

The next morning we fished hard and well and good as the ninny Hemingway would say while my wife prepared a big roast of wild pig and a cocotte of Cuban beans. We had marinated the pig meat in olive oil, lime juice, garlic, and fresh sage. We ate it with many wines including a not-so-simple Chassagne Montrachet.

Such food is to drink from the Great Mother's breast. After taking Peter to the airport I had a half dozen naps in the next two days. My prodigious napping is caused more by my love of unconsciousness than fatigue. It has occurred to me that our nitwit presidential candidate McCain might better spend his remaining days eating and napping rather than leading the putative Free World, which is only a soccer ball for satanic economic forces. Thirty years ago one super mogul I know was obsessed with animal fats and teenage prostitutes. He still is. He's untouchable in his forty-room condo in Dubai from which he zaps the world's poor with his electronic bullets.

To be sure it is a little easier to feed the body than the soul. Eating is an admission of mortality. Thirty years ago I was having dinner with a model who was thought to be the most beautiful woman in the world at the time. As she feasted on a single oyster and a single shrimp, I errantly told her that her lovely body would lose the argument with a five-buck Chinese wristwatch and that her future wattles were genetically ordained. My sharp tongue didn't further our friendship. If more writers would restrain their wit and simply talk about spirituality they would be far more likely to reach home plate. The idea of "reaching home plate" troubled me when young as I hadn't detected anything in a woman's physiognomy that resembled baseball.

Writers should be meteorologists of the soul, or spirit, whatever we may wish to call the unshakable core of our being. The absence of certain things reconstructs our reality. If you're without wine or toilet paper or have lost your spirit you are skewered like a pullet. Last winter during a number of physical difficulties I called my surgeon, nicknamed Che, to make sure I wasn't bleeding to death through my pecker during post-op. He kindly said it was unlikely. A few weeks later I was in San Francisco having an atomic MRI where they inject searingly hot radioactive fluid into your veins and slide you into an immense metal doughnut the innards of which are whirring at the speed of sound, perhaps, I thought, to see if I had caught heartworms from my dogs, one of many zoonotic diseases nature inflicts upon us.

It is hard to maintain your spirit when you're in the state of fear brought about by the medical profession. I had a setback when I took a walk the day after my kidney procedure. My morning stroll in wild surroundings is a central part of my hodgepodge religion. I hadn't read the post-op instructions just like I hadn't read a pamphlet when I was penalized two hundred and fifty dollars for smoking a cigarette in an expensive room at a Marriott Hotel. Fear and extreme penalties are industries in the United States.

So I take my morning walk, which is comforting because I'm nature too, meditate for a few moments, and read—most recently ancient Chinese poetry where the poets not surprisingly do a lot of wine drinking and walking. One day years ago I had only rice for lunch but nothing special happened.

Oddly Great Britain came to my rescue. Two recent superlative books are Robert Macfarlane's *The Wild Places* and Roger Deakin's *Wildwood*. These books took me by the scruff of the neck and slowly lifted me out of the despondency of flunking every single medical test of dozens. (Could it be that gluttony, alcoholism, and heavy cigarette smoking have ill effects on health? I'll look into this at a future point.) Both Macfarlane and Deakin write superbly and I was once again amazed at the difference between English English and American

English, noting that the Canadians have staked a claim in the stylistic sense to the middle ground between the two. I love the eccentric density of the prose in these two books, the way the prose imitates the delicate but profligate nature of nature, revealing the mysteries sought by Blake, Smart, and Clare. Our own prose more and more imitates the hygienic sloppiness of our collective punditry. Sad to say Roger Deakin died prematurely last year, a literary failure of major proportion.

Writers should be meteorologists of the soul, or spirit, whatever we may wish to call the unshakable core of our being. The absence of certain things reconstructs our reality. If you're without wine or toilet paper or have lost your spirit you are skewered like a pullet.

You can have a soul if you want but it's easy to lose it. I suspect that only a few physicists comprehend the inconceivable vastness of the universe and the rest of us are left to perceive clues. If the universe has chosen to have ninety billion galaxies then I am obviously welcome to have a soul. It is fragile indeed and requires extreme care when we are molting. Meanwhile we must be careful about the androids who have chosen to abandon their souls and have accepted the predominant reality of television. For a while we seemed well behind the bleaknesses of Orwell's *1984* and Huxley's *Brave New World* but our dismal plutocracy has leaped ahead. It is clear that the brokers, bankers, and realtors who wrought our current havoc figuratively live in those underground palaces we ascribed to Saddam Hussein. They are anyway blind to the rest of us.

THE BODY IS A TEMPLE

Everything is going along fairly well except for my health and behavior. I am struggling with a half dozen fatal diseases but it is clear to me that my suffering doesn't equal that of half the world's population. It is popularly supposed that we do *battle* with our diseases but nothing is more inept than the military metaphor when dealing with the improbable complexity of the body. I'm arm-wrestling my brain tumor today? Give me a break, fools! Incidentally I am not concerned with the violence done to my modest retirement fund by low-rent chiselers. Only recently I lost interest in money when I truly perceived the limits of what it can buy. In contrast a renowned medical specialist recently said to me over a glass of pomegranate juice (seriously) that only the human body makes him believe in God. I asked, "What about the ninety billion galaxies?" and he replied, "That's peanuts."

In truth we are migrants who were never told where we came from and have no idea of our country of destination. The eternal question is that though a hundred thousand people came to Dostoevsky's funeral did he know it? It is altogether natural that we invented a future life because our minds are insufficient to imagine not being. Death is omnipresent and it comes as no surprise to soldiers, cops, rural people, and those in the medical profession. Recently Julian Barnes was strikingly original in writing about the fullness of his fear of death. Lucky for him he collects wine, which is a far greater palliative for fear than religion. I could not imagine going off on a crusade to the Holy Land if I had a good cellar back at the castle.

Back in the mid-1940s when the world was trying to recover from World War II and we were living in a peasant village in northern Michigan, we were forced to go to Daily Vacation Bible School after a full nine months trapped like fishing worms in a can by our education. In a democracy we are forbidden the word *peasant*, but that's what most of us are and I don't mind it a bit. I wasn't Vlad the Conqueror in a previous life, but the peasant boy who got his head cut off for stealing a drink of water.

Anyway, Daily Vacation Bible School was the first major injustice of my life, when I wanted to be at our little cabin on a remote lake built by my father and uncles. I can still burn with anger sixty-five years later over this matter. One June morning the florid blimp of a preacher tried to teach us that our bodies were holy temples and should be treated accordingly. I was seated next to a boy who had a purple face because his heart was bad. His nickname was Purple Face. On the other side of me was a pretty girl who would show you her bare butt for a penny, my first exposure to pure capitalism and the mystery of the negative space that signifies a butt crack.

As Emily Dickinson said, "To live is so startling it leaves little time for anything else." Which of us miserable tykes in the fetor of the church basement classroom could comprehend the biblical lesson that a body is a holy temple? On the way home I conversed

with a number of yard dogs about the matter while picking flowers to ingratiate myself to my savage mother who was vexed that
I had broken a dozen eggs under my sister's bed, an inexplicable
act. It was obvious that if the body is a temple the mouth is the
front door and the emergency exit or back door is the butt hole.
The preacher was a real big temple with a bulbous paunch below
his belt who disapproved of alcohol, dancing, sex, and movies.
My dimwit friend Bob had been caught playing with his weenie in
the choir loft, and the preacher told him he would go to hell if he
played with his weenie. Bob wept piteously. I wondered what part
of the temple is the weenie?

This theological quandary has followed me for sixty years even
into the precincts of my Zen studies. Are the bodies of our fellow
mammals holy temples and what of the famous question "Does a
dog have Buddha nature?" Our lives are permeated with a haunting
atmosphere of lingering dread. This phrase was used to describe a
movie I decided not to watch for obvious reasons. As an elderly
peasant from notably unsuccessful farm families on both sides of
my parentage, I'm giving up nearly everything, especially my vain
interest in abstractions. Along with Ungaretti I ask, "Have I frag-
mented heart and mind to fall in the service of words?" (*Ho fatto a
pezzi cuore e mente per cadere in serviti di parole?*) The answer in the
American language is "Yup." Is religion an abstraction? Our bodies
aren't. Of course it's the doctrine that is abstract and the practice
far less so. The practice of religion reflects like a vastly distorted
fun house mirror our mammalian nature. We discovered fire so it is
altogether natural that we burned a virgin witch at the stake under
the instructions of the priesthood and under the assumption that
God likes roasted food.

It is time to leave the eagle aeries of theology for the door, the
mouth of the holy temple. Many years ago on a dark night near
the Toronto waterfront I was leaning against a brown Taurus when
Linda Spalding asked me to do a food column for *Brick*, a fateful
night indeed. Looking back I have realized that I've been on a diet
for forty years and if I had even lost half a pound a year I'd be fine,

which I didn't. Last week Mario Batali was at my home and it is easy to see how my willpower fails. Here is the menu:

Monday ~ America
Carnevino rib-eye steaks
Potatoes with sweet garlic and truffles
Salad with Gorgonzola
Grilled onions

Tuesday ~ Spain
Boquerones
Kumamoto oysters
Manchego and morcilla and berberechos
Nantucket bay scallops
Fideuà with rock shrimp, octopus, and Dungeness crab
Torta de la serena and tetilla with arrope

Wednesday ~ Modena
Lardo bruschetta
Robiola ravioli with duck ragù
Veal chops modenese
Cipolline with vincotto

I should add that on Wednesday we had a light lunch of grilled wild quail and doves, a wild mushroom ragù, and the leftover truffled potato salad, the flavor of which had intensified with a night's rest. The wines were appropriate:

1996 Casters del Siurana, Miserere, Priorat
1994 Remírez de Ganuza, Gran Reserva Rioja
1997 Remírez de Ganuza, Reserva Rioja
A case of Vedejo
Bastianich Vespa Bianco
Bastianich Tocai Friulano
La Mozza I Perazzi Morellino di Scansano
La Mozza "Aragone" Maremma Toscana

It will be immediately obvious that these three days were a religious experience as the holy food marched into the open mouths of the temples. The massive bowlful of truffles were a sacrament grated by my grandson Johnny, who averred that he would do this job rarely in his life. I have a huge grill and we used mesquite, oak, and manzanita for fuel for the prime beef and veal chops, and a huge paella pan to make the *fideuà*. There is something particularly toothsome about baby octopus, which I have eaten in quantity in Zihuatanejo in Mexico. Of course a *fideuà* is similar to a paella but you use pasta moistened with a reduced Dungeness crab stock. The back of the grill is appropriately painted with a portrait of the Virgin of Guadalupe.

There. These meals required the courage of early Christian martyrs, something I wished to be as a boy preacher. There was an untoward, near-death moment when I fell asleep at the table with a full mouth. Luckily this was noticed and I was shaken awake. We can't forget what happened to Mama Cass, Jimi Hendrix, and John Bonham.

The day everyone left, my peasant roots activated and I cooked myself a hot dog and a hamburger without shame, but then the next day Chris Bianco who had assisted Mario sent over from Phoenix, where he makes the best pizza on earth, a whole prosciutto and ten pounds each of imported mortadella (from Modena) and provolone. This was to allow my holiness to taper off slowly. At his sandwich shop Chris cooks whole pigs and lambs, which ensures freshness and flavor.

The creepy liberal English major in me might ask, Why are we cooking expensive meals during a global financial collapse engineered by the satanic money community that should be summarily executed? Well, religion isn't cheap, which is easy to see when strolling through the Vatican or visiting Mecca. And we all felt in a celebratory mood over the election of Obama after eight years when you had to be a proctologist to appreciate Washington.

Politics is a toilet bowl in whose reflection we hope to learn how to treat each other well and not kill each other in a thousand ways. I am reminded again of Baron Wessenberg saying in 1814 at the Congress of Vienna, "Nothing in the world is more haughty than a man of moderate capacity when once raised to power." Bush has flown off to the hellhole of Texas but we need to be reminded that he didn't severely bruise his country and world on his own. He had a legion of helpers in his sole interest of further enriching the members of his own class. This is still going on in the trillion dollars for business and nothing for uninsured poor children.

Wrens are helping me organize a new life for myself after a long period of writing too much fiction, four novellas in ten months to be exact. Life is mythology. Work is reality. Recently however, wrens have piqued my interest partly because of our similar builds, squat with ample tummies, and thus I am embarked on a voyage of discovery into the somewhat limited kingdom of wrens. We both suffer though I admit I suffer from hunger and thirst infrequently. Mario

It will be immediately obvious that these three days were a religious experience as the holy food marched into the open mouths of the temples. The back of the grill is appropriately painted with a portrait of the Virgin of Guadalupe.

left behind fourteen magnums of red but I have the courage to make my way through to the bottom of each bottle. I learned courage in my teens when despite my unkempt hair, blind milky eye, and twisted leg I rose to the top as a young night janitor. I was fourteen, had my work papers, and made fifty cents an hour. This caused certain lacunae in my education as I slept through much of high school. Back to wrens. My religion led me to them as I recently dreamed that God was a great brown bird and no one can disprove this.

Living as remotely as I do in Montana and on the Mexican border I only rarely take a peek into the peevish dumpster of literary activity, but I have noted recently that the "acknowledgments" sections of literary books are growing longer and longer. I am innocent, having offered only minimalist versions like "Thanks, Bob, for the loan." Feeling left out I offer this:

To my best friend Odin who forgave the ravens who sat and shat upon his shoulders. To all the girls I left behind because they were too far ahead of me. To my agent Myrna who navigated the pus-slick streets of Gotham in her fuchsia air shoes on my behalf, and allowed me to stay in mega-tropical Missouri with my children Frances, Francis, and Francine, and our beloved Yangtze cat Goober Pie. And to the rehab folks at Hazelden in Minnesota, and the vegan community of Café Girardeau who made my morning mirepoix of okra, Jerusalem artichoke, kohlrabi, and parsnips, not to speak of the magic of kelp. Yes, literature is the brutal but vital offal that fuels us on our void-bound journey. And to the Cedar Rapids, Iowa, drumming group the Night Kittens, who raised me from a recent narcosis. Big girls. Big drums. Those lassies in rabbit pelts got rhythm. And to the young Indianapolis couple I'll call Mimsy and Whimsy who showed me several sexual routes and side roads far from the banal Interstate. Not incidentally, the book you have in hand wrote itself.

FOOD AND MUSIC

I've been spending the summer thus far in the guise of a house wren though trout fishing a lot within a three-hour range and feeling sorry for the billions of planets in the universe that apparently don't have rivers. I had hoped to discover and discuss the relationship between music and food but there isn't one. This, of course, shouldn't and doesn't stop a writer. I've never heard of anyone demanding to hear Mahler while eating flan and many have died speed-eating barbecued chicken wings while listening to the babble of rap.

I am preternaturally nervous this morning because at dawn I pulled two corned tongues from the brine. I have never corned tongues before and this item is not available in Montana. A couple of years ago the publisher of this magazine tried to send me a corned tongue from a Jewish delicatessen in Toronto, but the permit for its entry into the States would have been five hundred bucks. In terms of geologic time no writer is worth this much money. The beef tongues, oddly enough, are from Mexico, presumably from Spanish-speaking cows in the province of Veracruz where they daily gazed at the vast mountain, Orizaba, and listened to the mauve songs of Caribbean wind.

The tongues were corned in one of Mom's crocks from the old farm where it usually held pickled herring, one of the family's few culinary triumphs. Dawn-to-dark work usually equates food with fuel to assuage the hunger of manual labor, rather than with elaborate fare to pique the interest of those who aren't truly hungry. For reference I used *The River Cottage Meat Book* by the estimable food writer Hugh Fearnley-Whittingstall. The name doesn't sound Jewish, but the rich brine he had devised reminds me of when I was a skinny young goy in New York City, and how desperately I searched for food I could afford aside from a fifteen-cent herring sandwich. When I managed to get a buck together for a dinner I'd head for a Jewish delicatessen, I think it was the famed Essex, where the counterman would bellow at me, "Hey, kid, you're too fucking skinny" and give me a vastly overloaded corned beef sandwich with plenty of life-giving fat, a substance now avoided in North America but which much of the world craves for survival. I would eat slowly, marveling at the beauty of life for a young artist in Gotham, knowing that back home friends and relatives were eating at Aunt Patty's Squat and

Imagine Ferran Adrià serving up a bowl of pistachio foam to a construction worker from Lyon or a rugby player from Toulouse. Of course all food may be reduced to its liquid essence and thence by our technological gizmos turned into foam. Suffice it to say foam is not the best part of the ocean.

Gobble restaurant, which featured Big Sonia at the Wurlitzer. Sonia also made a dozen different Jell-O desserts every day plus her signature dish, chicken à la king, which included a scant quarter of a teaspoon of garlic salt per five-gallon batch, plus the mucus-textured béchamel that contained nuggets of raw flour. Sonia would play "Hello Dolly" and grin with her prothagonicious jaw reminding me of those huge machines used in remaking highways that gobble and grind cement. My Aunt Vera once slapped my face in this restaurant when I asked how Sonia managed to center her ponderous butt on the toilet. The pain of the slap turned my scientifically inquiring mind toward the arts. Once I put my thumb out to hitchhike to New York City, I vowed to forever turn my back on green Jell-O with bananas and peas, and chicken à la king and its dark freight of soggy celery.

Arguably "Hello Dolly" is a perfect accompaniment for many low-life casseroles featured at church or community potlucks, but it is an error indeed to try to extrapolate principles from culinary septic tanks. Perhaps every effort should be made to keep the arts separate from one another. A noteworthy mudbath of the 1960s was poetry readings with jazz accompaniment. Back then when I'd give a public reading there was also a nitwit minstrel wanting to strum his guitar with my poems.

I admit that my thinking is susceptible to disarray during hot weather and my already limited vision can become further blurred. One blistering afternoon on the river I actually asked a friend and fishing guide if what I was seeing in the distance was a Sandhill crane or a yellow Volkswagen, but then Blake said, "Pray God keep us from single vision and Newton's sleep." In a proper mood this defect can make all women attractive. An ancient Chinese Zen man insisted that the fastest horse cannot catch a mouse as well as a lame kitten. Added to this muddy sight and thinking is the acceptance that aesthetically and biologically I am both a Mozart lover and a stray dog within the same skin. On a coolish Toulouse night it is better not to wolf down a big serving of daube or cassoulet before going to a chamber music concert. Frilly Debussy is better suited to a Parisian foam café than a bistro in Lyon. Imagine Ferran Adrià serving up a bowl of pistachio foam to a construction worker from Lyon or a rugby player from Toulouse. Of course all food may be reduced to its liquid essence and thence by our technological gizmos turned into foam. Suffice it to say foam is not the best part of the ocean.

It is a good thing that Schubert's habitual gluttony didn't enter his music. And poor drunken Henry Purcell could create the ethereal "Come Ye Sons of Art," which has little purchase among screen-writers. Purcell's wife locked him out of the house one hideously cold London night when the cloacal Thames froze nearly solid. Pur-cell died within a few days at thirty-six, and his wife is reported to have said, "Win some, lose some." The world has always been full of those who enjoy punishing others. Recently the Pentagon and the Department of Veterans Affairs decided the armed services should be a totally nonsmoking entity, including the war zones of Iraq and Afghanistan. Secretary of Defense Robert Gates overturned the war-zone smoking prohibition. It is easy here to construct an image of a dying soldier, the last of his blood leaking out on alien soil, being denied a final cigarette because of regulations. The boundlessness of zealotry is amazing but stifling to what we have left of the spirit. Just when I am thinking I'm totally right I prove myself partially in error. Yesterday our first tomatoes from the garden went well with the Spanish composer Soria, and the first peas (with capellini) were made even more perfect by Beethoven sonatas.

The other evening while discovering once again that vodka is not a health elixir, something I first noted on a trip to the U.S.S.R. in 1972, I recalled the TV trays and tables used back before peo-ple owned multiple TV sets. The single massive set, though small-screened, would be in a living room and the extended family would gather around with their TV trays eating Kraft Macaroni and Cheese that Mom had mixed up in a washtub. Dvořák's Ninth in E Minor would be on at max volume while a mile-long wagon train with ten thousand pioneers would be attempting to cross the very wide Mis-souri in a hurry because they were being pursued by ten thousand Lakota warriors. At the same time ten thousand buffalo on the other side were trying to cross to get at the usual greener grass that seems to imperil all creatures. Not incidentally buffalo are poor swimmers and there are records of herds of thirty thousand dying together while fording a river. In this case both the buffalo and all the settlers drowned in time to Dvořák's booming thud, except for a baby girl who floated downstream next to a rattlesnake on a buffalo carcass where she was found by the famed Indian killer Kit Carson. The baby later became the Queen of California, to be followed by many ten thousands of other queens who were to save the movie business from death by general pure male suppuration. Not incidentally the ten thousand Lakota warriors survived because they stopped for a few days to observe the rites of the summer solstice, then detoured to avoid the odor of deliquescence. An ex-marine and writer friend, Phil Caputo, told me that you can smell a battlefield miles away, another reason to light a cigarette.

Perhaps the most pleasant aspect of being a poet is trading poems with other poets by whatever means. The process is without the taint of ambition and the sodden feelings of publication. With poetry you have to sit around Sardi's restaurant a year or so waiting for reviews while playwrights get the bad news by closing time.

Recently I received what I feel is the best food poem in the history of the planet; by Merrill Gilfillan, one of our finest writers but not widely known:

The Good World

> For a full day after the kettle of Anasazi beans—creamy
> white, cumulus whorls of terra red—our heads were
> startlingly clear, tireless, ranging at ease, happy, the
> good world cast in cool civil light, magnified in the quietest
> way: We smelled the chiles roasting miles to the north,
> heard the cattle far from town, felt their heat, and long
> after midnight, giving up on sleep, walked out, under
> the box elder, tireless: calm skies, a moon like sugar
> in the mouth.

I read this poem in the steamy lassitude of mid-July and immediately set about making a pot of Anasazi beans despite the inappropriate weather. Beans and pork brought our country's people west, usually salt pork as wagon trains were short of refrigerators. I use

ground Chimayo, a high-altitude chile from New Mexico, arguably the most flavorful. The best beer for beans is either Pacifico
or Negra Modelo, the best music Linda Ronstadt singing Mexican
songs. You have to be careful as on a recent car trip to Nebraska I was
listening to Leonard Cohen while eating a small bag of Fritos and
began to choke on my emotions. For the same reason I can't listen
to Aretha Franklin or the blues singer Robert Johnson while driving,
let alone eating. The advantage of a pot of beans for a devout liberal
is that they may be eaten without guilt, which is not true of the five-
thousand-dollar dinner I once ate in Paris with some show business
acquaintances (Francis Ford Coppola, Danny DeVito, Russell Crowe,
and a few others), or the twelve-hour lunch of thirty-seven courses
but only nineteen wines I enjoyed with friends in Burgundy. As a
poet I didn't pick up the tab for either. Metaphorically the poet is
in a cage high above the cultural disco with the crowd below him
chanting, "Dance, fool, dance." Baudelaire claimed that the poet
couldn't walk so borne down was he by his giant wings—*Ses ailes de
géant l'empêchent de marcher*—which earlier in my career I used as
an excuse for bad behavior. Success in bad behavior is guaranteed.

Over the years I have made an extensive but informal survey
among the young, inquiring as to why they listen to tens of thousands of hours of loud rock, particularly of the heavy metal variety.
My conclusions proved obvious; to wit, such music is an effective
anesthetic for drowning out reality. It goes with fast food, which is
akin to shoving the gas nozzle in your mouth for a quick fill-up. It
might be a stretch to also conclude that bad music is destructive to
the palate but the evidence is there. I am unable, however, to connect
a particular type of musician to certain cultural phenomena such as
the implanting of huge breasts in recent decades or the tendency of
men to bench-press until they develop freakishly large breasts. And
in the past few years eating contests have become popular, hot dogs
being the most frequent item, with the winner downing sixty-eight.
This is beyond my ken, as one has always been enough for me. I
have never attended one of these contests but have been told that
the music is usually the triumphant theme from *Rocky*. According

to *Gourmet* magazine a man recently ate eight chickens at a Rhode Island restaurant that specializes, not surprisingly, in chicken. No mention was made of the mood music for the feat, but it was likely a clone of Sonia playing "Yes, We Have No Bananas" on the Wurlitzer with flotsam strains as if a patch of hollyhocks could groan.

I am assuming that our bad national news has crossed the border to the land of the maple leaf. Our country is in dire straits and every-where we hear the keening and howling of the unemployed. Seniors who have seen a severe drop in their retirement incomes have been turned out of managed-care facilities and stand on the curbs waving their arms at the silent heav-ens, their little potbellies shrinking from lack of apple-sauce and cottage cheese, their historical staples. One can only pray that their col-lective curses will doom the financial community to the hell it has blatantly earned.

The best beer for beans is either Pacifico or Negra Modelo, the best music Linda Ronstadt singing Mexican songs. You have to be careful as on a recent car trip to Nebraska I was listening to Leonard Cohen while eating a small bag of Fritos and began to choke on my emotions.

As I write this, Michael Jackson is still dead. He continues to die daily on CNN for forty days now, the examination of his bad habits revealed in a relent-lessly racist display of our dim view of black people. Today at dawn when I arose to make a chalupa, a generic border dish, then walked the dogs, I found myself wishing that I could prance across the pas-ture like M. J. did the stage instead of my bleak and burly shuffle. Incidentally, if you wish to restore your health, take out your larg-est iron pot and put in two pounds of pintos, ten pounds of pork shoulder, serrano and pasilla (fresh chiles), onions, cumin, lots of garlic, ground Chimayo chile, chopped cilantro, and water. Bring to heat on stove, then put it in the oven at 300°F for four hours, after which you jerk the pork and remove the bones. Serve on tortilla chips or Fritos with condiments of chopped onions, cilantro, and grated cheese. Eat a lot and then nap.

I am mindful of late of the notion of health. The late Anthony Burgess said that writing is the most unhealthy of professions. In truth you can wake up feeling fine, and writing all day turns you into a pile of dog doo-doo. It's not only the coffee, the cigarettes, the faux elixir of vodka, and the bottles of wine, but the unnaturalness of the act of writing shared with no other species. Led by birds many species sing, but writing is as suspect as collecting doughnut holes or using cell phones.

My corned tongues turned out well and I must salute Hugh Fearnley-Whittingstall. If Michael Jackson had only taken a few hours a day cooking his own food he might still be with us like B. B. King or Buddy Guy. My corned tongue is getting me over a long-held prejudice against the Saxons that I acquired thirty years ago while living in London in Jack Nicholson's household while he was filming Kubrick's *The Shining*. The chinless, sputtering upper-crust visitors were absolutely certain I was the bodyguard and hence I was invisible. I still hold a wan hope that they will translate my American novels into English. Meanwhile during this financial collapse I am surviving due to the generosity of the French. We all need to eat well in order to dig the graves of stockbrokers.

THE ARTS VERSUS FOOD AND BIRDS

Of late I've had the feeling that I may have lived too long, a state of mind the nature of which is impossible to determine. For financial reasons we keep our thermostat at fifty degrees (ten Celsius). This has the side effect of decreasing the number of visitors to our home. My Swede grandpa never wore a coat out to the barn unless it was below zero. He was made hot and strong by a diet of pork fat and herring and bowls of Wheaties with heavy cream. We've recently invested our savings in various lotteries to give God a chance to help us. We so hope that the Big Guy in the sky comes through for us so that we can afford complicated and expensive medical procedures as I'm having problems with my head, lungs, stomach, and right leg. My wife is fine except for severe asthma and crippling arthritis. I have abandoned my Art who is a cruel mistress, a seven-hundred-pound dominatrix with rhino feet and hair of ten thousand thin, virulently poisonous black snakes. I've been doing backflips and somersaults for this old cow for fifty years and want to seek other opportunities in the private sector.

Forgive me this mordant prelude that is not quite true. I admit I paid $246 for our prime roast for Christmas dinner and also drank twenty-year-old Domaine du Vieux Télégraphe Châteauneuf du Pape and Domaine Tempier Bandol La Tourtine, not exactly budget liquids. And recently before we left Montana we finished a dinner prepared by Mario Batali with an 1850 Madeira, said to be Abraham Lincoln's favorite though when he called out for it on his deathbed none was available. It would anyway have leaked out of his bullet wounds.

It seems that I'm a fact of limited nature. Since I emerged from a long lineage of peasantry I most often feel poor even though my J. P. Morgan broker says that this is not true. My empathy abounds. On my last trip to Toronto I wondered why that immense Harbourfront complex couldn't be turned into a giant, budget sausage restaurant for the Canadian peasantry.

Is it any wonder why I drifted away from Art to the world of food and birds? Food and birds are in Technicolor while writing is in anemic black-and-white. I had written ten books in ten years before a specific collapse occurred in mid-October. I couldn't walk out to the mailbox, drive anywhere, fish or hunt—do anything—without continually making up sentences, often very involved, about what I was doing. This was maddening indeed and I sought professional help from my mind doctor in New York City by phone and letter. As the weeks passed it became apparent that I was incurable except for a brief period while watching birds or eating, with neither activity lending itself toward our livelihood. I couldn't very well watch birds or eat every waking hour or could I?

I began a largely incoherent journal that reminded me of trying to screw a maple floor without a hard-on. The novel I had just completed was a deranged act of hubris in which I had fictively tried to figure out the connection between religion, sex, and money, only to conclude that the three composed a metaphoric bowling ball that could not be disassembled for clarity. No wonder I became a gibberer. In fact I didn't recognize the first indication of deliverance when it arrived in the form of Mario Batali and two other chefs, Loretta Keller of San Francisco and Michael Schlow of Boston. I had finished drafting the novel that Saturday at 10:17 A.M. and by mid-afternoon I was eating fennel salami and sipping from a sixteen-ounce glass of La Mozza Aragone, a current favorite. Meanwhile a friend from Seattle, the author and restaurateur Peter Lewis, was concerned that I was speaking in elaborately constructed paragraphs. For reasons of modesty I won't talk about what we ate for three days but will add the menu as a postscript. Who would want to hear about someone else's weighty bag of white truffles while they're eating bratwurst and kraut at Harbourfront?

The road back was tortuous and occasionally silly. A signal event happened at the Calgary Zoo. I had begun planning a return trip to Italy for our anniversary, but my wife decided we should drive to Calgary from our home in southern Montana. This meant savings of $25,000, as I like to be comfortable when I travel to Europe. We found Calgary to be an intensely agreeable place, with four days of fine restaurants and a cozy suite at the Fairmont Palliser. It was, however, too warm for me to try out the enormous ski jump built for a previous Olympics. The signal event and satori came at the zoo. A very young female giraffe was standing near the fence and I spent a long time looking at her eyelashes, which were the grandest eyelashes in creation. I actually shuddered at her *otherness*. I walked toward the howler monkeys I could hear in the distance, wondering about what I had been doing since I had last seen giraffes in Kenya and Tanzania in 1972 other than writing thirty-two books. Not much. The shattering din of the howler monkeys meant that they were obviously transmogrified writers. For reasons of humility every writer on earth should visit a cage of howler monkeys. The only disadvantage of the Calgary trip was the nine hundred miles of wheat we drove through on the round trip. This made me boycott bread for a couple of days.

Liberation comes in particulars. After the fact I noticed all sorts of cues in my notebook. When we reached our *casita* on the Mexican border in November, I was lucky enough to see an indigo bunting and blue grosbeak staring at each other as I had done with the giraffe. Not far away was a green-tailed towhee. Was there any language for what they were talking about? The natural versions of my favorite colors were overwhelming. I had been studying the sacramental miscellanies of Canadian writer Graeme Gibson, which had put my mind in the proper state of vulnerability to this otherness. Gibson is a mage of birds and beasts, combining modern science with ancient sensibilities.

Of course I backslid. One morning I couldn't help myself and wrote, "They found her in a bathtub full of blood the color of water."

The literary content of my mind was reduced to zero as I browned the oxtails and chorizo and started my sofrito in another pan, but then my mind was suddenly nagged by the fact that Flannery O'Connor was only kissed once in her life, while Wilt Chamberlain bragged that he had made love to twenty thousand women on his expensive bedspread made of wolf noses.

Not a bad first sentence but I immediately abandoned it and made a simple soup out of seven pounds of short ribs, a large head of garlic, cabbage, barley, and rutabaga, all of them the fruits of earth rather than the dithering mind.

Your carelessly kept journals will often tell you things but mostly in retrospect. "We often feel that part of us is in another place, that's because it is." Of course! Even the characters I was inventing were getting a little tired of me. They kept behaving against my intentions for them. I began to think that my slack short circuits were due to my age and immediately started a project with my mind doctor of thirty-seven years, Lawrence Sullivan, who has saved me from divorce, drug addiction, alcoholism, and suicide among other things. We're going to discuss at length the nature of what we have decided to call *The Last Act*. What are the precise mental changes that occur with advanced aging?

Frankly, many of our concerns vaporize. Ambition drifts away like a floating casket in a severe flood. The contents and scheduling of meals become far more important than bad reviews. The literati are slow to admit that what their god Kafka really wanted to do was to start a restaurant. His mistress was a fine cook and he was excited about being a waiter rather than a beetle with an apple stuck in its back. You publish a novel then sit around naked and unarmed waiting for what I call "the attack of the air guitarists," those who flail you with metal ships and burn your house down. It reminds one of that science fiction movie where New Zealand is under attack by genetically altered sheep. Of course I have to keep writing poetry. Poets are star-crossed lovers of themselves and their language. You can't fall out of love with poetry just because like Thomas Hardy you binged on writing too much fiction. Hardy made a lot of money and further consoled himself by writing only poetry and chasing a young woman hither and yon, an activity for which I have no time. Of late my main adulterous activity since I don't care for pornography is reading Anne Carson's (translation of) Sappho, which makes me shiver with delicate lust. In a footnote Carson talks about the Greek word *beudos*, which is the same as *kimberikon*, which means a short, transparent dress. A fine idea that should be obligatory summer wear.

I wrote in my journal, "I am at the command of ten thousand mastodons and at dawn Nebraska will be mine." What could this mean other than the errant frippery of the mind? It was followed by, "Our best work is always behind us due to the vagaries of time." Well of course, but why does the mind seek to pinpoint absurdities? "Jungles remind one of the creator's rather dreary overuse of the color green." After this sentence I immediately set about making a rather involved oxtail and Spanish chorizo stew and watching two male Gila woodpeckers fight out by the feeder. The other birds, including bridled titmice in close proximity, totally ignored them. The literary content of my mind was reduced to zero as I browned the oxtails and chorizo and started my sofrito in another pan, but then my mind was suddenly nagged by the fact that Flannery O'Connor was only kissed once in her life, while Wilt Chamberlain bragged that he had made love to twenty thousand women on his expensive bedspread made of wolf noses. Yes, wolf noses. As with billions of others it is unlikely that Flannery and Wilt ever met. "I've continued my life on the thoroughly careless presumption that when I die all questions will be answered." I wrote this down at night after dinner when I couldn't watch birds or eat. The grim content of this pathetic thought was allayed by watching Carlos Saura's marvelous film on fados, those haunting laments of love. The next evening I wrote, "I'd like to posit that gravy is the most important substance in the world and that toilet paper far exceeds the significance of the computer." This dead-end flotsam dropped away when I watched the film of Leonard Cohen's recent London concert. This great bird of night is my favorite troubadour. After the movie I had a bracing three pieces of matjes herring. Here's a scenario: a pretty girl doesn't know about the matjes herring you've just eaten. She French-kisses you and simultaneously upchucks and does a backflip from the peculiar smell.

"It is altogether possible that every wife in the world is married to the wrong man." Another promising beginning that I must put aside until my mind is thoroughly healed by food and birds. "I don't miss the life of the circus, the hoops of fire, the hermaphrodite bears from the Caucasus, the clowns on break reading the *Wall Street Journal*." This is too esoteric. The circus is on the wane and is no longer an active metaphor for our hopes and desires.

To say *the arts* is too much for any mouth to honestly manage. I practically faint from irritation and must run to the refrigerator for a snack or to the window to see a dickcissel. Even worse is the NEA motto, "A great nation deserves great art." They got that one backward. This phrase makes me flee outside and walk up a cold creek barefoot looking for a dead fish to chew on to clean my sinuses.

"How well I remember milking the cows when it was thirty below zero, reaching out for those warm teats as if they were owned by a lover. If they were cold and hard it meant the cow was frozen dead upright and would stay that way until spring when she would fall when her joints thawed." I've already covered this sort of material in an early novel called *Farmer* that sold poorly. Middle-class readers think that the hardship they've never experienced is banal. They love their reality which is a video game with the texture of Camembert.

I nearly included sex fantasies to add to the food and birds as a nostrum against the destructiveness of the arts but convincing sex fantasies are hard to create. In the new *Sports Illustrated* swimsuit calendar the January photo of Jessica at first made me tremble, but eight days into January the simpering Jessica looks down at me as if to say, "Your desuetude repels me." Short of offering her $10 million, which as a thousandaire I don't have, I doubt if I could turn the trick, unless maybe we went to the tropics and she became feverish and deranged from malaria.

No, birds and food will have to do and perhaps poetry. I have held fiction at bay for three months but I am weakening in winter's dim light. I wrote a little verse that works equally well for fiction writers.

Poet Warning

*He went to sea
in a thimble of poetry
without sail or oars
or anchor. What chance
do I have, he thought?
Hundreds of thousands
of moons have drowned out here
and there are no gravestones.*

Here as an appendix is the recent menu. The artful chef, Mario Batali, said, "My art turns to shit by the next day."

Carte di Paradiso

October 19–21, 2009
Paradise Valley, Montana

An extravaganza prepared by
Mario Batali
Loretta Keller
Michael Schlow

Noche primera: Madrid

Chorizo y prosciutto
Spicy sausage & cured ham

Bodas
Smoked, sweet & pickled anchovies with chiles & lemon zest

Gambas à la planxa
Grilled spot prawns with olive oil, garlic, parsley & serrano peppers

Cocido con guindillas en salsa verde
Madrid-style chickpea stew with lamb bacon &
spicy peppers in green salsa

Chuletas de cordero y morcil/a
Grilled lamb chops & blood sausage

Dos tartas: manzana y uva
Apple butter & grape tarts

2007 Bastianich Tocai Friulano
2005 Aragone Maremma Toscana La Mozza 1.5 L

2005 NaiadesVerdejo 1.5 L
2003 Torre Muga Rioja 1.5 L

Sera seconda: Modena

Mortadella al refano
Finely ground pork sausage with freshly grated horseradish

Gnoccho fritto al lardo, testa & culatello
Fried dumpling served with pork fat, headcheese &
the "heart" of prosciutto

Tortellini al tartufi bianchi
Pasta stuffed with mortadella, turkey & rabbit, tossed in butter
with Parmigiano-Reggiano & topped with shaved white truffle

*Zampone e cotecchino con pure di patate e Aceto Balsamico
Tradizionale Extra Vecchio*
Stuffed pigs' leg & pork sausage with potatoes puréed with extra-
virgin olive oil & drizzled with very old balsamic vinegar

Crostata di mela
Open-faced apple tart

2007 Bastianich Tocai Friulano
2005 Aragone Maremma Toscana *La Mozza* 1.5 L

1990 Produttori del Barbaresco Centenario 1.5 L
1990 Bruno Giacosa Barbaresco 1.5 L

1850 D'Oliveira Madeira *Verdellio*

Sera terza: Firenze

Finocchiona
Fennel salami

Due bruschette: cavolo nero e acciughe
Grilled rustic bread with lacinato kale & anchovies

Bistecca alla Fiorentina
Grilled Tuscan Porterhouse

Fagioli "al fiasco"
Beans oven-baked with lardo, prosciutto, garlic, thyme & fresh sage

Insalata verde
Mixed greens with radish, scallions & toasted almonds dressed
with a marjoram garlic vinaigrette

Pan di zenzero
Ginger cake with whipped cream
2007 Bastianich Tocai Friulano
2005 Aragone Maremma Toscana *La Mazza* 1.5 L

1990 Castello dei Rampolla *Sammarco* 1.5 L
1990 Giacomo Conterno Barolo Riserva *Monfortino* 1.5 L
1989 Ceretto Barbaresco *Bricco Asili* 1.5 L

1850 D'Oliveira Madeira *Verdellio*

WINE AND POETRY

Give me women, wine and snuff
Until I cry out "hold, enough!"
You may do so sans objection
Till the day of resurrection;
For bless my beard they aye shall be
My beloved Trinity.

—John Keats

This must have been written when John Keats was young and a bit of a rowdy. Underneath each old poet wherever he goes is an immense reservoir of sentimentality about his life as a young poet. When I was nineteen in Greenwich Village one stew bum bar to the east of Bleecker past MacDougal offered a glass of simple red for a quarter. On a possibly morose day this single glass was capable of producing literary ecstasy. Occasionally in extremis my nifty budget was a dollar a day for food, another for wine, and the last was for my seven-dollar-a-week room without a window. This austerity did not quell my obsession at the time for Rimbaud and Keats, the latter being the most singular lyric poet in English letters. As a mediocre student I wasn't in the least interested in critical assessments and more than fifty years later still am not. I was drawn to what made my heart sing in what my father called "this vale of woe." This meant wine and poetry.

Wine crawls in the window of your life and never leaves. A young poet is at a loss because his calling has set him outside so many comforting boundaries the culture offers and wine easily offers itself as a liquid fuel, making him think he might belong in this hostile country. Even Virgil's father chided him about becoming a poet, saying, "Homer died broke." Of course any young geek can think of himself as a dark orphaned prince from another country. Whatever works to keep the ego inflated without evidentiary fuel. One invariably becomes a poet long before writing actual poems. It begins with a general reverence for life and its intensely detailed existence, for women, trees, fish, dogs, rivers, birds, and of course for wine. As the great philosopher Wittgenstein said, "The miracle is that the world exists."

Li Po, perhaps the grandest of all Chinese poets, said,

> *If the heavens were not in love with wine,*
> *There'd be no Wine Star in the sky.*
> *And if earth wasn't always drinking,*
> *There'd be nowhere called Wine Spring.*

Only yesterday did the circle of wisdom close more completely with a science factoid from NPR. We are genetically related to yeast! One would have thought so. We are fermented and naturally enough we ferment. The gods slipped us this gift in prehistory, noting our hardships, our cold and hunger and our battles with wild beasts. "Oh no, another glacier is headed our way, let's drink some wine," one imagines them saying. Way back then in southern France in the locale of many great present vineyards there were one-ton bears running around at top speed on their hind legs, an unattractive fact.

It has been said by anthropologists that perhaps the Neanderthals lost out to our species because they drank too much. Alcohol presents obvious dangers. The guards of ancient Scandinavian kings had to be half bear and when drunk would errantly kill a king in their enthusiasm. Just recently there was a convention of seventy thousand AA members in San Antonio who must have been a disappointment to local restaurateurs whose profit margins depend on alcohol. Of course, one cannot question the legitimacy of an organization that saves so many from dying. Of my many poet friends, many have died from drink, though predominantly from hard liquor. One friend, the luminous Nebraskan poet Ted Kooser, for two years our poet laureate, told me he had to quit drinking decades ago so that he'd stop falling down stairs.

We are genetically related to yeast! One would have thought so. We are fermented and naturally enough we ferment. The gods slipped us this gift in prehistory, noting our hardships, our cold and hunger and our battles with wild beasts. "Oh no, another glacier is headed our way, let's drink some wine," one imagines them saying.

This seems a valid reason indeed. I had to moderate in my midforties so that I wouldn't have to quit. I had a fine cellar at the time and the thought of not drinking it was unbearable. I also didn't want to spend the rest of my life not doing something. As the French poet Gérard de Nerval said, "One must drink or someone will drink in their place." Obviously, though, one must give up a beautiful woman if you are abusing her.

Ikkyū, the renowned Zen master of the fifteenth century, was a bit unorthodox in saying that the Buddha can also be discovered in wine and in brothels. He wrote:

Dead winter but our poetry glows:
Drunk after downing cup after cup.
Years since I enjoyed such sweet love play.
The moon disappears, dawn breaks, yet we hardly notice.

For a number of years in my late teens and early twenties I worked on a horticulture farm and part of my duties involved pruning grapevines. Pruning time is usually cold, wet, and muddy but in a vineyard you become intimate with the mystery of wine. The vines and soil look dead and half frozen and you doubt the future of everything, including yourself. But then spring comes and the vines leaf out and you are lucky enough to have a girlfriend who likes to drive with you into the countryside with a blanket and a bottle of seventy-cent Gallo red and make love in a pasture or grain field. The wine, however cheap and it's what you can afford to carry in your 1947 Dodge, allows you to ignore the mosquitoes.

Wine produces memory. If I drink a Brouilly in Montana, the wine inevitably reproduces my sitting at Le Select on Montparnasse in Paris dozens of times drinking the same wine trying to recover from a day of interviews on a Paris book tour. When I drink a bottle of Domaine Tempier Bandol in our *casita* near the Mexican border, I invariably revisit my many meals cooked by Lulu Peyraud in Bandol in southern France. My memory helps me eat them again. If I drink a Bouzeron on a warm summer evening, I'm able to revisit some of the best trout fishing of my life on a lovely river when we would finish our floating on the last mile of river or so by opening a bottle of Bouzeron. We are delightfully trapped by our memories. I can't drink a bottle of Châteauneuf-du-Pape Vieux Télégraphe without revisiting a hotel bistro in Lucerne, Switzerland, where I ate a large bowl of a peppery Basque baby goat stew. A sip and a bite. A bite and sip. Goose bumps come with the divine conjunction of food and wine.

An initial glass of whiskey might be helpful after a cold October day of bird hunting but I've tended to stick to wine in my hunting and fishing. Also, the sudden jolts offered by hard liquor lessen the possibility of making a good dinner, while the gradual all-suffocating warmth of wine tends to increase one's cooking attention.

More than thirty years ago I wrote a "Drinking Song" that begins with:

> *I want to die in the saddle. An enemy of civilization*
> *I want to walk around in the woods, fish and drink.*

I'm presenting this not necessarily as an article of faith but close to it, like Keats's Trinity of wine, women, and snuff. Sad to say, Keats died at age twenty-eight of tuberculosis, a disease that cheated the world of many potential glories. I close with a glorious note on Claret from his letters.

> *I never drink now above three glasses of wine—and never any spirits and water. Though by the bye, the other day Woodhouse took me to his coffee house—and ordered a Bottle of Claret—now I like Claret, whenever I can have Claret I must drink it,—'t is the only palate affair that I am at all sensual in. Would it not be a good speck [speculation] to send you some vine roots—could it be done? I'll enquire—If you could make some wine like Claret to drink on summer evenings in an arbour! For really 't is so fine—it fills one's mouth with a gushing freshness—then goes down cool and feverless—then you do not feel it quarrelling with your liver—no, it is rather a Peacemaker, and lies as quiet as it did in the grape; then it is as fragrant as the Queen Bee, and the more ethereal Part of it mounts into the brain, not assaulting the cerebral apartments like a bully in a bad-house looking for his trull and hurrying from door to door bouncing against the wainstcoat [wainscot], but rather walks like Aladdin about his own enchanted palace so gently that you do not feel his step. Other wines of a heavy and spirituous nature transform a Man to a Silenus: this makes him a Hermes—and gives a Woman the soul and immortality of Ariadne,*

for whom Bacchus always kept a good cellar of claret—and even of that he could never persuade her to take above two cups. I said this same claret is the only palate-passion I have—I forgot game—I must plead guilty to the breast of a Partridge, the back of a hare, the back-bone of a grouse, the wing and side of a Pheasant and a Woodcock passim. Talking of game (I wish I could make it), the Lady whom I met at Hastings and of whom I said something in my last I think has lately made me many presents of game, and enabled me to make as many. She made me take home a Pheasant the other day, which I gave to Mrs. Dilke; on which tomorrow Rice, Reynolds and the Wentworthians will dine next door.

—John Keats, from Letter to George and
Georgiana Keats, February 18, 1819

CAREGIVER

Will carbohydrates be the downfall of Western civilization?

This sentence cribbed from the back of a cereal box (organic flax and raisin bran) is not the less poignant for its source. I'm even using my most loathed word, *caregiver*, which summons up the image of serene but slack-faced busybodies so intrusive in our lives of late. Everywhere we are imperiled and fear burbles in us like the third stomach of a cow fed on noxious weeds. Around the clock the media smothers us with war, famine, disease, and widespread sexual mayhem, and even the animal kingdom is pestered minute by minute by faux scientists demanding more money for research. There is clearly a worldwide conspiracy to drown us in fear. Even the solace of food and alcohol is suspect not to speak of the cigarettes so valued by Albert Einstein, James Joyce, and me.

Oddly, before I am free to help others I'm struggling to ascertain my own specific relationship to the ninety billion galaxies out there. No information on the matter has been forthcoming and I'm itching to get on with my new job as a caregiver. One of the more remote galaxies, M109, is said to possess a trillion stars which is half again too many. It is difficult to get your head around these ninety billion galaxies but until we learn our connection we're only whistling in a cemetery.

Meanwhile I need this alternative career as a caregiver in order to make a quick mil and retire. Any writer naturally fears elimination in the last round, the end of the third act, as it were. Miracles are possible. I read that the Cleveland Clinic can remove a five-foot section of colon through a one-inch incision. This is astounding. Presumably something was wrong with the colon or they wouldn't willy-nilly remove it.

I concocted a couple of quick showbiz ideas but no one has bitten yet. How about retelling the story of Anne Frank starring Lindsay Lohan? Instead of Nazis we would have apostate Mormons and locate the story in Utah. Mel Gibson is the evil ruler bent on murdering all non-Mormons. Lindsay is being hidden in the basement of a pharmacy/liquor store, perfect for her behavioral issues. Of course she is discovered and Mel is ready to cut her heart out on an altar in the Tabernacle when she escapes, running nudely through the desert, jumping on a horse that in turn jumps off the rim of the Grand Canyon where Lindsay is swept by the Colorado River south to safety in the arms of a poet who heals her dependencies. Another, perhaps more marketable idea is a simple TV series to be called *Guess the Disease*. Each segment would have a succession of terminally ill patients with a rare disease giving measured symptomatic clues to a panel of doctors who try to guess it. In addition to solving my money problems this would offer much-needed help to prizewinning doctors. A dear friend was recently charged $50,000 for a three-hour neck surgery and who can live on that? They put in long days and need a new car to drive home.

Meanwhile I want to retire and live in a willow grove beside a lilting stream with Dawn Upshaw singing to me. I have not yet determined the chef or wine steward. If I only have five minutes left to live I'll simply pet my dogs as that's not time enough to prepare and eat a proper meal.

I'm a bit fatigued from spinning fictive fibs for the few remaining readers of literary fiction. Next week I have to fly to Paris and do twenty-seven print, radio, and television interviews in five days. I'm told by my French publisher, Flammarion, that there might not be any time for me to eat. I'll pack a few sandwiches in my duffel and hope that they don't deliquesce. In my childhood we poor kids often took lard sandwiches to school and many of us grew big and strong, mostly big. Luckily in my fridge I have a block of Mario Batali's lardo. It is wonderful melted on French bread. I won't have an oven in my Paris hovel but can encase the lardo in bread and keep it in my underarm until it melts. This is the much-wanted American ingenuity.

Sergei Yesenin wrote:

> *Here on earth I wished to marry*
> *the white rose and the black toad.*

What an accurate metaphor for our lives. The white rose is our ideals inextricably wound together with the black toad of our actual lives. How much can I help you, gentle reader, when I'm mostly only a forensic pathologist of a dying culture, a morgue that has only recently discovered it's a morgue not a five-star hotel? And I'm a poet and what is a poet but a wandering trollop with a weak smile, a bareback rider without bridle or reins? That preposterous aesthete Rilke actually insisted that everyone should eat Quaker Oats. Did this help in war-torn Europe when Verdun claimed 800,000 casualties in ten days? Perhaps. Camus maintained that the critical decision was whether or not to commit suicide and that once you assent to your own survival you must commit to life with your full energies. As an irrelevant aside I must observe that while millions of humans have committed suicide, dogs avoid this act, except for that famous Eisenstaedt photo of the Pekingese, bored with Paris, leaping himself from the top of the Eiffel Tower. This was definitely a black toad moment.

Of course it's presumptuous for me to think I can help you when my own life has been a model of disorder, but then because of the structure of time I can't very well go back and scrub the paving stones I've walked upon. And I must be honest. I can't tell you to lessen your carbon imprint by riding a bicycle to work when I don't own one. And I have severe shortcomings. Last year an observant doctor told me that I didn't know how to breathe. When I was young, members of my family would yell at me while I was reading on the sofa: "Breathe!" I've observed that I didn't breathe adequately while talking and writing but then scientists have proved that there is no more unhealthy profession than writing except for dump picking, which exposes one to trillions of malevolent bacteria daily. I chatted with some Mexican kids who were dump picking down on the border where I live in the winter, and these kids were covered with ulcerated sores while the writer's disfiguring sores are interior. Oddly children can be fine if their parents don't cut off their legs and blind them with their own disappointments. In the interest of honesty I should add that I'm blind in my left eye from an injury and my right leg is slightly crooked. Mom only told me this when I was in my fifties: "We were sorry we couldn't afford to fix your leg when you were a child." I also have gout, high blood pressure, type 2 diabetes, and severe kidney stones. I have also had some success that I have learned to view as a disease.

However, I have a healthy diet and it is here that you might find my value as a caregiver. I don't short myself at the table because I have learned that it is more fun to eat than not to eat. Michael Pollan, a food genius, has pointed out that we'd be better off to adopt the eating habits of our grandparents and great-grandparents. The invention of the supermarket has been generally disastrous for human health, though of late there has been a specific improvement in food options. France and Italy have also suffered from supermarkets but there open public markets still abound. I regularly visit a half dozen in Paris, preferring as I do markets over cathedrals and museums. There are grand markets in Arles, Narbonne, and Lyon, and in Italy my favorite is in Modena. It occurred to me that the giant pig's head for sale in Lyon was far more beautiful than the Statue of Liberty, not to speak of the smarmy Mona Lisa. At this moment at eleven A.M. in Montana my wife is picking raspberries, green beans, scallions, tomatoes, and new potatoes for lunch. If you don't have a garden it's not my fault. Cities should have gardens in every vacant lot and on rooftops.

Some health points are obvious but we still can't see them. If you're emotionally distressed drink a big glass of French red wine. It's easy and works immediately. While the wine does its job you are free to watch the lovely clematis flowers and vines work their way up the branches of the small dead plum tree in the garden.

Of course our individual, sociological, and political problems are so immense that all palliatives are slightly pathetic. I write about food as it is clearly the largest of problems, especially to the couple of billion people among our population who don't get enough. There is also the question in the United States of whether bad food is better than little food. Something in addition to our sodden educational system is making us stupider and stupider. There has been immense political and media effort to make our minds smaller and smaller. There seems to be a severe evolutionary glitch unless you view our whining, indolence, fear, and ignorance as the easiest adaptation to reality. We have a clear oligarchy of the very rich and when you slip down the food chain a notch you have what H. L. Mencken called a *booboisie*.

Back to Michael Pollan and the food of our parents and grandparents and great-grandparents, so far from the supermarkets exuding their stale poisons. I have to travel a great deal and it would be complicated to stow Grandma Hulda Wahlgren's pickled herring and homemade butter in my carry-on, or those huge crocks of confit of pork or sauerkraut by Grandpa Arthur Harrison. The easy solution is to quit traveling and stay home and raise my own pigs. As a child I would hear, "Jimmy, slop the hogs," and I would carry a huge pail of kitchen leavings out to the pigpen, watching with a great admiration the way these burly creatures ate with fabulous energy.

Even a poet as deranged as myself can't quite offer raising your own pigs as a solution, though it is an obvious step in the correct direction. There is also the somewhat embarrassing fact that I can afford to buy specially raised pork, chicken, beef, and lamb. In France they call such people as myself the members of the *gauche caviar*, or the Armani Left, but then I've already said that success is a disease that diverts one from the more graceful qualities of life such as nature, love, and fishing, submerging the unlucky soul in narcissism. A famed mega-mogul in American business said on his deathbed, "Why do I have to die?"

Only humor and humility allow you to endure life as a senior with its clear view of a mile-high, neon-lit exit sign. I offer suggestions in the spirit of one building a rickety bridge across a deep ditch full of venomous snakes. At dawn tomorrow drop your cell phone in the toilet during your morning pee. In 1944 people averaged forty phone calls a year and now they're over five thousand. Your cell phone time can be spent growing vegetables and learning to cook. Keep your lights turned off. All these electric lights are heating up innocent nature. Look out the window on a night flight and so much is ablaze for no valid reason. The world is running out of potable water, or so we are told. When you pour a glass of water finish it even if you have to add whiskey to manage. Fire a large-caliber bullet into your television screen. Avoid newspapers and magazines and movies, all of which have been unworthy of our attention. I will allow fifteen minutes a day of public radio news so you won't lose track of the human community. I want to say to give your excess money to the poor but other than being generous to my larger family and friends I can't seem to manage this, so ingrained is my greed. Naturally we all fail. Just last night I watched a few minutes of a BBC program about how women as young as fifteen in England are having plastic surgery to make their vaginas more attractive. Seriously. I kept hoping that the cast of Monty Python would pop out of the woodwork but no such luck. What chance does a fiction writer have in such a world?

Mom, now deceased, told me to try to light one little candle in the woeful darkness of this world. I have a blue chair in the yard in front of my green studio where most often I have neither candle nor match. I watch the clouds move this way and that. Over the top of my wife's garden, which has a high fence for protection from deer and elk, I see the Absaroka Range of mountains, part of the cordillera of the Rocky Mountains, that start up in Canada and descend to our winter home on the Mexican border. When I sit there every day, even in the rain and wind, I dwindle into absolute humility at the world's disarray. Yes indeed we are suffocating under three feet of spin-dry lint mixed with goose shit. However after looking at the gardens and the mountains for a while, the birds flying left and right, up and down, I think of the ancient Lakota saying, "Take courage, the earth is all that lasts."

I offer suggestions in the spirit of one building a rickety bridge across a deep ditch full of venomous snakes. At dawn tomorrow drop your cell phone in the toilet during your morning pee. In 1944 people averaged forty phone calls a year and now they're over five thousand. Your cell phone time can be spent growing vegetables and learning to cook.

For morale reasons it behooves us to live vividly. While I was having a little lunch of breaded pork steak, potatoes, green beans, and tomatoes, also some scallions and tiny carrots dipped in aioli, I remembered that on his deathbed Unamuno cried out not for more light but for more warmth. People should try freshly picked potatoes, a pleasure of a different order. Today we're having fresh Japanese eggplant with yogurt and mint. I was thinking momentarily of becoming a missionary of food with a semitruck containing a living diorama of a cow, a pig, chickens, a couple of lambs, and dozens of vegetables, then quickly discerned I should leave this project to the young.

Cooking vividly offers mental equilibrium. We've been using a lot of buffalo lately, gotten from Wild Idea in South Dakota. Poached buffalo tongue with garden beets and salsa verde, altered from a recipe by Fergus Henderson (a brilliant man), was splendid, and so were buffalo ribs cooked slowly Chinese style. Having once watched in Nebraska a battle of two buffalo bulls weighing a ton apiece, I find it impossible to imagine how the Lakota hunted them with bows and arrows off horseback.

Yes, heat is more immediately valuable than light. I've been cooking largish pork shoulders off to the side of direct coals for five hours. You make a marinade invented by J. S. Brown of Tallahassee, Florida, composed of a quart of apple juice, lots of garlic, a handful of black pepper, a bottle of Frank's Louisiana Hot Sauce, and three-quarters of a pint of cider vinegar. Don't worry, you soak the meat overnight, you don't drink the marinade. With long cooking the pork, an immense gift of the gods, becomes soft and tender, and you slice it onto toasted onion buns, with a thick slice of onion and your own favorite swabbing sauce. I recently read that two men who have reached a hundred years both attributed it to daily onion sandwiches. Not wanting to live that long I'm backing away from this idea.

I owned Clifford Wright's *Some Like It Hot* for years, but only lately became attentive to this compendium of peppery recipes that is sure to become one of my bibles. I'm planning to do rabbit in adobo sauce to prepare my loins for next week's trip to Paris. When I return, to restore myself, I'll try Wright's Peruvian pork roast, which contains a full cup of cayenne in its thick marinade paste. Yes, a cup! This should raise my brain temperature to a fervent level.

In Blaise Cendrars's *Panama* there is an intriguing line: "Like the god Tangaloa who was bottom fishing and pulled the earth up out of the waters." Wouldn't it be nice to think so?

Meanwhile, I offer a small recent poem that helped me temporarily counter the expanding borders of the ineffable.

Broom

To remember that you're alive
visit the cemetery of your father
at noon after you've made love
and are still wrapped in a mammalian
odor that you are forced to cherish.
Under each stone is someone's inevitable
surprise, the unexpected death
of their biology that struggled hard as it must.
Now go home without looking back
at the fading cemetery, enough is enough,
but stop on the way to buy the best wine
you can afford and a dozen stiff brooms.
Have a few swallows then throw the furniture
out the window and then begin sweeping.
Sweep until you've swept the walls
bare of paint and at your feet sweep
the floor until it disappears. Finish the wine
in this field of air, go back to the cemetery
in the dark and weave through the stones
a slow dance of your name visible only to birds.

CHEF ENGLISH MAJOR

"Nobody can tell you nothing," my dad used to say to me. He was actually well educated but regularly used a remnant of rural bad grammar for emphasis. The off-the-wall arrogance that allowed me to become a novelist and poet didn't pan out in the kitchen, and it has taken me nearly fifty years to become a consistently acceptable cook.

There are obvious and somewhat comic limitations for the self-taught golfer, tennis player, or cook. With the last it's not all in the recipe, but that's a start. About forty years ago when my eldest daughter was ten and my wife was taking late-afternoon tennis lessons, my daughter said, "Dad, don't you think we should follow the exact recipe, at least the first time out?"

What a preposterous idea! Was my own daughter quelling my creativity? Of course. And of course she was right. I was blundering through one of Julia Child's epically complicated seafood dishes while she was studying the recipe in careful detail. Here we were stuffing sole with crab when the mortgage payments of $99 a month on our little farm in northern Michigan were a struggle.

I still have grand lacunae: I have never successfully baked a loaf of bread or made a soufflé that rose higher than its liquid batter. I do well with fish, wild piglets, chicken, elk, venison, antelope, doves, grouse, woodcock, varieties of wild quail, and sharp-tailed grouse but not so well with Hungarian partridge in our present home in Montana. The key to any failures has always been arrogance and perhaps too much alcohol. Once while I was having an after-lunch drink with the famed chef André Soltner of Lutèce, he said that when he hired the young for his kitchen, within a day they wanted to create a salsa of their own devising. "As for myself I have invented nothing. I cook only French food," he said. This seemed not quite true because in answer to my question he rattled off a half dozen possibilities for Muscovy duck, a large fowl and difficult to master. My problem here is an errant creativity that befits the page rather than the kitchen.

Poverty can hinder, but it can also help. In graduate school I was struck by Arnold Toynbee's notion that great cuisines come from an economy of scarcity. By common consent we are dealing with the cuisines of the Chinese and the French, throwing in the Italians as third. By extension this is why it's hard to get a good meal in Iowa or Kansas, where they have everything. In our own case it was a long period of near poverty averaging about twelve grand a year for fifteen years during my apprenticeship as a poet and novelist. We ate very well because my wife has always been a far better cook than I. My specialty was food shopping and studying recipe books. My wife had the specific advantage of not cooking with her ego. As a fisherman and hunter I was always good at "bringing home the bacon." In the rural areas in which we lived wild game and fish were in plenitude, and since I learned how to hunt and fish early in life, wild food plus what we grew in our big garden was a large part of our eating. Luck plays a goodly part in hunting and fishing, assuming you've mastered the technique. I recall one cold spring evening coming home from nearby Lake Michigan with five lake trout that had a combined weight of sixty pounds, and one day during bird season my French friend Guy de la Valdène and I came home with nine grouse and seven woodcock. The next day he was startled when a local friend of mine stopped by and gave me an "extra" deer. A gift deer in France would be a very large gift indeed.

For the man who cooks perhaps twice a week the prime motive in cooking is to have something to eat worthy of your heart's peculiar desires. In my own critical view 99.9 percent of restaurants in America are in themselves acts of humiliation for someone with exacting tastes. When you live rurally and remotely good restaurants are rare, and there were these long periods when if a good restaurant did exist in our area it was rarely visited because we couldn't afford the tab. It was the same when I lived in New York City at nineteen and my weekly salary of $35 was split evenly among room rent, food, and beer, and the recreation other than chasing girls was to walk the streets reading restaurant menus pasted to doors or windows. The restaurants were so far out of the question that I felt no envy. One evening in the White Horse Tavern I won two bucks in an arm-wrestling contest and turned the money immediately into a large corned beef sandwich. There was a place near Times Square where you could get a big piece of herring and two slices of rye bread for fifteen cents. When you're nineteen you're propelled by the non-calorie fuel of hormones so much so that when I'd return home to Michigan, my father would regard my skinniness and say that I might eventually return home weighing nothing. At that age you're always hungry but are too scattered to figure out how to address the problem.

Cooking is in the details and is not for those who think they must spend all of their time thinking large. This morning I burned my Jimmy Dean hot-pepper sausage patty because I was on the phone speaking with a friend about another friend's cancer. Yesterday morning I ruined a quesadilla by adding too much salsa because I was busy revising a poem. How can I creatively and irrelevantly interfere with a proper quesadilla? It's easier to screw up while cooking than driving, both of which suffer grossly from inattention.

You start with hunger and then listen to the chorus, small, of two daughters and a wife. If the weather is fair you look out the window at one of your several grills and smokers and then head for the freezer or grocer. When I was cooking solo at the remote cabin we used to own and sadly lost, everything depended on my captious moods, which in turn depended on how well the work went that day and the nature of the news from New York or Los Angeles. Your immediate survival can depend on the morale boost of a good dinner. I recalled a day when I got fired (for arrogance) yet again from Hollywood and the murk of the dismissal was easily leavened by grilling a baby lake trout, about a foot long, over an oak fire, basting it with dry vermouth, butter, and lemon. Minor disappointments over an inferior writing day could be allayed with a single chicken half basted with a private potion called "the sauce of lust and violence." This recipe is hard to screw up, so you can easily consume a full bottle of Côtes du Rhône during preparation.

I've talked to a couple of prison wardens about how food is the central morale item for us caged mammals. At the cabin I'd even walk a couple of hours to ensure a sturdy enough appetite to enjoy a meal. I have regularly observed in both New York City and Paris that intensely effete cooking is designed for those without an actual appetite. You have to be a tad careful about your excesses because you can't make a lasting philosophical system out of cooking, hunting, baseball, fishing, or even your sexuality. Life is brutal in its demand for adequate contents, but the very idea of leaving out cooking mystifies me. Life is so short, why would you not eat well or bring others to the pleasure of your table?

Men learning to cook often start with the BBQ grill, perhaps because they have been roasting meat over fire for a couple of hundred thousand years. Of course women do it equally well, but then they must think, Let the dickhead go at it; I'm tired of doing all of the cooking. There is no better insurance for a long-lasting marriage than couples who cook together or a man who engineers the meals a few times a week to release his beloved from the monotony.

It is quite impossible for a man to do anything without a touch of strutting vanity, and as the years pass a man will trip over his smugness in the kitchen or at the grill. A friend who is normally a grill expert got drunk and literally incinerated (in a towering flame) a ten-pound prime rib in front of another friend, who had laid out the two hundred bucks for the meat, which ultimately tasted like a burned-out house smells. And there must be hundreds of thousands of instances of the one dish a neophyte can cook. You hear "Wait until you try Bob's chili" or "You won't believe Marvin's spaghetti sauce!" as if there were only one. Bob's chili had a large amount of celery in it, which exceeds in heresy the idea that God is dead, while Marvin's pasta sauce had more oregano in it than a pizzeria would use in a week.

Currently the overuse of rosemary among bad cooks in America must be viewed as a capital crime. The abuse of spices and herbs is a hallmark of neophyte cooking and enjoyed only by those with brutish palates. I admit my guilt early on in this matter, recalling the upturned faces of my daughters and their glances: "What in God's name did you put in here, Dad?"

I admit to obsessions that by definition can't be defined, as it were. Once on my way north to the cabin I stopped in an Italian market in Traverse City, Folgarelli's, which helped shape and enlighten the eating habits of the area, and told the proprietor, Fox, that I needed seven pounds of garlic. Fox was curious about which restaurant I owned, and I said it was just me at my cabin, where the nearest good garlic was a 120-mile drive. To start the season in Michigan's Upper Peninsula, where many years there still was remnant snow on the ground in May, I needed to make a rigatoni with thirty-three cloves of garlic in honor of the number of years Christ lived. Fox Folgarelli seemed sympathetic to my neurosis as he built my sandwich out of mortadella, imported provolone, salami, and a splash of Italian dressing. Food lovers are not judgmental of one another's obsessions. Many years later when I sat down in France with eleven others to a thirty-seven-course lunch (only nineteen wines) that took thirteen hours, no one questioned our good sense. Nearly all the dishes were drawn from the eighteenth century, so there was an obvious connection to the history of gastronomy, though in itself that wouldn't be enough to get me on a plane to Burgundy.

The biggest corrective in my cooking was to become friends and acquaintances with a number of fine chefs. Early on it was Alice Waters and Mario Batali. My friendship with Mario led me to Tony Bourdain. When my seventieth birthday came up, Mario, April Bloomfield from The Spotted Pig, and Adam Perry Lang came out from New York City and Chris Bianco from Phoenix. We had a dozen lovely courses, ending with 1937 Château d'Yquem, 1937 Madeira, and 1938 Armagnac to get close to my birth year. On another trip Mario brought Loretta Keller from San Francisco and Michael Schlow from Boston, the fastest knife I've ever seen.

The immediate lesson of being in the kitchen with a fine or great chef is humility. You properly want to go hide behind the woodpile until the dinner bell. You are a minor tennis club player from South Dakota in the presence of Roger Federer. What astounds you other than the product is the speed and dexterity with which they work. You feel like a sluggard because you are a sluggard. I can truthfully say that I wrote my novella *Legends of the Fall* in nine days, but by then I had twenty-plus years of practice. The same with chefs. There are no accidents or miracles, there is just hard work accompanied by taste.

It is a somber situation with the best home or amateur chefs. When I watch my elder daughter, Jamie, forty years after our first forays into French cooking, I am aware that I have fallen behind her until I'm around the corner out of sight, but then after university she worked in New York for Dean & DeLuca catering. When I cook and learn from my friend Peter Lewis from Seattle I remind myself that he owned the restaurant Campagne for about fifteen years. In France my friend the writer and book dealer Gérard Oberlé, who hosted the thirty-seven-course lunch, can bone a lamb shoulder in minutes, while I take a half hour. And who else makes a lovely sixteenth-century stew out of fifty baby pigs' noses? The owner of the vineyard Domaine Tempier, Lulu Peyraud, now in her nineties, has cooked me a dozen meals, and a few courses of each have caused goose bumps. You watch closely and hopefully manage the humility of the student again.

Cooking becomes an inextricable part of life and the morale it takes to thrive in our sodden times. A good start, and I have given away dozens of copies, is Bob Sloan's *Dad's Own Cookbook*. There is no condescension in the primer. Glue yourself to any fine cooks you meet. They'll generally put up with you if you bring good wine. Don't be a tightwad. Owning an expensive car or home and buying cheap groceries and wine is utterly stupid. As a matter of simple fact you can live indefinitely on peanut butter and jelly or fruit, nuts, and yogurt, but then food is one of our few primary aesthetic expenses, and what you choose to eat directly reflects the quality of your days. Your meals in life are numbered and the number is diminishing. Get at it.

THE LOGIC OF BIRDS AND FISHES AS IT RELATES TO SHINGLES

I admit I'm not often found browsing ancient Sufi texts. You take your chances but come willing for your life to take a radical shift. This isn't helpful but the confusion always comes with my lame sense of order. I had anticipated (wrong) a dulcet spring watching our migrant birds arrive, walking the dogs, good hygiene, and no apocalypse, donating Lady Gaga and the Tea Party rubes to the proctologists. Instead I've had forty-nine days of shingles thus far, the feeling of which is to be bound in tightly stretched hot barbed wire and to be treated generally like Gustave Doré treated Dante's hell-bound travelers.

Since this is by nature a food column I'm beginning this ritual by eating two junior buffalo tongues, much lower in fat and tastier than beef tongues. They were raised not far from Crazy Horse's home, to which I ascribe great meaning. Our trail of butchery followed east to west and is still continuing. We are as pathetic as the plastic in which we survive. There's an immense section of the Pacific dense with plastic, which is our heritage. We have spent our history shitting in the sandbox and giving ourselves rewards for it.

Nothing new here, dumb people are dumb people. Sad, though, when they're proud of it. Much care must be spent diverting yourself from irritation. For forty-nine days I've had no problem, what with having this severe case of *zona*, as they say it in Europe. The pain is relentless and I've spent a lot of time trying to make sense of it without success under the heading "The Theory and Practice of Pain." You can read all you need to know in an hour and come up empty-handed except for your jolts and spasms. Doctors are some-what embarrassed because there's not much they can do beyond the pain pills, which I stay distant from except minimally because they're soul deadening. It is here that I finally understood Rilke, who denied himself pain pills while dying because life was too precious to waste on nothing. Naturally older people go through streaks of illness that are plain bad luck, though I was told mine was likely nervous exhaustion precipitated by writing at least fifteen books in fifteen years. It isn't fun to be obsessive but I've always been what they call *fugal*. Coincidentally my wife fell victim to an incurable skin disease called *bullous pemphigoid* a few months before my shingles, though it can be contained. It had never been diagnosed in Montana but can be treated at the University of Arizona Medical Center in Tucson, near which we live in the winter.

Now for the interesting stuff. Other people's illnesses are a tough go. Thank God it's not me, we think. Or we say, "Why me?" to a doctor and he says, "Why not you?" I once wrote in a poem, "Our bodies are women who were never meant to be faithful to us."

My plan was a bit scattered at first, but it made my experience endurable, if barely. During the first week my mind got totally hooked on a new book by the young Turkish writer Elif Batuman (she is an American born in New York City to Turkish parents), *The Possessed*, *possession* being, ostensibly, what happens to people who spend too much time reading Russian literature. Since this happened to me between eighteen and twenty-five I found the book darkly comic and anxiety-provoking. I had read that Dostoevsky drank fifty cups of tea a day so it seemed in order to buy a teapot. The drawback was to be spending most of your time peeing. For a break *Finnegans Wake* was wonderfully sexy.

However, fifty years later, these books do not add much in the way of clues to my own true nature. Three doctors have attributed my infirmity to nervous exhaustion, something the Russians were good at. When you get the idea of writing it doesn't mean that you have to do it fifty years without stopping and neither does it mean you should try to memorize *Notes from the Underground*. It has occasionally occurred to me that if I hadn't gotten interested in cooking early on I'd be a goner. The same way with fishing. If I write for four hours then go fishing there's a semblance of calm, as fishing replaces the writer's black lung disease, drinking.

There was a gift this time. I had to stop writing because of the somewhat electrical jolts and spasms of pain. I couldn't flow. I recalled that when Suzuki Roshi was dying of cancer he thought of the pain as a caboose trailing off behind him. In my case my curiosity had to drive me ahead with nothing for the pain to feed on. Mind you if the emotions aren't there to feed on, the sense of pain is far less brutish. It's pain, but it's pain unadorned, less acute, of course, than gout and kidney stones but more tolerable if your brainpan is active. I have lived fairly actively with birds and fishes all of my life and once my mind had released me to live with them moment by moment a great deal of pleasure arrived.

This easily could be misunderstood as sleight of hand but I welcomed them as distant relatives in behavior and the logic that fueled their lives. I could at least abandon my largely worthless nomenclature as long as I was ill.

There was a radical event one day at dawn. It was two degrees for the first time since 1879. "This is abnormal," I said. "This was a radical event," I said loudly. "My sores hurt."

Another day. Before dawn. Loud crashing sounds in our brushy front yard next to the creek. I felt weak and old so didn't investigate. It wasn't light enough to shoot. At mid-morning I took the dogs for a walk and there was what was left of a large buck deer in three pieces. A couple dozen ravens. I imagined the battle, the leaps, the twisting. By evening it was largely gone and the bones turned from red to white. For the two (mountain) lions, it was a Michelin three-star.

Perhaps the worst pain today but the best recent meal, a lavish lamb tagine with a simple wine that wouldn't be canceled out. Odd that wine was devised in southern Iran thousands of years ago.

Pain is causing the nature of my curiosity to change. It is a far more intense need to find out why I hurt, which is at best simpleminded because you hurt because you hurt, a medical explanation that without a doctor at your elbow presumes you know a thousand physiological details and terms. It's more likely that the pain amps up the whole system, which subconsciously feels threatened, thus science was invented. One grand scientist I know, Danny Hillis, has posited that his position as a prominent inventor is a sexual boost. Women in the tribe turn to the inventor because he makes their lives more gracious and easy. The hunter of course keeps their tummies fed. When the medicine man tells the attractive female patient exactly what shingles is she yawns and bobs her hair because she metaphorically is going to get her ass kicked for weeks.

I can't recommend anything about life indoors. On several occasions in the past few years a group of Chihuahua ravens, fifteen plus, decided to take a walk with me and the dogs. They were noisy, as if giving me a lecture while guiding me up a steep canyon. My Scottish Labrador tended to ignore them but they made my wife's English cocker intensely irritable, like one of those jaw-flapping English politicians one sees on TV. It was clear that Mary the cocker wanted to kill a raven but she never came close. Then she pretended she didn't want to kill one but in any event never came close. I sat on a log and began to think of a splendid eel stew I ate in Narbonne with a Côte-Rôtie. It was my first eel stew, a natural match with this feeder. I had been feeling a little poorly because my books had become successful in France and I was convinced something was wrong. Why should my books do that much better in France than America? Early in the morning before the stew I had been wandering around Montpellier and found where Rabelais went to college. This made me feel better as I had revered Rabelais in high school, thinking he would be a perfect friend. Occasionally while cooking I'd think of something Rabelais might like, say a duck and rabbit cooked in a barbecue sauce my wife makes from fresh plums. We had a petite miracle wandering, looking for food. An American woman from Tennessee had a little restaurant on a side street. Her name was Whitney Blanc and her husband was a French chef but they had moved back to Montpellier, a wise choice as I love its spaciousness. The chef had made a young turkey fricassee that had surpassed anything I have had of that order. Meanwhile at the next table they were having a birthday party for a hundred-year-old woman who was drinking a good deal of wine and flirting with us, one of those pure, gorgeous interludes. We stayed an extra morning for an equally fine lunch. The next evening we were way out in the country where an ex-croupier was cooking us peerless sardines *a la plancha* on the route of the new Paris-to-Barcelona train I'll take this May.

Unrestricted travel is to take yourself by surprise with otherness. In Villeneuve-lès-Avignon outside Avignon by the river, there is a little three-star hotel called de l'Atelier, the back of which is in a thicket and near a splendid wine bar and restaurant, the AOC. After dinner we sat out in a soft rain under a big umbrella listening to dozens of chatting birds and my vertebrae were humming. There had been very few birds in Paris, Lyon, Nîmes, Arles, though of course many out in the Camargue, where I try to visit every time I'm in France, and also see the Mediterranean. And in a garden restaurant, La Chassagnette, a friend was at a nearby table with Canut Reyes, a member of the Gipsy Kings, who played guitar for an hour, a wonderful substitute for a bird. In hopefully the waning days of my *zona* I am at least in the heaven of birds, this being the apex of northward migration with many exotics and rarities. One day while grilling a baby goat I saw a lazuli bunting and four different orioles, and one day while finishing a novel I saw an elegant trogon three feet out the window.

Of course our curiosity brings us to beauty, without which we couldn't bear up under pain. When you are covered with sores you naturally wonder why but then you don't pursue the question because you know that pain is in grand supply. I certainly had no urge, no matter how dramatic, to see the mountain lions kill the deer. I like to turn the volume down to the equilibrium of the ordinary. On my many trips to Paris on publishing business I visit the bistro Le Bon Saint Pourçain as much as five times because everything about it suits me, including the terrier Vickie who hangs out there. The food is superlative and I don't get drunk or stay sober. It urges me to the middle whether I am eating *brandade* or beef with olives.

We miss nearly everything. Yes, I got my work done to the tune of thirty-five books but more pain arrives with the obvious lacunae in botany, physics, mathematics. The odds were against me camping with Marilyn Monroe in a pup tent at fourteen.

PAIN

Pain (2)

Pain is at the steering wheel
swerving left and right for a year now.
It costs a fortune, which I don't have,
to try to get rid of pain. Maybe a girl
could help or more vodka but I doubt it.
Or a trip to the tropics where the pain would boil away
like the hot cabin last summer where you awoke
and thought you were a corned beef boiling in a pot.
You want to give up, throw in the towel but you
can't give up because you're all you have.
Maybe they should put you down like an old dog
like our beloved cocker spaniel Mary who is nearing

the end with paralysis. But unlike me
she's happy much of the time. On walks
she keeps falling down and I pick her up
to get her started again. She seems to smile.
Neither of us wants to die
when there's work to be done,
other creatures to be snuck up on,
food to be eaten, a creek to wade,
though I hope to eventually ask God to fully
explain the meaning of Verdun where 300,000 died.

I begin with this frolicsome poem to try to clear the air of any literary particulates, the pollution of pretty sentiment. Pain is really about the struggle of drowning and it has been the primary fact of my life, occasionally removed by a chicken tagine or some other fascinating dinner or say a drink on the veranda. The birds are attentive because one of their own is being cooked, a distant cousin also of the dinosaur.

Pain is all in the details. When you awake with alarm at four A.M. you are not suffering from an abstraction. Since you are unable to remove this fact of life you do what you can to lessen its severity. For me this doesn't include powerful drugs because I become too loopy to write—my livelihood, important because I'm at least the partial support of eleven people. I recall reading that Faulkner's family in Mississippi would put him on the train for Hollywood whether or not he wished to go. I don't mind my life. I never expected to make a living as a writer and the fact that I do startles me. This is mostly true because of the generosity of the French toward my work rather than the citizens of New York.

It's been my experience that gluttony and public drunkenness help allay pain.

So I'm not really whining. At least I am not a wee child blasted in the gut in Syria. Those with shingles and the following post-herpetic neuralgia form quite a voting bloc. We don't like anything or anybody except occasionally our children, dogs, and birds. We vote "NO" in thunder. I recently in desperation had an expensive trip to the Mayo in Arizona but nothing happened in terms of a cure. When I entered, there was a large pool of bloody vomit on the front sidewalk which was off-putting. Someone wasn't feeling well. I had the perhaps erroneous conviction that the dead are liquefied and piped directly to hell. Why not? Or to the desert as organic fertilizer.

My new plans include a trip to Mexico to see a witch, or *bruja*, and if this doesn't work a trip to France where the medical community, unlike America's, is motivated far less by profit. There's a paucity of BMWs in France. I have the feeling if shingles produced more profit we would have solved the puzzle by now. There's the local case of a girl whose mouth was engorged by shingles. Her weight got down to fifty pounds and her parents threw her away by mistake during spring house cleaning. She was found barely alive at the dump and taken in by a pedophiliac foster parent. Not surprisingly Kafka was a lifelong victim of shingles.

My trip to the Phoenix Mayo was not without its pleasures. The famed chef and friend of mine and Mario Batali's, Chris Bianco, has several restaurants in the city. It's been my experience that gluttony and public drunkenness help allay pain. We had a quick four pizzas washed down by an equal number of rare vintages. In my opinion the famed La Casaccia is the best of all breakfast fruit juices if a little pricey. The next evening after an afternoon of getting pawed over we had four pastas and then a marvelous Ligurian fish soup and five excellent wines. A prime cause of illness is the failure of people to hydrate during meals. A slight difficulty was finding my room. My ace secretary had gotten me a suite at an immense golf resort full of Republicans dressed in golf fashion like Kansas pimps. I was bilious and sobbing by the time I got to bed to Fox News announcing that God was changing his name to Fred.

The most difficult thing about pain is that it's so domineering you can't get out of reach of its relentless body blows. Fly-fishing is diverting enough to lighten the load doubled with being in a beautiful place. Hunting less so, as you can't forget that you're trying to blast a supposedly lesser creature into eternity, where it is apparent their speedy attempts at escape they don't want to go. Visiting foreign countries is also helpful. Your imagination is captivated enough that you're not feeling the infirmity. Soon enough I hope to go to Arles, France, and simply sit in the empty coliseum built at the time of Julius Caesar. It would be nice to also listen to Arlésien bullfight music without the bullfight. It would also be pleasant if pretty girls would chase one another around the arena but I've not yet seen this phenomenon. After the sitting has exhausted me I'll return to my hotel room which is huge, rare for France. I'm told that both Dominguin and Picasso always stayed in this room. Before lunch Picasso would sit on the balcony and search the village square for girls to invite up for a bite to eat. What a kind fellow! I am not quite short enough to get away with this behavior. Picasso was too short to join our Marines. After a nap and coffee I'll take a brutally long walk and then have dinner and several bottles of wine at Le Galoubet, and perhaps a nightcap in my room. Early to bed, early to rise. I'm up usually at five A.M., admittedly a stupid habit. I took my Joycean vows as a writer at age fourteen and sixty years later I'm still doing it every day. Is this wrong? No, merely the path of an obsessive. Of course there was the occasional day off for illness or fishing, nothing dire certainly.

Having read a lot of silly historical novels in my youth I've always wanted my own poultice and then to recover and take up with the general's winsome daughter. We'll swim nude in a river and then who knows what will happen? It's tattooed on her back that she's 100 percent protein.

There has been the odd suggestion that shingles can be precipitated by psychic exhaustion as long as you had chicken pox as a child, the home of the virus that can hide half a century before it reveals itself like Babe Ruth swinging a bat. Most get over it in a month or two while with an unlucky few, less than 1 percent, it develops into post-herpetic neuralgia and the sores on the flesh retain their vigor.

I haven't mentioned the largest weapon in the pathetic arsenal against shingles. Not certainly the dozen lotions that were purportedly surefire and I was the gullible boy that spread them wincing with each stroke. The biggest gun is, pure and simple, the brain. Soon after the onset you accept the simplest of facts: the disease is random and your suffering quite meaningless. This is definitely against the texture of the popular culture of our time and its bizarre mavens who try to skew all of the traceries of our lives into something consequential. This is the back wall and the answer is no. Man's hardest work is hope and belief. Some of us who have done a lot of reading are hard to convince. The meaning of the great suffering of Mandelstam is the incredible poems it produced. What is the exact feeling when you are being escorted to your execution? What was the nature of Anne Frank's last day on earth? Read her and you can imagine even if you can't bear her forgiving nature. Remember that you're pissed off back in Toronto on your sofa.

I can't tell you why the idea of the logic of birds and fishes diverted me. It's the whole person led this way and that by its brain. I have spent as many as thirty days in a row in extreme heat, fishing and observing sea life in the Florida Keys with emphasis on the latter, and ninety days in a row trout fishing on a lovely river in northern Michigan. There, landscapes utterly engage the imagination so that pain becomes muted. If you can't go anywhere you can resort to what Ouspensky and third world shamans called flying or traveling. I have slowly walked the floors of remote oceans and softly flown through the Himalayas and across Africa. You won't leave this pain behind but you'll considerably lessen its intensity.

All you want is for the pain to go away when you first pick up one of at least a dozen of supposedly miraculous salves or lotions. Today's variety is called Swedish Bitters which I'm trying because I'm half Swede and still have a sense of humor. My wife applied it at breakfast. It works a little though under the skin there's still a kind of pulsing or thumping. It also comes in the form of a mud poultice which I've ordered. Having read a lot of silly historical novels in my youth I've always wanted my own poultice and then to recover and

take up with the general's winsome daughter. We'll swim nude in
a river and then who knows what will happen? It's tattooed on her
back that she's 100 percent protein.

Lately I've taken to visiting an MD who is also a hypnotist. He
has successfully banished the pain albeit temporarily and is trying to
teach me how to hypnotize myself. I recall as a teenager wanting to
learn this art to get girls. I bought a couple of books through men's
magazines. One brash young woman seated in my 1947 Plymouth
said, "What the fuck are you trying to do, Jimmy?" She was one in
a long line of failures. My single success was false in that a cousin
had also tried to hypnotize her for sex so she was hip to what was
going on. She was amused and took off her clothes in a trice. The
car was dusty and she had a sneezing fit. She said afterward that she
was "horny as a toad" and was just pretending to be in a trance. She
did look slightly like a toad but at that age I wasn't too critical. We
relieved each other's pain for several months until she found a boy
who was less "silly" than me.

Surely language is a frivolous way to spend a life. Almost as
bad as being a general in Afghanistan. I spent a couple of spring
months at age nineteen studying *Finnegans Wake* and the damage
was irreparable. I still hear parts in my dreams. My last birthday I
was concerned that I was one hundred and seventy-four. My wife was
driven batty by this and finally convinced me to knock off a hundred
so I was only the age of the grief-stricken Goethe when he couldn't
convince the eighteen-year-old neighbor girl to marry him. It would
be fun, or so he apparently thought. Yummy! Older writers are those
about whom it is written "There's no fool like an old fool."

Back to pain. It works poorly as a focus for life. You're certainly
not going to write yourself out of it. Most of the doctors I've seen,
a dozen or so, maximize the aspects of psychic exhaustion as a con-
tributor to the disease. Why am I writing more than a book a year?
Beyond my frivolities they advise a sabbatical but then I can't afford
it. The big grants go to the academics. I should have saved more from
the salad days but I didn't. I do know that in the entirety of human
history pain is by far the biggest question mark. We humans sit in a

beleaguered circle rotating toward our ends knowing that whatever pain we've had we're likely to get more toward the end. We are protein for the gods and are devoured by the wholeness of earth. The specifics are always unthinkable. During a recent illness of my wife I visited her in intensive care for sixty days. The feeling in this ward is one of total incomprehension. My shingles became not much more than raindrops until I went outside and saw pain descending like a thousand firebirds. Once on the way back home to care for the dogs, one an old cripple, I stopped by a huge river, got naked, and threw myself in but then I'm too good a swimmer to go this way. Besides, the dogs would become depressed by their hunger as they do.

COURAGE AND SURVIVAL

I'm simply not the sort of guy who throws himself on a live grenade to save the lives of his buddies. Think of the tombstone inscription: "His guts were blown out so that others may live." A few months later a medal would be sent from the Pentagon in Washington to my home lauding me for "extraordinary courage."

Courage is an antique word, more suitable to the nineteenth century, and does not apply to killing the enemy with drones. And I'm not talking about the plenitude of male courage of the cheesy variety. At my cabin during bird-hunting season a friend said, "It takes balls to drink three bottles of wine before dinner, then eat two whole chickens with more wine, and still go to the tavern for a couple of nightcaps." He awoke hollering from suffocation later that evening. He had spilled the bottle of wine he took to bed and was now purple and his three English setters were sleeping on top of him. True, he walked as many as ten miles in a day of hunting, but our admiration for sheer consumption is limited. A petite girl at a bar in Rockford, Michigan, ate thirty-two hot dogs one day, but that certainly doesn't mean I want to marry her even if she ate ten pounds of foie gras at a sitting.

My sense of courage is to continue struggling against unassailable odds. Say the last few months of Anne Frank, or Lorca standing there on the mountainside waiting for the bullets. Or Mandelstam wandering in winter in Russia with the Stalinists giving chase in order to kill him. He felt lucky to have a bulky, warm overcoat and was able to sleep in ditches, invisible because he was covered with snow. He would peek out from the drifts. This is a far cry from an American poet on a grant in Europe, wishing he had the money for a fancier hotel. There is a new and wonderful edition of Mandelstam's poetry translated and edited by Christian Wiman. Of course Mandelstam is a heartbreaker who some hockey fans can't handle. On a recent morning I awoke at first light, around 4:30 A.M., with the notion that poets were anthropologists of the soul.

It is a shimmering hot, glorious Fourth of July, a national holiday in which I do not participate because of crowd fear, and my wife, Linda, just drove me the sixty yards to my studio, my art shack as I call it. I can't walk that far because I have recently been diagnosed with spondylolisthesis. It's troublesome to have an infirmity you can't pronounce. The hardest part about not being able to walk is the melancholy look I get each morning from my dog. My profuse apologies to her are so much blather as she really doesn't understand English other than a few words. I can no longer run down our gravel road holding a football, but then I have never done so. The gridiron is anathema to me. Don't worry. I'm not going to write about pain as I have in the last two issues. Since diagnosis I have been sitting and brooding for a month in my studio like an infected mushroom. I'd like to be writing a madrigal but I don't know how, a sixteenth-century Roman madrigal in honor of the exquisite Italian lamb shank recipe my wife made for me from a Batali book. With it I drank a simple Brouilly, a French light red, a bistro wine designed for summer months. Humble as they are I favor the shanks over the leg because the flavor is more intense.

It is my hope that lying down can be construed as courageous. I nap three times a day and find the prone position very good for thinking. I suspect that consciousness herself requires courage because it is easier and more pleasant just to play dumb but it can get you in a mess. My own physical downfall was partly due to the slump I can fall into after publication. Last fall I published both a novel and a book of poems, after which my head went to sleep and I totally lost my attentiveness to my shingles, not that there was anything to do, or so said the Mayo Pain Clinic, and this back infirmity was creeping up. Now some surgeon will play tiddledywinks with my vertebrae. When you're older you know your body is going to shitcan but you never see what form it's coming in.

This morning when I was driven the hundred steps to my studio I saw two baby wrens wrestling like puppies under the apple tree. With wings it's awkward to wrestle but that's what they were doing: flapping, flopping, jumping in battle. Not that far away in the honeysuckle bush in the raspberry enclosure there's a nest of transcendently beautiful yellow warblers. The infants are said to weigh one-twentieth of an ounce, the size of honeybees. In a couple of months when they reach the size of bumblebees they will take off south to Costa Rica or a neighboring country where they, of course, have never been. How they'll find their way is still somewhat of a mystery. There is an implicit, unconscious courage here. Some will flag and drown in the Gulf. In the spring when we used to fish off Key West, returning warblers would occasionally land on our skiff for a rest. Migrating Australian finches are said to stop for nine-second naps, not nearly enough for me. When I sit in my cheap plastic chair in front of the studio I'm brought to a dazed stop pondering the natural world. Here's a little poem about sitting in this chair, staring at the garden:

Galactic

Sitting out in my chair near Linda's garden
a mixture of flowers and vegetables, pink iris,
wild poppies, roses, blue salvia and veronica
among tomatoes, green beans, eggplant and onion.
I think that I sense the far-flung galaxies
and hear a tinge of the solar winds,
maybe not possible but I think it so.
With so many infirmities I await the miraculous.
Galaxies are only grand thickets of stars
in which we may hide forever they say.
Where is my dead brother I want to know?
The universe is wilderness. No one answers the phone
because no one has hands, just minds.
The hands have been forgotten back on earth.

Having been brought so low by my body I've been working on a survival plan, a bit absurd like all lists. Imagine Caesar's:

- Trash Egypt.
- Conquer Great Britain, including Greenland.
- Order a thousand barrels of wine for next year.
- Order fifty Tunisian girls. I like their complexions.

That sort of thing. Mine is simply:

- Get back your driver's license. I wrote *Legends of the Fall* in nine days, but I can't write *Legends of the Yard*. I had a reckless driving charge last fall and demanded a jury trial. This spring they dropped the charge. I had to take a written test. They looked at my license and kept it. They wouldn't give it back. I told them I had driven sixty years and got only one traffic ticket. They seemed not to hear.

- Write poetry. This is the only thing that raises my spirits amid the sodden pain I am experiencing. I sit in this studio during our prolonged heat wave feeling lucky that I am not Mandelstam trying to outrun Stalin in the Russian winter or Lorca standing on the hillside waiting for the high-powered 30.06 bullets to hit his back and ass, designed that way because he was known as gay. When in doubt, work on poems, the only thing that levitates your mood. It is your calling. Your money work—novels, etc.—doesn't reward your soul. The poet is an anthropologist of the soul.

- Banish the fantasy of moving back to a remote cabin in the Upper Peninsula of Michigan. It wouldn't be helpful to become a faux Canadian, which I already am. I wanted to be born in Churchill and have a baby polar bear as a pet. I could save my money and come down to the wondrous strip clubs of Sault Sainte Marie, get drunk, and embrace the beauteous strippers who come all the way from Montreal with prime French butts.

- Pay attention, as Zen master Deshimaru said, "as if you had a fire burning in your hair." Or as D. H. Lawrence said, "The only aristocracy is that of consciousness." Sort of "He who notices most lives the most," a slight vulgarization. Just now I noticed a tiny wren baby crawling through tall grass through the lattice construction of the garden fence. He's doubtless hungry, the most powerful motive.

- Cook more. This is difficult because standing is difficult. However I must humbly follow the example of the baby wren. Crawl, kiddo. You have a high stool near the stove and counter, and it's not asking too much to crawl across the room to the pantry for ingredients. A wren could do that. Pull down thy vanity, O man. The effect of good cooking on morale is high indeed. I have never been good at humility but occasionally I find it gives you a boost. Despite more than five decades of marriage, if you are both devout cooks, a certain amount of contentiousness arises during cooking. In this case your best sous chef is not your wife. Why is this? The lumps should have been flattened over fifty-two years, but there is something so deeply personal about cooking that the irascible ego easily pops up with a frown. I used to mostly cook late in the evening for the next day. This offered maximum freedom for me to overplay my hand. Yes, I like seven pounds of short ribs and twenty-three cloves of garlic in barley soup. Some will settle for less but they're not writing barley poems.

Obviously I need courage to deal with my current dysfunctional body. And religion? The Bible says that the kingdom of God is within you. If so, I haven't noticed it lately. I'm not making light of devotion or a mother praying to bring her baby back to life after it's been cut out of the stomach of an anaconda in Venezuela. Human suffering has to be the largest of all question marks. You must beware of hope, a radically dangerous emotion. Hope can roll over and crush you. I went to a dozen doctors last winter in Tucson for shingles relief and each time I had a wide-eyed midwestern hope and faith that was promptly smeared. Hope is a bourgeois Tinker Bell that can transform into a guard dog of the most vicious nature. You raise your expectations then are gutted like a deer. However, if you need to say a little prayer, go ahead and moisten your lips for the deaf gods, although it's like fly fishing in a sewer: "Raise your chin, O son of man, your doom is around the next corner on the left."

Yes, I like seven pounds of short ribs and twenty-three cloves of garlic in barley soup. Some will settle for less but they're not writing barley poems.

These infirmities have been mounting up to a degree that I can't help thinking I'm close to cashing out. Tomorrow at seven A.M. I get a steroid shot in the spine that might offer some temporary relief, then a booster in August in order to go to Paris. I'm desperate at the idea of missing the Paris trip, though it's a book tour and I'll mostly sit on a balcony near the Odeon and do interviews. Interviewers are muttonish but part of the game. Yes, I write longhand with a pen and tablet. This is hard for people to believe but to me the computer is the spawn of Satan. Then again, I've always been a Luddite, much saddened by the invention of the auto. Many people think a Ferrari is beautiful but it isn't if you compare it to a horse.

Of course we are loaned this life, then suddenly one day it's overdue. This is a little tight and nifty but so was La Rochefoucauld. I fully expect to take a long walk to Virgo to see the clusters of a trillion stars. I wonder how they counted them. I had worried about reaching the year 2000, at which I've been successful. All my dark dreams about dying young like so many in my humble trade never happened. Hundreds warned me I was going to die young from smoking and drinking but I disappointed them.

Returning to earth, my favorite place after all, at least for the time being. This evening we're having our first pesto of the summer, what with the basil having matured. I love this dish. It is the taste of early summer eventually overtaken by garden ripe tomatoes. The garden is huge, the vegetables mixed with dozens of species of flowers. It is visual splendor. I stare at it for hours in an effort to forget myself. When the Lakota used to ride into battle they would say, "Take courage, the earth is all that lasts." I am notably not a Lakota though I have visited Wounded Knee several times to kneel and pay my respects, also the site of the death of Crazy Horse, which reminds you of the utter shabbiness of Washington now. When his three-year-old daughter died he climbed the tree to her burial platform and stayed there for three days, playing with her toys.

I am not a Lakota warrior in the nineteenth century. I tease my mind knowing if I didn't have a wife and two daughters and grandchildren, I would have offed myself during this period when life offered so little except pain, occasionally a courageous act. Also in these dire times I am a partial support of eleven. You ultimately don't want to disappoint others or make them feel they failed you. Nothing failed you except your body. I once wrote long ago in a prophetic poem, "Our bodies are women who were never / meant to be faithful to us."

SAN RAFAEL

Just recently, last fall in fact, I had extensive spinal surgery for a condition called "spondylolisthesis." If you can pronounce this you likely have it. To give the surgeon a better view of my interior carcass I was slashed from neck to tailbone. Recovery was slow and I had to go to the famed Mayo in Minnesota to help it. I loathed the Mayo, the vast Pentagon of medicine. I wouldn't feed their food to a starving migrant. It was very hard on my tender empathy to see so many hopeless cases. There was a truly beautiful girl who was paralyzed for life. This meant that I could never take her camping, which girls really deserve.

My real desire for surgery was so I could resume walking my dog Zilpha every morning. When I was immovable she would stare at me with melancholy, never to know what was wrong. I have to take a little walk every morning to compose my mind for writing.

This is a bit odd but necessary. Montana was not good for recovery because there was way too much snow so I made my way to our small *casita* down on the border. The chief neurologist at the Mayo had told me, "You can walk your way out of this." So that's what I work on. I went through dove and quail season on my friend's San Rafael ranch without firing a shot. The doves were in the thousands last year but almost none this year. We speculated that they had been killed by Muslim terrorists farther north. There were plenty of quail but I only shuffled along and couldn't keep up with the dogs. My mood was always corrected by spotting an oak log to sit on and staring hard at the landscape. If you do this it will enter your dream life, which is better than your mom beating you or running from the grizzlies in Montana.

I made some notes on log sitting. There are Emory oaks felled by forest fires or weakened until they eventually fall. I worked so hard on this because I had lots of time stuck there in the near wilderness. Naturally I thought of franchising my concepts and touring the nation and Canada and making a retirement income. The problem is the oak trunks weigh tons and right away I'd have to use the very American method of faking it, creating a lightweight version to follow me in my travels. There were dreams of fame and fortune before I put on the brakes. Why not give my modest *Brick* audience the sacred technique for free? Besides I can no longer bear public appearances. Here goes perhaps nothing:

In that case if you see a poet stumbling down the street offer him some red wine.

Approach the log cautiously with proper reverence as if you were entering a French cathedral or the bedroom of a nude girl or a nude man if you're a girl. If it's warmish, over sixty, inspect the lower sides of the log for a Mojave rattlesnake. They can kill people, horses, and cows. You don't want that, or do you? Just recently I have been reading a natural history memoir of my friend Harry Greene, a herpetologist. An appalling number of herpetologists have been killed toying with these creatures. Vipers don't want to be our friends.

Now examine the log closely for the most comfortable place to sit, usually away from the sun. Sit down and stay for forty-five minutes to an hour. Empty your mind of everything except what is in front of you, the natural landscape or the canyon. Dismiss or allow to slide away any aspect of your grand or pathetic life. Breathe softly. Avoid a doze. Internalize what you see in the canyon, the oaks and the desert willows, the rumpled and grassy earth, hawks flying by, a few songbirds. When you get up bow nine times to the log.

Easy does it. Three logs a day is generally my maximum. When you get in your car it will seem as wretched as it is. A horse would be far better. For hours your mind will still be absorbed in the glory of what you saw rather than mail, e-mails, cell phones, TV, etc. Hopefully log sitting will allow you to change the contents of your life. You will introduce yourself as a "log sitter" rather than a poet, novelist, or mortician. You will walk more slowly and perhaps your feet will shuffle like mine.

There. If all *Brick* readers send me a nickel a month I'll buy some life-giving red wine. Maybe they don't have nickels in Canada? In that case if you see a poet stumbling down the street offer him some red wine. We are all brothers though I wouldn't throw myself on a grenade to save any of them.

I have traveled widely and intensely in the west and the San Rafael is the most beautiful ranchland I've ever seen. It is five by seven miles, more than twenty-two thousand acres of good grass in an area without much good grazing, but then the previous owners, the Greene family, took care of it. Ross runs only about six hundred cows when the land could easily handle three times that. I was on the Gray Ranch, 321,000 acres, when they shipped out nine thousand cows. A previous owner had run nineteen thousand but that was too hard on the land.

Despite being from an agricultural family—my father was an agronomist and county agent—I have never been much interested in land, whether farm or ranch, in terms of productivity. Instead of following in my father's footsteps I became a poet and novelist, so consequently it is altogether natural that my primary impulse toward land is aesthetic. I do make careless estimates on productivity. Up near Jordan, Montana, I thought on the vast Binion Ranch that it would take more than three hundred acres to graze a single cow and at dinner in a local diner found out this was true. Ten acres of my farm back in Michigan would equal a thousand acres in many places in Montana in terms of available grazing. I had plenty of rain and rich soil. When I could get only twenty bucks a ton for my alfalfa I bought forty Scottish Highlanders and fed them at my neighbors', who had good pasture cut by a creek. They were worrisome cattle. I built a storm shed for them so they could get out of the fierce Michigan winter but they wouldn't enter it. They stood around shaggily in belly-deep snow trying to reach the ground for grass. They were tasty beef which I had never eaten before except in the British Isles. Some of the most beautiful farms in America are to be seen on the way west in mid-Minnesota, or out near Fergus Falls. There are both beef and dairy operations, the houses look comfortable in the rolling green land. There are often immense ponds, really lakes, with rowboats parked in the reeds, evidence that you have fishing to go with the fat cattle.

I can readily imagine buying a small ranch I'd call "The Log Ranch." I'd truck in thirty-three logs and arrange them on the property like the stations of the cross. This could soothe me in my perhaps limited time in the twenty-first century which has been coarse indeed. I've been lately fixed on Syria which is like getting scalped every day. I also can't bear that we're in Afghanistan when next door Mexico so desperately needs help. We'd save a lot of gas money and wouldn't have all of those suicides of men returning from Afghanistan.

It was quite interesting not to hunt. There was the thought that I'd killed enough game birds in my life. I missed eating them because properly cooked they are as good to eat as anything on this earth. I remember my mock hunting in Michigan's Upper Peninsula, an unknown part of Canada, toward the end of the season when I knew I should slow down my shooting. I'd let my English setter go on point. I'd flush the bird and yell, "Bang" and off it went to continue to live. The dog didn't mind. It was all fun and after a long afternoon of mock hunting you felt good.

On my little log ranch there will be no livestock except dogs and one Jersey cow. I will have made a pet out of the cow and allow her to follow me in the house. Don't worry, she'll be toilet trained. As a child I made pets out of certain cows and they'd take walks with you hither and yon, including the dense woodlot. Cows don't have a lot of fun before they're shipped off to die so it was nice to give them some human companionship. Come to think of it I prefer the company of a cow to any literary festival or reading I've ever endured. They have such pretty eyes and think of you as a leader, a gross mistake. In my limited time in Washington, D.C., or the United Nations I made little sense out of these piles of ninnies. The U.S. Congress had only a 10 percent approval rating because they are largely malicious dolts and feebs. I'm all for making politics a "women only" profession to see if they can't improve on our enfeebled condition. Back to cows. It is largely known that Jerseys give the best milk and the heavy cream I need for my French recipes, and which is not available except in a pasteurized form which ruins it. So there I am on Log Ranch sitting before the fireplace with my sleeping cow and dogs. Not surprisingly she moos loudly when she needs to go outside to the toilet, a little startling in the middle of the night or to drunk girls stopping in for the usual love who did not notice the cow. "Holy shit!" they scream to the shatteringly loud moo. They calm down with more drugs and alcohol like they do in any country.

I've begun yet another novel and I find myself in a mood similar to my post-op trauma from spinal surgery. The sky has descended and darkness prevails. You feel like you're driving an old used car trying to get out of China. You finally hit the coast and the Pacific only to discover there are no bridges to America. You turn around with difficulty on the beach, running over several swimmers but they are strong and can withstand the tires. You head west across China and Asia including Mongolia's dreaded Gobi Desert. You earn gas money working in the fields and selling your body to the usual eager priests. You finally hit Cornwall in the British Isles but there is no bridge there. The English have lied about bridges again. You fall asleep in the filthy car with priests knocking at the windows. You wake up in Montana after the toughest trip of your life and you're still only on page 145, about a third done.

With or without spinal surgery writing novels is brutal yet I don't want an ounce of empathy or sympathy. After all I'm writing at our little winter *casita* in Patagonia, Arizona, not far from the Mexican border. Wonderful food is available in my home and at the Wagon Wheel bar cooked by Susi. Her enchiladas are the best I've ever had and she makes her red chile sauce from scratch out of big ristras of peppers.

One can't chicken out on food. The day before at a Japanese restaurant he had eaten a spoon of wasabi through lack of concentration. That will get your attention.

Also my logs on the San Rafael are a half hour away for my delectation. Also the birds are ten feet away. One April my mother counted one hundred nineteen species in two days. This is a prime spot on the migration route.

We end with a serene still life with no names: a man sprawled on the rug before the fireplace with his beloved cow and dog. The dog is nestled against her tummy down near her teats, the warmest place, nestled the same way they are out in the yard where the dog imitates her, a friend, eating grass. The cow has unfortunately pooped on the porch. This is a cognitive problem in addition to being a clean-up problem. She thinks the porch is outside where she has freedom to defecate. But the porch is really half inside, half outside. How to teach the cow this nicety? The man is diverted from this animal complexity by his stirring appetite. The surgeon had told him to eat a lot to restore his strength and weight. Lately he had favored Moroccan food including a recent lamb tagine though the harissa his wife made was too hot, causing him to weep sweet tears as he continued to eat it. One can't chicken out on food. The day before at a Japanese restaurant he had eaten a spoon of wasabi through lack of concentration. That will get your attention as you sputter desperately, "We won the war why are they doing this to me?" There is a world of food out there but some of it is dangerous. If you eat a square yard of roasted pig skin or the skin of an entire goose you're going to pay for your crimes. The dog will also eat saltines but what's in a saltine for a dog? She eats them because she sees me eat two every night to comfort my tummy. My friend's dog eats live fish.

EAT WHERE YOU LIVE

Moving to Patagonia for the winters twenty-five years ago was a considerable revelation. I had visited Tucson a number of times but didn't catch on to the cuisine. I had been to Mexico City on the way home from Cozumel but had settled for French food in a hotel that was pointlessly expensive.

When I was at Michigan State University, our late night college hangout was a Mexican place with what I later recognized as Tex-Mex food. I had eaten the wonderful roast cabrito at Mi Tierra in San Antonio. It took a while to recognize my limitations. A flash point was eating grilled baby octopus in Zihuatanejo on a fishing trip. This is Mexican food? Of course. We northerners are perversely misinformed. Without question, Mexicans cook seafood much better than we do in the States. I don't mean border food, far from it. I have been in the Veracruz area several times where you can get wonderful whole roasted robalo (common snook). The same is true on the west coast in terms of roasted fish. We ate a nine-pounder one evening in Tulum with many bottles of good Mexican white wine.

Closer to home, we're within twenty miles of Nogales. I've eaten at Las Vigas perhaps a hundred times, most for the superlative machaca sonorense. I had them organize a banquet when I paid off the mortgage, and it included a wild pig shipped from Florida, and also a large snapper, some enormous wild shrimp, and a mariachi band, of course. I'm hoping in the future to travel around Mexico and hire housewives to cook me their favorite bean dishes.

The other half of the year we live in Montana where food choices are distinctly limited. You can't even buy an edible tortilla in Montana and my past experiences trying to make them were a disaster. You can't buy a calf's foot in Montana to make menudo, an obsession of my taste. Millions of calves and no feet for sale. This was also true in northern Michigan where I began making my own menudo. It's clearly against the law to wander into a pasture and cut your own.

So here we are happily for half the year. I've been given both javelina and mountain lion sausage but didn't care for either. We eat lots of doves and quail roasted over wood fire and my ace urologist, Dr. Alfredo Guevara, cooked a wonderful cabrito last year. Down here much of my taste for American food wanes. Eat where you live is a far better practice.

GRAMPS LE FOU

There had been certain slippages of late that he chose not to dwell upon. He had mistakenly used the cortisone cream his wife applied on her ankle rash as toothpaste and had wondered at the blandness of the flavor. Perhaps he was losing his taste buds? This was not as serious as squirting Neo-Synephrine in his eye instead of Visine, which had temporarily disturbed his already limited vision. He filed these simple-minded mistakes under monkey brain, the Zen question of whether one part of the brain can accurately assess slippages in another part of the brain.

He offered an easy pardon to himself for these errors because when he had recently passed his seventieth birthday he had decided that life was a liquid rather than a solid. People created grievous errors when they treated their lives as a solid, and this was his own downfall when several months before a neurologist had diagnosed

him as having "acute mental exhaustion." His wife had driven him
to the doctor knowing that left to his own devices he would only
pretend to have gone to the doctor. He was a talented fibber and
fully capable of recounting a visit to a neurologist having read Edel-
man's *Neural Darwinism: The Theory of Neuronal Group Selection* and
Robert Martensen's lunar *The Brain Takes Shape: An Early History*.

Some few days our lives have their own intact stories and he
was about to live an utterly bruised tale of love and loss that would
lead him to radically imperfect conclusions.

The day had started poorly, Thursday to be meaninglessly exact,
with a five-mile drive to the village's corner grocery to pick up the
Tucson paper and a jar of Best Foods mayonnaise. He enjoyed hearing the Spanish frequently spoken in the store. Their winter *casita*
on a creek in the mountains was a scant fifteen miles from Mexico
and thus border life offered the pleasant air of living in a foreign
country without the wretched experience of a long plane trip and
the inevitable delays spent in terminals that had become crosses of
dog pounds and enormous toilets.

Unfortunately he had returned home with a jar of Kraft Miracle
Whip salad dressing and his wife had immediately noticed. In his
defense he said that the mayonnaise and salad dressing were next to
each other on the shelf and had the same off-white color. "Darling,
wear your glasses. Each product in the store has a different name.
It's sort of like books. Books can look similar, but the titles are all
different."

He watched the dogs leave the room, which they always did
when he and his wife spoke sharply to each other.

Back in the car he was diverted by a dream he'd had about
exactly where his Scottish Labrador, Zilpha, had lost her collar. He
could "see" the collar in a particular side ravine off Paloma Canyon.
He murmured, "Eureka" to himself and drove right past the grocery
store, turning right to follow the winding road to San Rafael Valley a
half-hour distant. Dreams had always offered vital information to him
in contrast to the thorough junkiness of his mind, which included
all the names of the basilicas in Florence, the lyrics of "Tell Laura I

Love Her" and an improbable number of Protestant hymns from his childhood, the alphabetical names of the kids in his second grade, and the complete menu of his seventh birthday dinner (pickled herring and baked beans and a German chocolate cake). He had told the neurologist that it would be nice if he could get up in the morning, start the coffee, and slice a mango without saying, "Dawn found him carving a mango." The neurologist seemed slightly alarmed and wanted to make an appointment for him with a psychiatrist. He tried to stomp out of the office, but he had hurt his knee while bird hunting and couldn't stomp.

Dreams offered a liquid clarity unavailable in daily life. Once, in New York City at the Carlyle Hotel he had heard the alarming news from home that their neighbor's three English setters had been lost running off in a northern Michigan blizzard. That night after a troublesome fourteen-hour script meeting, and eating a full roasted chicken ordered ahead at Elaine's plus two bottles of sumptuous old Barolo and an ample Calvados nightcap, he had dreamed the exact location of the lost dogs. They had crossed a country graveyard about seven miles south of home where a human friend had been buried the summer before, then headed southeast to a place where they liked to hunt grouse and woodcock. He flew home the next day still burdened with wine and chicken and drove directly from the airport to the location where he had dreamed the dogs would be. They emerged happily from a huge snowdrift where they had burrowed for protection from the weather. When he delivered the dogs to his hunting friend he decided not to mention the dream. The experience was far more pleasant than getting five hundred thousand dollars for a screenplay that after five drafts had been reduced to the usual chatty desuetude. Unfortunately his prescience was limited to dogs. A couple of years before he had visited with an interpreter in a Mayan jungle settlement where they were challenged by three enormous guard dogs. When they visited the jefe, who was without legs due to diabetes, his own leading disease, the jefe asked him through the interpreter if he was part dog. The interpreter advised him that this was a serious question and he replied that there was some canine in the blood in his mother's side of the family. When they left, the jefe told him to be careful about the local jaguars, which hated dogs more than people. Jaguars always tore the heads off dogs.

When he reached the gate to Paloma Canyon on a friend's ranch it was a few minutes before he could remember the lock's combination because his mind had drifted back to a girl he had seen in a Key West dress shop exactly twenty-seven years before. She had been stooping before shelves of blouses in her white shorts and her butt was a perfect Anjou pear. He had felt the kind of involuntary shudder usually experienced only in fiction. And what's more, when she stood her face was the twin of Botticelli's *Venus*, a peculiar antique beauty he had rarely witnessed.

When he opened the gate he wished very much he had brought Zilpha along. He had never been here without a dog or a friend, and the absence of either seemed to make the canyon fearsome and impassive in a way that reminded him of the twenty-ton Olmec heads he had seen in a museum in Jalapa, which was a mountain city north of Veracruz. The other unnerving aspect of the museum had been the hundreds of small statues of women transmogrifying into jaguars. They had made him rethink the nature of women, but more important to the day was the recent publishing of a book that showed a number of jaguars caught by motion-sensitive cameras in this area. To ranchers the jaguars were even less welcome than wetbacks. However, he didn't feel particularly threatened by anything except Washington, D.C.

To leaven the brooding atmosphere with black humor he walked several hundred yards out of his way to reenact his heart attack. The June before when he had revisited a cardiologist friend in San Francisco for three days of tests the doctor had told him that he had experienced it and did he remember the experience? Why lie about such matters? He didn't know, but now he collapsed to the ground, flapping his arms in mock dismay. The actual event had involved his vision crinkling like aluminum foil or, better yet, blurring geometrically like an amok DVD.

Now he lay smiling on the comfortably warm earth and watched
a daddy longlegs spider trot by as if bent on a specific destination.
He had read that this spider was virulently poisonous but its mouth
was too small to bite a human, a delightful metaphor the meaning
of which he hadn't determined. He was mindful that a teaspoon of
the soil beneath his cheek contained a billion bacteria and that a
teaspoon full of a black hole in the cosmos far above him weighed
three billion tons, a strong teaspoon indeed. This was a slightly higher
level of the junk in his head he wished to get rid of. A lovely little
rock wren was flitting around not twenty feet away, which made him
wonder why only one of Goya's twenty children reached adulthood.
He pondered the possible connection between Goya and wrens,
coming up with the rather lame idea that the infant mortality of
songbirds was disappointing.

He steeled his geezer body to get to its feet on a lame leg. His
immediate mission in life had been limited to mayonnaise and finding the attractive dog collar he had bought Zilpha the year before in
Denver. If he had taught her the word *collar*, she would have found it
herself when they backtracked. She knew many words, like *kitchen*,
walk, *sit*, *quail*, *woodcock*, *grouse*, *Linda*, his wife, or *Mary*, Linda's
cocker spaniel, but there hadn't been a need to teach her *collar*, which
was another not very meaningful indignity humans put on dogs.

Back on his feet he set off for a side canyon to the southeast,
thinking of an old friend who had amassed a collection of thousands
of raised-skirt photos. The man was a bit of a porn addict on the
lighter side, as it were. His own tastes were more refined. There
was a girl who worked in a coffee shack in a vacant lot in Butte,
Montana, who wore braces and her tongue appeared to be too large
for her mouth but other than that her appearance was decidedly
Florentine. This taste had arrived in his hormonal college career
during the single year he had changed his major to art history. He
had invented elaborate sexual fantasies about Lucrezia Borgia. In his
thirties it was Lauren Hutton (a bit Florentine) and Emily Brontë
and more recently Clara Schumann. It was apparent that the leading
cause of Elvis Presley's death was constipation, an errant thought.

A side effect of his impaired vision was that he only imperfectly perceived inclines and declines. The real tip of inclines was when he became winded. In the car the tachometer was the indicator. When he reached a flat area that held a Hohokam fire ring, he paused for a much needed cigarette in this place where ancient Indians a thousand years before had warmed themselves and cooked dinner. In another place a dozen miles away near a spring he had found a flat granite rock with a half dozen metate holes, where they ground their acorns and other seeds presumably to make unleavened bread. Around the metate holes the granite had been worn smooth by centuries of bottoms sitting there grinding seeds. This was slightly erotic, though he was discouraged when he had read that male chimpanzees will give up lunch in order to look at photos of female chimpanzee butts.

He had dreamed that Zilpha's collar was in a rock formation a couple of hundred yards up the ever-steepening ravine. Except in periods of extreme drought there was a rock pool that gathered a fair amount of water and he was now painfully thirsty in the late morning heat, not having had the sense to carry a canteen from a belt loop. When he and a friend, or friends, hunted quail in the area he could gaze up the steep ravine to watch the dogs drink from and wallow in the rock pool. It had rained an inch, rare for late February, two days before and he decided to chance a sip, possibly dangerous because of the intestinal parasite giardia that could come from the droppings of javelina, deer, or mountain lions that might be in residence in the water. Since rock pools were so rare in the area he suspected it might be a trinchera, a catchment built by ancient farmers to collect water that they would slowly release for their crops.

The climb was quite the struggle for a seventy-year-old and he paused a dozen times to catch his breath and to calm the pulsing twinges in his bad knee. This led him to worry about his wife's asthma, which after one incident had kept her in intensive care for several days. They cajoled each other about what are now called "health issues." It is far easier to suggest that your wife visit a doctor than to go yourself. His visit to the neurologist was a horrid case in point. She had worried about his recent misidentifications of so many of the birds that gathered at the patio feeders. More striking was the way he had asked her a dozen times in a month who painted the Milton Avery print of three chickens on the dining room wall. This had also worried him, but then he assumed that it was vodka or copious amounts of French red wine that had destroyed the cluster of neurons that had held Milton Avery's name. They were both thinking Alzheimer's, though neither of them mentioned the disease out loud. His brain scan, however, revealed nothing in particular. He told the neurologist that he had learned that heavy smokers don't get Alzheimer's and the doctor sputtered, "No comment." Over the years it had become apparent that antismoking zealots thought the habit more contemptible than baby raping. A few years back at a cocktail party in New York City he had been smoking out on a fire escape and a lovely woman with tears in her eyes asked, "How can you do that to yourself?" and he had quipped, "I'll think about quitting if you show me your butt." She fled and he was a little embarrassed at his crudity. New Yorkers didn't care for the rough country humor he had grown up with.

Nearing the top his mind began to play the music "Theme from Rocky." He was sweating profusely, amazed again at the local weather. When he arose at six A.M., which was his pointless habit, the air had been below freezing and now nearly noon it was at least seventy, giving him a little concern about possibly emerging crotalids. The area was the only place in the States with seven varieties of indigenous rattlesnake. The species called Mojave gave him the most concern as it had poison so strong that it could kill horses and cows and the snakes were common in the immediate area.

He knelt and drank greedily from the rock pool then vomited convulsively on seeing a large dead rattler at the bottom of the shallow water. He shook while wiping his face with a handful of dry grass, remembering a similar event in the Absaroka Mountains in Montana when he drank from a creek only to discover that there was a dead elk close by around a bend upstream. He studied the swollen dead snake and determined that it actually was a crooked branch that had fallen from the widespread branches of the Emory oak above them.

He laughed, thinking that life is not what it seems. There was also the serious thought that a type 2 diabetic couldn't afford to lose his late breakfast of a bowl of Anasazi beans. A couple of times while driving he had begun to doze off and had to stop and eat a few bites of a candy bar to raise his wavering blood sugar, which could be either too high or too low. He had taken his eight pills that morning for his various infirmities, but his diabetic pill was time-released and he had lost it to an imaginary snake.

Luckily the car was downhill, but he wouldn't even attempt it for a while. He cleared a bed in the grass, scraping away stones for a long snooze that would restore his equilibrium. He made a pillow out of his vest and drew out his pocket watch. It was just after twelve noon. Squinting his eyes in the last moment before sleep he noticed a brightish color under a bush no more than ten feet away, which he thought was likely a candy wrapper discarded by one of the hundreds of illegal migrants who made the difficult passage across the canyons and ravines of the valley. No, it couldn't be, he thought. He scrambled over with a hearty wince for his bad knee. Sure enough it was Zilpha's collar. "Victory in our time!" he shouted, with the shout echoing down the deep ravine. His first impulse was to attach the collar around his own neck so he wouldn't lose it but he settled for drawing it up his arm to his shoulder. If he died the presumed searchers could call the local number on the dog tag to give his wife the news. His mission was now reduced to mayonnaise. He fell asleep with a specific glow warbling in his body, counting on his earwax to repel a tiny bug making its way up his neck toward his ear. He hadn't the strength to squash it.

Two hours later he was making his painful way down the ravine while trying to decode two dreams that had arrived during his nap. Why should his knee hurt more going downhill than up? In the second dream he was in a room with a half dozen brown women drinking wine. They were fairly big women, not to his taste, and one was nude like a beige Rubens. They were all jolly and he woke up with an erection, a reassuring event for an old man. Did this mean that he should travel into Mexico in search of big women? The first dream was awkward and dismissible compared with the pleasures of the second. It was brief and he was floating down the river that adjoined a cabin that he used to own in Michigan's Upper Peninsula and where he would swim on the rare hot days. It was a remote place, but the river's surface was covered with ugly flotsam that was passing him on its way to huge Lake Superior. After a few dream minutes he recognized the flotsam as all of the thousands of pieces of junk in his brain.

When he reached the bottom of the ravine he turned the wrong way on the two-track, east rather than west, because he was irritated at the psychological aspects of the flotsam dream. Trash is trash. He corrected his course and was pleased to spot his white SUV perhaps two miles in the distance down the big canyon so lavishly landscaped with the canyon walls decorated with green Emory oaks, juniper and manzanita, and umbrous grasses. Nature still looked more than a bit ominous without a dog or a companion or a gun for that matter. He tried to dismiss the feeling as primitive, which of course it was, but so was this lone old figure wandering in the wilds. When he passed the now less funny heart attack scene, he recalled Marlowe's "O lente, lente currite noctis equi" (run slowly, run slowly, dark horses of the night).

The sun had come back out and he was sweating hard when he reached the water tank near his car. He doused his face in the icy water and said hello to the curious Angus cows and calves on the other side of the tank. Now he was thinking that the flotsam dream supported his contention that life was liquid rather than solid. Maybe written language isn't natural, thus his profound mental exhaustion? He had merely floated for six weeks now and it was much more pleasant than working despite the occasional panic over money, which he shared with the world at large. Maybe if he continued floating all of his brain junk would disappear around a bend in the river. Only a week ago he had announced to his wife that he intended to spend the rest of his life studying wrens, which he loved for their pretty heads and tubby bodies. "That's a wonderful idea," she replied. He was supposed to go to France on business within a month and he thought of canceling when he learned that there was only a single species of wren in Europe. As a liberal Democrat he was often disturbed by the inequalities in nature, the total lack of parity. The marsh wren had two hundred songs while the canyon wren had only ten. Was that fair? But then the canyon wren had the loveliest song in nature along with the loon. It was apparent that in his wren study he would have to let wrens be wrens and let nature be non-Jeffersonian.

On a nearly hour's drive back to the village his mind was empty and the mountain landscape looked more interesting than usual and somewhat mysterious. It could be Tibet or western China even though it wasn't. He was unconcerned about heaven or the afterlife and would settle for being a tree in which possibly wrens would nest. For a moment he wanted nothing, not even time.

When he entered the village he slowed to follow a pretty Mexican girl on a blue bicycle, her lovely butt cocked upward as if aiming at him, which it wasn't. At the grocer's the woman clerk he liked looked quizzically at the dog collar around his shoulder and told him that his wife had been in earlier and had bought the mayonnaise. He decided to buy another jar to round out his day.

TRULY OLDER

When you're seventy-six, as I am, you can die in ten minutes, ten hours, ten months or maybe ten years, or every minute in between. About fifteen years ago I had intuitions of doom and wrote a memoir. Now fifteen years later I have noticed that I'm not dead yet. There is a temptation to bring the memoir up to date in the form of a novella. I am fiction anyway, lock, stock, and barrel. I made myself up from scratch and started fibbing as a baby.

This February I had to cancel a book tour trip to Paris because I was feeling poorly. I thought that maybe I had been feeling poorly for seventy-six years, though in my thirties and forties I walked a couple of thousand miles in wilderness forest. I hated to miss the duck and goose fat I need to keep going in this woeful life. Also the oceans of wine across the wine-dark sea. But to be frank I didn't want to go to Paris and feel ill in the middle of winter when the body craves fuel. My publisher, Flammarion-Gallimard (they recently united), had promised to build me a little temporary igloo in the Luxembourg Gardens to save hotel money. Frenchwomen love to rub their hot butts against chunks of ice or so I've heard around the quad. Also you don't want to be sick without your momma and she's been dead twenty years and is no longer available. Of a family of seven there are only three of us left. Life is like that.

I am fiction anyway, lock, stock, and barrel. I made myself up from scratch and started fibbing as a baby.

Unfortunately my illness isn't faked to get out of a book tour, which I've done here in America. My doctor found it inscrutable that my blood pressure had dropped to ninety over fifty which is perilously low. I am drastically lethargic though I still write every day like a good Scout. I suppose I am losing specific density and might blast from earth into an azure haze.

Somehow I remain roaring with largely irrelevant ideas and plots. Instead of living in a confused state of what I call the "high whine" why doesn't the Republican Party settle down and figure out how to recycle toilet paper? It would save hundreds of millions to build prisons to house the poor, who they loathe. You dunk water and Clorox along with the toilet paper into the oil barrels that they love. On a hot day you dump them on the neighbor's tennis court. Voilà! By evening you scoop up the detritus with snow shovels and you have precious toilet paper. Naturally I should patent this brilliant idea but as an artist I don't have time to deal with legalities.

That's just a starter in a list that includes using atomic cannons to fire tens of thousands of condoms into poor neighborhoods from a distance of thirty miles. Keep that population down by every means.

I'm also in favor of a high tax on poets for their poetry. We abound in the mediocre and somebody has to do something about it, though it might deliver us into the hands of rich poets.

Stop women from denying dates by saying, "I have to wash my hair and do my nails this evening." Any idiot can do this in ten minutes. It hurts bad to take second place to grooming.

Of late I've been rereading John Keats. He is where I started at age fourteen when I first contracted the disease of writing. I read "The poetry of earth is never dead" and was utterly won over. I've never stopped writing poems since then, though early on I worried how I was going to make a living. My first volume, *Plain Song*, came out in 1965, just short of fifty years ago. Recent to that date I had been flunked out of graduate school for what a professor called "arrogance." Imagine that! Anyway they changed when I got a book published by a New York publisher, W.W. Norton, which had never happened to one of their students before. I got a job at a university on Long Island on the basis of this slender book of verse. This was a mixed blessing indeed as I did not thrive in an academic atmosphere. It made me drink too much. Again, imagine that. Sadly I could not thrive in that atmosphere which was too fustian and pimpy with its craving for tenure. By the grace of two years of grants we moved to a small farm back in northern Michigan and stuck it out. For a period of ten years I never quite made ten grand a year, short rations with two kids. We had a huge garden and ate a lot of venison and fish that I caught. I wrote a novel, *Wolf*, which did so-so, and one called *Farmer*, which failed, but then struck pay dirt with a novella, *Legends of the Fall*. Unfortunately I got mixed up in Hollywood with which I didn't deal well. Now as an old man I have published thirty-six books and I'm tired indeed. I wish I could afford a fishing sabbatical. Philip Roth quit everything and I was a bit jealous but then he's real famous and could afford it, which I can't. However it's gross to complain when I've done fairly well as a writer, and any writer who makes close to a livelihood is fortunate indeed.

Any fool knows that red wine is the best energy drink if you keep it within two bottles.

Was it that nitwit Edna St. Vincent Millay who said, "Life must go on I forget just why"? Try to remember, kiddo, the reason for life is simply life.

The part that is barely endurable is that I was an epic walker in my life but two years after spinal surgery I'm now what you must call a "shuffler." There are worse things. Before surgery I couldn't walk at all so I was quite grateful when I learned to walk again. So was my dog who was terribly melancholy in my inoperable stages. Now I take her down to our creek early every morning where she flounders with delight. The other emotional mainstay on the Mexican border where we live in the winter is the virtual flood of birds that migrate through our property on the creek, beginning in late February through March and April. The profusion of these songbirds is consoling.

I was so sorry to miss my trip to Paris. My behavior there seems a bit peculiar to some of my local friends. I get up very early and walk three or four hours, often having an omelet full of *lardons* to fuel my effort. I usually walk through the Luxembourg Gardens, first stopping to look at *le jardin fruitier*, a small fenced garden of fruit trees that was begun in the seventeenth century. For reasons of energy and hydration I stop at cafés for a *verre de rouge*. Any fool knows that red wine is the best energy drink if you keep it within two bottles. A light lunch and a nap and I'm ready for my ceaseless interviews in which I extravagantly fib about the past. Each evening I have an elegant dinner with my publisher or the usual lust-crazed actress. French actresses invariably ask me, "Can you help me off with my undies," and I always say, "Not today, I am doing my hair." They weep, of course, but I maintain my impeccable standards in foreign countries. I nearly got thrown out of Russia for lying on my visa but I begged them to let me stay until I saw the tomb of Dostoevsky.

The peculiar thing about Paris for me is that I always keep the same schedule as in the Upper Peninsula of Michigan, that depleted and over-timbered wilderness. Up very early, walk my bird dog for several hours, back to the cabin for breakfast, a little nap, then work inventing a new universe.

Luckily my books do very well in France. The surge came at a time when I had just quit screenwriting. It was a time of financial insecurity as I had to make enough to feed my savagely hungry daughters. The French saved my little family for which I'll always be grateful. I had many bestsellers over there but never in America.

I didn't want to drop dead in the middle of Hollywood and have producers rape and rob my body. I got a couple of productions off the muddy floor out there but nothing of the quality to write Mom about. She was convinced the place was *immoral* and that I was daffy. She was right on both counts. So much alcohol, drugs, money, and beautiful women. I told Mom that showbiz wasn't built as a cathedral. I was relentless and never got a dime from the profits of *Legends of the Fall*. I have recovered by fishing, hiking, and watching birds, and writing poetry, taking countless naps, and talking to my dog. Maybe I could write a bestseller about naps, then move to Montreal and eat.

REAL OLD FOOD

I have spent a great deal of time in the past six months researching the archaeology of food, sometimes in later dates lapsing into the more known history of food. The purpose of this work is a book I am doing with the chef Mario Batali to be called *On the Track of the Genuine*. To ensure our freedom in the writing we have not presold this book, though a worldwide auction is coming in the future, perhaps in coordination with the Keeneland horse sales in Kentucky in the spring. I have been lucky enough to never have learned the computer so I escape the loneliness of the writer by having twelve satellite researchers, all attractive young women. By never touching a computer I saved thousands of hours of precious time. Do we really need to read a long article on how Russian prostitutes are shipped to Spain in blue oil barrels?

I come from generations of backwoods people adept at fishing and hunting. This was never thought of as *manly*, an invention of some later feminists in attempt to ridicule people who betimes go outside. In fact, my mother was an excellent angler, though I had to row the boat, an arduous task as it was brutally heavy holding six passengers in the humble craft made of water-soaked pine. A farmer had made it for my dad for thirty-five dollars, oars extra. I had to bait my mother's hook as she couldn't stand big, squirming night crawlers, possibly a Freudian glitch. Let us readily admit that the preponderance of outdoorsmen are jerk-offs, pure and simple. Canadians must ban the New Brunswick habit of breasting woodcock that you've shot. It's a criminal waste. Roasted, the legs and thighs that are thrown away are the finest thing God allows you to put in your mouth. Pluck them. It only takes minutes. I suspect these non-pluckers go in the bathroom after the hunt and look at their dicks in the mirror or do the John Wayne strut around the cabin to get ready for the bar. Sad to say these people are generally pathetic cooks. I have heard dozens of times in my sporting life, in both Canada and America, how they'll skin several grouse, put them in the Crock-Pot with three cans of Campbell's mushroom soup, and cook for hours. This is ghastly treatment of a creature. It's too bad you can't train grouse to shoot hunters. Canada should ship these people to that island where they can be clubbed to death with seals and their bodies ground into sausage and sent to China.

In the mythology of north central Africa, the savanna from which we all emerged, there was a heroine known in story and song as Irma Warmgut. She could chop into a dead elephant faster than any man and secure the hundreds of pounds of kidney fat for her family. The fat was useful in preserving other meats just as it is in contemporary French-made confit to preserve ducks and add flavor. My grandparents on my mother's side were very poor farmers but rich in big stone crocks. You could fry up fifteen pounds of sausage patties, put them in the crock, and pour over them ten pounds of melted lard. The sausage would still be good for several months.

We hear much these days about the war against fat. To the eye it is not yet successful. I know several blimpish people, men and women, who average ten bottles of Pepsi a day while eating their chocolate cookies. All sugar pure and simple, despite the strict diets they say they try. Not liking sugar or pop myself, I don't get it. I collect huge paunches at our local grocery stores and supermarkets. Some real big ones, in both Michigan and Montana. I don't have a camera, but all I have to do is stare and blink my eyes a few times and the record paunch is indelible. I did this with game animals in Africa forty years ago and still have hundreds of mind photos on record. You use the same method if you have the luck to look up a pretty girl's dress. You blink and are home free. You blink and now you have a permanent record of what makes life valuable. Naturally I also do this with food. Some of us remember the food in that wonderful, edible movie *Tom Jones*. I can still see a wild piglet in France roasted and stuffed with truffles and a lamb I cooked over coals after my daughter had inserted sixty cloves of garlic. No California wine was allowed on the property.

Three famed physiologists at Harvard did spadework on the universal problem of odors. All fat people, even myself when I occasionally get overweight, have crevasses in the manner of glaciers in their fat, out of which emerge unpleasant odors. The physiologists point out that the problem can't be attacked without the military and a well-organized gestapo. This is a fearsome choice, but a solid democracy can make a wise decision. If you doubt me, take a Fat Boy's Steam Bath. This chain is in every city and you can find it by odor.

I am in the middle of a crushing experience that almost, but not quite, affects my appetite. It is the publication of my new novel, *The Big Seven*. America novelist William H. Gass pointed out that there is no more sodden time for a writer than publication. No one asked me but I agree. In fact, many fellow writers tell me that I'm on easy street. Here I am making a living as a writer and I'm only seventy-seven years old. Obviously, it could have been otherwise. It looked grim when I quit writing screenplays so as to avoid dying in Los Angeles. This preemptive decision cut my income by more than half. Luckily the French stepped in and decided they liked my stories. Who knows why? I do know now that dozens of trips to France have given me the opportunity for enough to eat. I can be a little hard on chefs. One evening in the Camargue, a chef insisted on cooking me all the local seafood, plus roasting a small lamb in the fireplace, plus a dozen bottles of wine. Midnight found us both sleeping on the stone floor, having traded shirts in new friendship. As Mom would have said, "It was a learning experience." No, it wasn't. Too much wine steals my judgment that was never very good in cold sobriety.

The hardest thing lately has been the deaths of two good writer friends, Peter Matthiessen and Charles Bowden, plus the death of the insane book collector Beef Torrey. With Matthiessen it was the grandeur of this bird of passage disappearing. I had known him well for more than forty years and he and the poet Gary Snyder were models of behavior for me. Neither did the vanity jitterbug in New York City. I always advise humility to young writers because no one has the ability to invent the destiny of their ambition. If any, in spades. Both Matthiessen and Snyder were and are naturalists of some repute, amateur, often the best kind, rather than professional. This helps. A several-hour walk in the forest heals more wounds than any doctor of my experience.

> *You, as a writer, must mix your essential gluttony and writing carefully. Despite your complaints you have lots of time to do so. Good food is so much more important than the mediocre writing that pervades the earth.*

I'm not allowed to say "Woe is me" minutes after I was faxed a review saying I was a hero of American literature. I wonder what one actually is. Luckily it doesn't involve throwing yourself on a grenade to save your friends. The death of a friend is the strongest pointer possible to the clarity of your future. In a world in which Anne Frank dies, it is easier for me to lose interest in the inevitability of my own.

In times of extreme stress like book publication I crave herring. It is much more comforting than the drugs and alcohol favored by so many. When heart and brain feel like a jackhammer at play, I turn to herring, the food of my people on my mother's side, the Swedes. Since where I live my several lives is somewhat inaccessible, I depend on others. This time Mario Batali sent eight containers of different herring from Russ & Daughters, the herring capital on East Houston in New York City. Since you don't drink good wine with herring I poured a simple eight-ounce glass of vodka. As I dabbled in the containers, waves of glorious warmth suffused my body as if I were sleeping with Venus, fresh from the sea.

I sang a simple hosanna, knowing that if I write novels, it's my business. Just buy the book, chumps. Button your gobs to criticism.

With the right things to drink and eat you can have a nice life. It behooves you to find out what they are. You can obviously eat better in France than in Michigan or Montana or Arizona or even the fabled Ottawa in Canada, though Calgary is a better choice. You, as a writer, must mix your essential gluttony and writing carefully. Despite your complaints you have lots of time to do so. Good food is so much more important than the mediocre writing that pervades the earth.

EVERYDAY LIFE:
THE QUESTION OF ZEN

I often think that because I am quite remote up here in northern Michigan from others who practice, and am intensely stubborn, I learn so slowly that I will be dead before I understand very much.

But "Who dies?" is a koan I posed for myself several years ago. To know the self, of course, is hopefully to forget the self. The especially banal wine of illusion is to hold on tightly to all the resonances of what we see in the mirror, inside and out. In our practice the self is not pushed away, it drifts away. When you are a poet there is a residual fear that if you lose the self you will lose your art. Gradually, however (for me it took fifteen years!), you discover that what you thought was the self had little to do with your own true nature. Or your art, for that matter.

When I learned this I began to understand that the period of *zazen* that lays the foundation of the day is meant to grow until it swallows both the day and the night. Time viewed as periods of practice and nonpractice is as fanciful a duality as the notion that Zen is Oriental. The kapok in the *zafu* beneath your ass is without nationality. The Bodhidharma and Dogen saw each other across an ocean river that is without sex, color, time, or form. What is between Arcturus and Aldebaran?

I was wondering the other day about this body that wakes up to a cold rain from an instructive dream, takes its coffee out to the granary to sit on a red cushion. The body sees the totems of consolation hanging around the room: animal skins, a heron wing, malformed antlers, crow and peregrine feathers, a Sioux-painted coyote skull, a grizzly turd, a sea lion's caudal bone, a wild-turkey foot, favored stones, a brass Bureau of Indian Affairs body tag from the Wyoming Territory, a bear claw, a prehistoric grizzly tooth. These are familiar, beloved objects of the earth, but the day is not familiar because it is a new one. The bird that passes across the window is a reminder of the shortness of life, but it is mostly a bird flying past the window.

"The days are stacked against what we think we are," I wrote in a poem. The point here, albeit blunt, is that when you forget what you are, you truly "see" the day. The man who howls in anger on the phone an hour later because he has been crossed is a comic-figure dog paddling in a sump of pride. He wasn't conscious enough at the moment to realize that there is evil afloat in the land, within and without. This condition can be called "self-sunken." A little later, when he takes a walk on the shores of a lake, he does himself a favor by becoming nothing. He forgets being "right" and "wrong," which enables him to watch time herself flickering across the water. This is a delightful illusion.

The hardest thing for me to accept was that my life was what it was every day. This seemed to negate notions of grandeur necessary for an interest in survival. The turnaround came when an interviewer asked me about the discipline that I used to be productive. It occurred to me at that moment that discipline was what you are every day, how conscious you are willing to be. In the *Tao te Ching* (in the splendid new Stephen Mitchell translation) it says, "Act without doing; work without effort." So you write to express your true nature, part of which is an aesthetic sense that reflects the intricacies of life, rather than the short circuits devised by the ego. Assuming the technique of the art has been learned, it can then arrive out of silence rather than by the self-administered cattle prod to the temples that is postmodernism.

After this body eats a tad too much for lunch it returns to the granary, stokes the fire, and takes a nap with its beloved dog, who, at eleven, is in the winter of her life. A distinct lump of sorrow forms, which, on being observed, reminds the body of the Protestant hymn "Fly, Fly Away," and we are returned to the fragility of birds. The sense of transience is then embraced. When the dead sister reappears in dreams she is always a bird.

On the body's waking with a start, because it is the dog's nature to bark on occasion at nothing in particular, the body resumes the work. There has been an exhausting effort in recent years through the form of poetry and novels to understand native cultures. The study of native cultures tends to lead you far afield from all you have learned, including much that you have perceived and assumed was reality. At first this is disconcerting, but there are many benefits to letting the world fall apart. I find that I have to spend a great deal of time alone in the natural world to be of use to anyone else. Above my desk there is a wonderfully comic reproduction of Hokusai's blind men leading each other across a stream.

Whatever I have learned I owe largely to others. It was back in 1967 that I met Peter Matthiessen and Deborah Love, then Gary Snyder, though in both cases I had read the work. But in these formative stages of practice the *sangha* is especially important. George Quasha introduced me to the work of Chogyam Trungpa—*Cutting Through Spiritual Materialism* is an improbably vital book. Shortly thereafter I met Bob Watkins, a true Zen man, who had studied with Suzuki Roshi and Kobun Chino Sensei. The work of Lucien Stryk has been critical to me, though I have never met him. Then, through

Dan Gerber, I met Kobun himself, who has revived me a number of times. Through all of this I had the steadying companionship of Dan Gerber, who is currently my teacher. Without this succession (or modest lineage!) I'd be dead as a doornail, as I have been a man, at times, of intemperate habits. I'm still amazed how the world, with my cooperation, can knock me off Achala's log back into the fire. There is something here of the child who, upon waking, thinks he can fly, even though he failed badly the day before.

There is an urge to keep everything secret. But this is what Protestants call the sin of pride, also greed. They have another notion relevant here, that of the "stumbling block," wherein the mature in the faith behave in such a way as to impede the neophyte. There is, sadly, a lot of this among Buddhists, the spiritual materialism that implies that I have lived in this town a long time and you are only a newcomer. This is like shouting at a child that he is only three years old. It is also the kind of terrifying bullshit that has permanently enfeebled Christianity. Disregarding an afterlife, he who would be first will be last.

We should sit after the fashion of Dogen or Suzuki Roshi: as a river within its banks, the night sky in the heavens, the earth turning easily with her burden. We must practice like John Muir's bears: "Bears are made of the same dust as we and breathe the same winds and drink the same waters, his life not long, not short, knows no beginning, no ending, to him life unstinted, unplanned, is above the accident of time, and his years, markless, boundless, equal eternity."

This is all peculiar but quite unremarkable. It is night now and the snow is falling. I go outside and my warm slippers melt a track for a few moments. To the east there is a break in the clouds, and I feel attended to by the stars and the blackness above the clouds, the endless blessed night that cushions us.

Photo Credits

Grateful acknowledgement to Grand Valley State University for archival assistance and providing the photos on pages 1, 9, 141, 207, and 272; and deepest gratitude to all of the photographers for their work.

p. 1: Jim in Key West. Photo by Guy de la Valdène.

p. 9: Jim in Lake Leelanau, mid-1970s. Photo by Bob Wargo.

p. 22: Jim and Linda Harrison at a family wedding. Photo by William Campbell.

p. 39: Jim in France in 1971. Photo courtesy of the Harrison family.

p. 52: At Dick's Pour House, Lake Leelanau, Michigan. Photo by Bud Schulz.

p. 58: Jim Harrison and Gérard Oberlé. Photo courtesy of Gérard Oberlé.

p. 82: Making breakfast, mid-1970s. Photo by Linda Harrison, courtesy of the Harrison family.

p. 91: A spare hour a day for walking. Photo courtesy of the Harrison family.

p. 95: Jim Harrison and Peter Lewis. Photo © Don J. Usner.

p. 113: Nick Reens, Guy de la Valdène, and Jim Harrison. Photo courtesy of the Harrison family.

p. 141: Jim in the driveway to his Michigan house. Photo by Jurg Ramseier.

p. 147: Guy de la Valdène, Tom McGuane, Russell Chatham, and Jim Harrison in Key West. Photo by Stephen Collector.

p. 151: John and Jim Harrison with their mother Norma and a neighbor kid. Photo by Winfield Harrison and courtesy of the Harrison family.

p. 158: Lulu Peyraud and Jim. Photo by Peter Lewis.

p. 176: With Mario Batali. Photo by John Potenberg.

p. 183: Jim in his Boston years, early 1960s. Photo by Bill Corbett.

p. 207: Jim with his beloved bird dog Tess. Photo by Philip Newton.

p. 216: Jim, Anna, Jamie, and Linda Harrison, early 1980s. Photo by Dennis Gripentrog.

p. 223: Morning hike, Patagonia, Arizona. Photo by Judy Hottensen.

p. 236: Jim and grandson Silas Potenberg. Photo by Jamie Potenberg.

p. 243: Jim in the San Rafael Valley. Photo courtesy of the Harrison family.

p. 250: With chuck wagon, Patagonia. Photo by Peter Lewis.

p. 252: Morning cigarette outside his writing studio in Livingston, Montana. Photo by Amy Hundley.

p. 267: Lunch break at the Livingston "fish shack." Photo by Amy Hundley.

p. 272: Jim, Judy, and John Harrison with their catch. Photo courtesy of the Harrison family.